SHOCK ZONE

GAMES AND GAMERS

P9-ASD-916

THE AWESOME INNER WORKINGS OF VIDEO GAMES

ARIE KAPLAN

Lerner Publications Company • Minneapolis

NOTE TO READERS: Not all games are appropriate for players of all ages. Remember to follow video game rating systems and the advice of a parent or guardian when deciding which games to play.

Copyright © 2014 by
Lerner Publishing Group, Inc.

Lerner Publications Company
A division of Lerner Publishing Group, Inc.
241 First Avenue North
Minneapolis, MN 55401 U.S.A.

Website address: www.lernerbooks.com

Content Consultant: Crystle Martin, postdoctoral researcher, Digital Media and Learning Hub at the University of California, Irvine

Library of Congress Cataloging-in-Publication Data

Kaplan, Arie.
    The awesome inner workings of video games / by Arie Kaplan.
        pages   cm. — (Shockzone — games and gamers)
        Includes index.
        ISBN 978-1-4677-1250-7 (lib. bdg. : alk. paper)
        ISBN 978-1-4677-1779-3 (eBook)
        1. Video games—Design—Juvenile literature. I. Title.
    GV1469.3.K34 2014
    794.8—dc23   2013001160

Manufactured in the United States of America
1 – MG – 7/15/13

TABLE OF CONTENTS

UNDER THE HOOD

You love playing on the latest video game console, but have you ever taken a moment to think about **what's going on inside that mysterious box?** Ever wonder what goes through all of those cords? Or how Mario knows to jump when you hit the A button? Turns out, the answers to these questions are totally interesting. Even better, they're not as tough to understand as you might think.

console = a device used to play video games

Gamers buy millions of video game consoles each year. Ever wonder how those small boxes make your favorite games possible?

SONY.

PLAYSTATION 3

Blu-ray Disc

60GB

Believe it or not, whether you're using an Atari 2600 from the 1970s or a PlayStation 3, most game systems are basically the same. Sure, the graphics look better on more modern consoles, and the ways of controlling games have changed. But the same kinds of parts are found inside just about all of them. Pretty much every console has the following guts:

- Processors
- Software kernel
- Computer code
- Storage space
- Memory
- Outputs
- Controls

All of these parts work together to bring your games to life. But what does each part do, and how do they play nice together to bring games to your TV screen? Let's crack open the plastic and dive inside a game console to figure out how all the pieces work.

Surprisingly, the same kinds of parts are inside these two consoles.

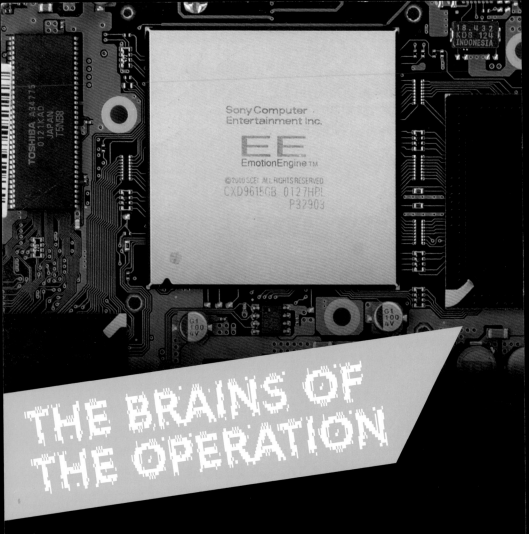

TOSHIBA A34775
0121KAD
JAPAN
T5N58

18.43.2
KDS 124
INDONESIA

Sony Computer
Entertainment Inc.

EE
EmotionEngine ™

©2000 SCEI ALL RIGHTS RESERVED
CXD9615GB 0127HPL
P32903

G1
100
4V

G1
100
4V

THE BRAINS OF THE OPERATION

Game consoles have to be able to think for themselves. Imagine you're playing a basketball video game and the other team is just standing around. Sure, it might be fun at first to run past them and leap into the air for a couple of slam dunks. But it would get boring pretty quickly. For the opposing players to fight back, we're going to need to give the console a brain. This brain is known as the central processing unit, or CPU for short.

Any kind of video game console or other computer needs a CPU. A console's CPU does three basic things. First, it performs math. Second, it makes decisions based on rules that the game creators gave it. And third, it moves information from one place to another.

The Wii U CPU has the power to send graphics and sound to two screens: one on the TV and one on the controller.

Let's go back to that basketball video game to check out examples of all three things. First, the math. When you shoot the ball, the console has to figure out where the ball goes. How far away from the basket were you? How hard was the shot? How good are the shooting skills of the player you're using? The CPU crunches all these numbers to decide how the ball flies through the air. The CPU also follows rules. Imagine you just hit the game-winning shot. The game creators have to give the CPU the following rule: the player with the higher score wins. Even basic stuff like that has to be spelled out for the CPU. Finally, the CPU moves information around. When you win the basketball game, confetti falls from the ceiling and a victory song plays. The CPU grabs the graphics and sound for these things and puts them onto the screen.

As you can probably tell, the CPU is the true brains of the operation when it comes to gaming. Without it, nothing would get done.

THE BRAINS OF THE BRAIN

CPUs contain amazingly tiny devices called transistors. The newest CPUs have more than a billion of them, each ten thousand times smaller than the width of a human hair. Each one simply switches on and off. By doing this in the right order, the transistors help the CPU do its three basic tasks.

A SOFTWARE KERNEL THAT REALLY POPS!

When you hear the word *kernel*, you probably think of the piece of corn that your microwave turns into popcorn. But it turns out that *kernel* is also a word for the core of any computer's software. And that includes the software inside video game consoles. Just be sure not to stick your PlayStation in a microwave.

software = any kind of computer program, including video games

The main job of the kernel is pretty simple. It helps the CPU talk to the software. Imagine the CPU is a sleek fighter jet and the software is the pilot. Without the pilot, the fighter jet is just sitting around the runway rusting its wings off. And without the jet, the pilot is just kicking rocks down the runway. Same thing with the CPU and the software. They're useless without each other. But when they come together, they become amazingly powerful. The kernel is what makes this teamwork possible.

But that's not all the kernel does. It also helps the software talk to the other important pieces of hardware besides the CPU. These include the memory and the controllers that make video games possible. In other words, no kernel, no game.

hardware = any kind of computer program, including video games

THE OPERATING ROOM

The kernel is the main part of what's known as the operating system, or OS. This is software that the computer uses to launch other programs, whether they're games, Internet browsers, or word processors. You might have heard about some of the operating systems on computers. Do Windows, Linux, or Mac OS ring any bells? Nearly all the world's computers run on one of these three operating systems.

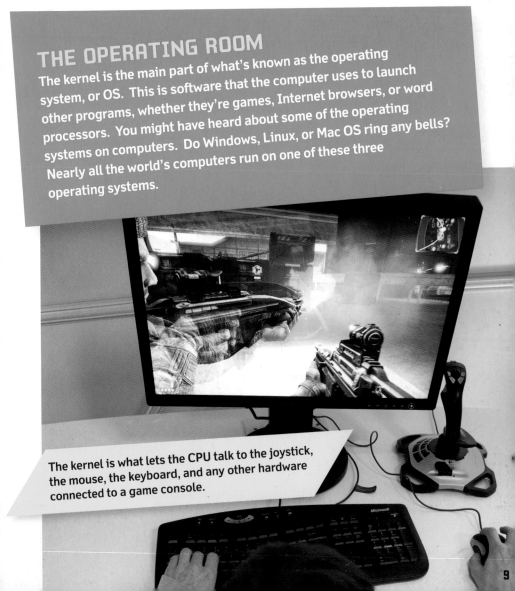

The kernel is what lets the CPU talk to the joystick, the mouse, the keyboard, and any other hardware connected to a game console.

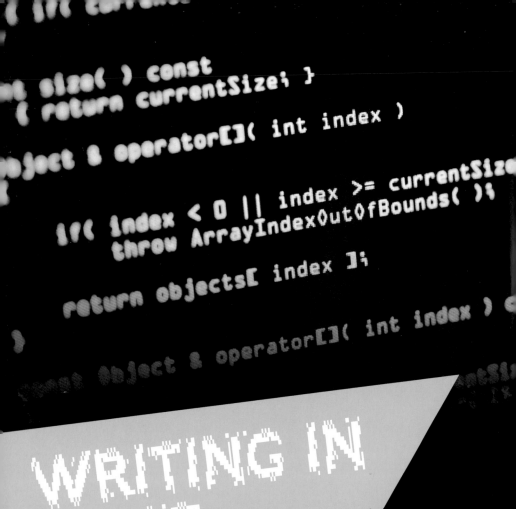

WRITING IN CODE

"If the player presses A, the character jumps. If the player presses B, he shoots a fireball. Here comes a bad guy! JUMP ON HIS HEAD!"

Unfortunately, game creators can't create their games by writing with regular words. Turns out, creating games is a lot more complicated than that. Games must be written in special languages known as programming codes. Here's an example of some

This code, written in a language called C, displays the words "Super Mario" on the screen:

```
#include < stdio.h>
void main()
{
    printf("\nSuper Mario\n");
}
```

Yikes. A bit tough to read, right? Why does programming code look so different from regular language? The reason is that the CPU is not really all that smart. You have to give it very careful instructions for it to do its job properly. A computer only speaks a specific language, and that language is called programming code. A programmer uses this code to give the computer detailed instructions. To make a game, a programmer has to write many thousands of lines of code.

The programming code tells the CPU everything about the game: who the characters are, what they look like, where they are, and how they move. The programmer also makes sure that everything runs smoothly all the way through the game. Any tiny mistake in the programming code and the game might stop working. Programmers don't want a herd of angry gamers stampeding down their door if they find a game-ending programming error on the final level.

Programmers spend long hours working on the programming code for games.

REVVING UP THE GAME ENGINE

Programming games is tough. Long hours, late nights, and tons of work go into writing all those lines of code. But think about it: lots of code might stay the same from game to game. If you're making a first-person game, chances are another programmer has already written some code you need. The basic instructions that tell the CPU how the character moves, what the enemies do, and how the levels are built are probably pretty similar. Why not just reuse those parts

first-person game = a game in which the player sees through the eyes of the character

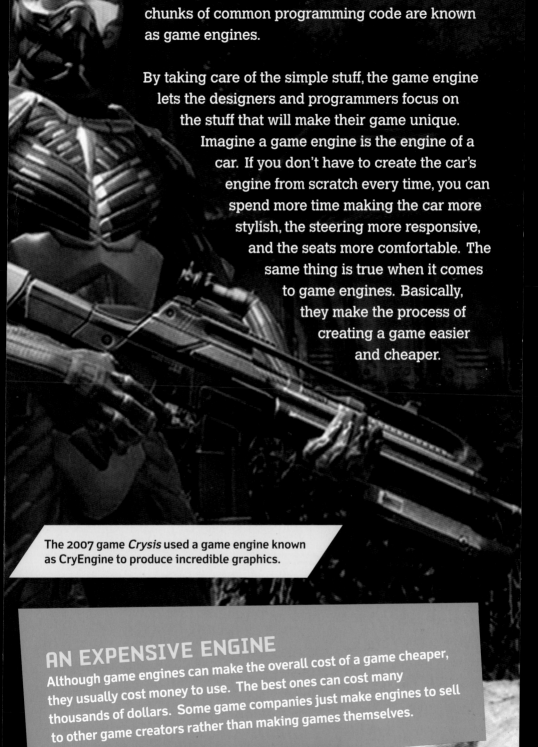

chunks of common programming code are known as game engines.

By taking care of the simple stuff, the game engine lets the designers and programmers focus on the stuff that will make their game unique. Imagine a game engine is the engine of a car. If you don't have to create the car's engine from scratch every time, you can spend more time making the car more stylish, the steering more responsive, and the seats more comfortable. The same thing is true when it comes to game engines. Basically, they make the process of creating a game easier and cheaper.

The 2007 game *Crysis* used a game engine known as CryEngine to produce incredible graphics.

AN EXPENSIVE ENGINE

Although game engines can make the overall cost of a game cheaper, they usually cost money to use. The best ones can cost many thousands of dollars. Some game companies just make engines to sell to other game creators rather than making games themselves.

WHERE GAMES LIVE

Just like people, games have to live somewhere. If the kernel and the CPU are going to use the game's code, they need to know where to find it.

From the 1970s to the 1990s, the most common home for games was on cartridges. These are pieces of plastic that contained computer memory chips. The memory chips hold the programming code that makes up the games. Along one edge of the cartridge, metal connectors can be seen. When this edge is plugged into the console, these connectors let the cartridge and the console talk back and forth to each other.

For the earliest video games, cartridges worked great. They were pretty cheap, and they didn't need to hold much information. Graphics and sound were simple, so they didn't take up much space. Back then, space was measured in bytes. Cartridges for the Atari 2600 held 4 kilobytes—4,000 bytes.

But by the 1990s, games were getting a lot more complicated. Amazing graphics and high-quality sound took up more and more space each year. Cartridges were able to keep up for a little while, but soon games were getting too big too fast. Fitting games into cartridges was starting to feel like fitting elephants into your pockets. The Nintendo 64, the last console to use cartridges, could hold up to 64 megabytes—64 million bytes. But one of its competitors used a new storage technology that held more than ten times that much.

bytes = single pieces of information

The PlayStation's CDs gave video game developers tons more space for their games.

This new competitor was the PlayStation. It used compact discs, or CDs, to hold its games. CDs could hold 700 megabytes, far more than the old cartridges could. This huge amount of storage space was available because CDs work very differently from cartridges.

A CD is a type of optical disc. On optical discs, information is contained in a long line that begins on the edge and winds around and around toward the middle. The line is extremely narrow and amazingly long. If you stretched it out, it would go on for more than 3 miles (5 kilometers)! Along the line are microscopic holes known as pits. By measuring the pits and the gaps between them, the game console can read the information on the disc.

But it didn't take long for this incredible new technology to become out of date. Soon games were filling up three or four CDs. Fortunately, scientists invented a new kind of optical disc with even more storage space. These were called DVDs, or digital video discs. They hold more than six times as much as CDs. A few years later, even newer optical discs called Blu-ray Discs came out. They can hold a whopping ten times more than DVDs. Many movies are sold on DVD or Blu-ray Disc. But did you ever notice that they're the same size as CDs? How did they cram even more storage space onto the same size disc?

The answer is in the pits. On DVDs and Blu-ray Discs, the line of pits is narrower than on CDs. This means that the line of information is even longer, so more information can be stored. DVDs and Blu-ray Discs are used on modern consoles. The PlayStation 3 uses Blu-ray Discs, and the Xbox 360 uses DVDs.

LASER DISCS

How do game consoles read the lines of information on CDs, DVDs, and Blu-ray Discs? The answer: very narrow beams of light called lasers. Consoles spin the discs at amazing speeds while shooting a laser toward the lines of information. DVDs use red lasers, while Blu-ray Discs use thinner ones. Can you guess what color they are?

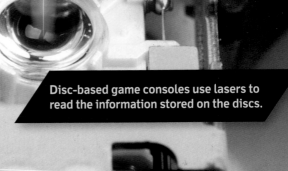

Disc-based game consoles use lasers to read the information stored on the discs.

A GREAT MEMORY

The CPU has to deal with a ton of stuff at once. It's constantly handling graphics, sound, enemies, and the buttons the player presses. In other words, the CPU is a serious multitasker. But it can't manage this juggling act all by itself. It's got a partner known as RAM. By the way, that's random-access memory—not a male sheep!

The game console's random-access memory holds onto programming code that is needed right away. It pulls the information off the cartridge or disc and then passes it to the CPU whenever it's needed. This speeds up the game and prevents long loading times.

Games that have a lot happening on-screen, such as *Civilization V*, need plenty of RAM to run smoothly.

Not having RAM would lead to some very unfortunate gameplay. Imagine you're in the middle of the latest *Halo* game. You're playing as a super soldier sent to defeat an alien invasion. You dash across an open field toward a giant alien crab and press the button to pull out your giant laser, and . . . whoops. Your laser cannon is still loading from the game disc. CRUNCH. Congratulations—you've gone from super soldier to appetizer.

RAM makes sure this doesn't happen. It loads everything—characters, weapons, backgrounds, and everything else—smoothly so gameplay isn't interrupted.

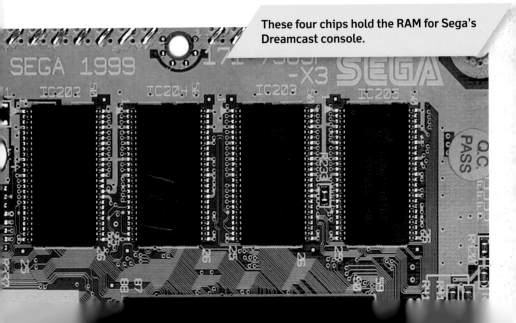

These four chips hold the RAM for Sega's Dreamcast console.

FROM CONSOLE TO TV

Getting your game from the console to the TV sounds simple, right? Just plug the cord from the console into the back of the TV. But it takes some serious technology to make it all happen. It's even more impressive when you find out what came before.

The cable that goes from the console to the TV is known as the AV output, or audio-video output. Early consoles used RF, or radio frequency cables. That technology was pretty much from the 1800s, and it showed. Graphics were blurry and fuzzy, and sound was just plain bad. But the consoles at the time weren't powerful enough to perform better than that anyway.

Later consoles used composite cables. This type of cable usually had three ends that went into the TV—yellow, red, and white. The yellow one carried the picture, while red and white carried sound. The quality was a little better but still not great. By the year 2000, console graphics had gotten amazingly good, but composite cables were making them look amazingly bad.

Finally, in 2006, the PlayStation 3 took AV outputs to the next level with HDMI. Using HDMI, consoles send high-definition graphics and ultra-crisp sound through a single cable. The latest and greatest consoles, including the Xbox 360 and the Wii U, also use HDMI cables. At last, AV outputs have caught up with the raw power of today's game consoles.

HDMI =
high-definition
multimedia
interface

HDMI cables helped PlayStation 3 games look better than any console games that came before.

PUSHING THE GAME'S BUTTONS

So you've got a great game running on your console. The graphics are awesome, and the sound is crystal clear. But guess what? If you can't control what's happening on-screen, all you're doing is watching a movie. To make this into a real video game, we need to figure out a way for the player to tell the game what to do. Enter the controller.

Practically every controller in gaming history has had one or more buttons. But how do they work? Think of each button as being a switch. Like a light switch, a button can be either "on" or "off." When you flick on a light switch, you're letting electricity flow through to the lightbulb, causing it to illuminate. Game controller buttons work the same way.

Imagine you're in the middle of an intense battle in a fighting game. You want your character to throw a knockout punch, so you hit the A button. When you press it, a tiny piece of metal in the A button touches another piece of metal inside the controller. Electricity flows between the two pieces and sends a signal back to the game console. The CPU figures out which button was pressed and checks the code instructions for what to do if the player hits A. The code tells the CPU to have your player swing his fist for the knockout. POW! Nice work. But really, the controller and the CPU did all the hard work.

Game companies had some seriously weird ideas for new controllers in the 1990s.

POSITION
6/6

HEALTH
99%
+0'03.50
TO RECORD

LAP
2/3

1ST WASHINGTON 0'18.
2ND EMERSON +0'00.27
3RD F. ALOHEW +0'00.63
4TH T. WHITE +0'00.85
5TH C. CAVALL +0'01.50
6TH ...EUA +0'03.17

TAPPED OUT

Buttons are great for some games. And they were the only way to play for many years. But nowadays, **millions of players are controlling their games in totally new ways.** If you've ever used an iPhone, a Nintendo 3DS, or a Nintendo Wii U, you're familiar with one of these new control technologies. Can you guess what it is? That's right: touch screens.

touch screens = screens that you can touch to control rather than using buttons

There are a few different types of touch screens. The technology is super advanced but surprisingly easy to understand. The first major type of screen uses resistive touch.

This is the kind used by the 3DS and the Wii U. These screens have two layers—plastic on top and glass below. When you tap the screen, the two layers touch. Electricity from the screen flows between them, sending a signal to the CPU that says where the tap happened. Resistive touch screens are very accurate, but they don't always respond quickly to touches.

The next cool touch tech is called capacitive touch. The iPhone and other smartphones use this kind of screen. Like the resistive touch screens, these have two layers. When you tap the screen, electricity from your screen goes into your finger. This CPU can tell how much electricity left the screen to find out where the screen was touched. Capacitive touch screens aren't quite as accurate as resistive ones, but they are super responsive. This responsiveness is part of what makes smartphone games like *Angry Birds* so popular.

The controller for the Nintendo Wii U console includes a built-in resistive touch screen.

A PLAYER IN MOTION

You turn on your game console and stand in front of your TV screen. Your hands are empty. There is no controller to be found. Suddenly, you move your hand. The on-screen menu follows your movement. Just a few years ago, this scene was a science fiction dream. But recently, games that use this type of control—known as motion control—are some of the most popular on the planet. You've probably had a chance to try playing a Wii, an Xbox Kinect, or a PlayStation Move. But how do these incredible new controls work?

The Wii and the Move use a different type of motion control than the Kinect. In these types, the player must still hold a controller. But make no mistake, these are no ordinary controllers. Looking a bit like TV remotes, they are packed with devices that can figure out where the controller is and how it moves. This information is sent back to the console. The result is that when you swing the controller like a sword, your character on-screen swings her sword too. When you hold it like a Ping-Pong paddle, you can knock the on-screen ball back to your opponent.

The Kinect is more like the sci-fi scenario from before. No controller is needed. The Kinect uses some seriously cool technology to pull this off. You put a small device next to the TV, and it shoots out thousands of infrared dots all across the room. The dots are normally invisible, but you can see them if you wear night vision goggles. The Kinect can tell how long it takes for the light from these dots to bounce back. Based on this, it can tell if there is a person in front of it and what that person is doing.

infrared = a type of light that is invisible to the naked eye

Gamers using the Xbox Kinect don't need to hold a controller.

BREAKTHROUGHS IN GAME TECHNOLOGY

Throughout the history of video games, some games took advantage of new advances in technology. The creators of these games had a great understanding of how games work. Not only that, but they knew how to transform this new technology into a fun experience for players. Here are five of these games. Each of them highlights a particular part of video game technology.

Controller: *Super Mario 64* (Nintendo 64, 1996)

Most games are designed with the console's controller in mind. But *Super Mario 64* might be the only game where the opposite is true. Nintendo mastermind Shigeru Miyamoto knew that the Nintendo 64's first game had to be amazing. So he designed the controller to work perfectly with the game. The result was that Mario's first 3D adventure had incredibly fluid controls. Earlier 3D platformer games had been clunky and hard to use. But the Nintendo 64's joystick let players control the portly plumber with ease.

Storage: *Final Fantasy VII* (PlayStation, 1997)

Square, the makers of the *Final Fantasy* series of role-playing games, originally planned to make *Final Fantasy VII* for the Super Nintendo. But they were concerned that the cartridges used on the Super Nintendo wouldn't have enough space for their epic game. When Nintendo announced that their next console, the Nintendo 64, would also use cartridges, Square decided they'd had enough. They made *Final Fantasy VII* for the PlayStation instead. The game ended up spanning three discs, and it became one of the most popular games in history.

RAM: *The Legend of Zelda: Majora's Mask* (Nintendo 64, 2000)
How do you follow the best game of all time? That was the challenge for *The Legend of Zelda: Majora's Mask*. It was the follow-up to *The Legend of Zelda: Ocarina of Time*, a game that many consider the best ever made. Finally, Nintendo figured out a way to top it. They would beef up the console itself. Along with the game, they introduced the Expansion Pak. Players could plug the Pak into the Nintendo 64 to double the console's RAM. The added memory allowed the game creators to make the game world larger and more detailed. Many gamers felt that *Majora's Mask* lived up to the previous game.

Engine: *Half-Life 2* (PC, 2004)
Half-Life 2 introduced Source, a new engine created by Valve Software. The engine featured advanced animation and lighting, creating stunning graphics. It also made it easy for gamers to play against one another online. The engine proved to be amazingly flexible. Although it was originally made for first-person shooter games, it was later used for practically every kind of game you can imagine. Almost ten years after it came out, it is still being used today.

Motion Control: *Wii Sports* (Nintendo Wii, 2006)
Wii Sports didn't feature amazing graphics or a stunning sound track. But it still became one of the most influential games of all time, all thanks to its innovative motion controls. The game came with Wii consoles, and it showed what the new system could do. Even people who didn't usually play games found *Wii Sports'* bowling, baseball, and tennis games crazy fun. Within a few years of the release of the Wii and *Wii Sports*, Nintendo's rivals Sony and Microsoft had both released their own motion controllers.

Atari 2600 Teardown
http://www.ifixit.com/Teardown/Atari-2600-Teardown/3541/1
The people at iFixit take apart all sorts of electronics to see what makes them tick. In this article, they take apart an Atari 2600—one of the earliest game consoles. If you want to check out what high-tech games looked like in the 1970s, take a look.

How Video Game Systems Work
http://www.howstuffworks.com/video-game.htm
Want more information about how game consoles work, including lots of technical details? Then this is the place for you.

Peckham, Matt. *Kinect Has a Thousand Eyes Viewed with Night Vision Goggles*
http://www.pcworld.com/article/209881/kinect_has_a_thousand_eyes _viewed_with_night_vision_goggles.html
You probably don't have night vision goggles just lying around your house. But don't sweat it—someone on the Internet does. They've taken pictures and video of a Kinect in action. Check out how Kinect uses thousands of infrared dots to capture players' motions.

Source Engine
http://source.valvesoftware.com/
Valve Software's website features tons of information on their influential Source game engine. Learn about how it handles physics, graphics, and audio, among tons of other stuff. Boatloads of cool screenshots let you see how these things look in actual games.

Super Scratch Programming Adventure!: Learn to Program by Making Cool Games. San Francisco: No Starch Press, 2012.
Want to learn more about writing your own programming code? Check out this handy book, and you'll be making your own games in no time.

White, Ron, and Timothy Downs. *How Computers Work.* Indianapolis: Que Publishing, 2008.
A video game console is basically a computer that does one thing: run video games. So if you're craving more information about how all the parts of computers work, check this out. Tons of great pictures and illustrations make the info fun and easy to read.

PHOTO ACKNOWLEDGMENTS

The images in this book are used with the permission of: © Yoshikazu Tsuno/AFP/Getty Images, p. 4; Evan Amos, pp. 5, 6, 8 (left), 14, 16, 19 (bottom), 22; © Mark Lennihan/ AP Images, p. 7; © successo/Shutterstock Images, p. 8 (right); © imagebroker.net/ SuperStock, p. 9; © RapidEye/iStockphoto, p. 10; © Tom Landers/The Boston Globe/ Getty Images, p. 11; © Fabrice Dimier/Bloomberg/Getty Images, p. 12; © NVIDIA Corporation/PRNewsFoto/AP Images, p. 13; © Tsugufumi Matsumoto/AP Images, p. 15; © Hemera/Thinkstock, pp. 17, 26; © iStockphoto/Thinkstock, p. 18; © 2K Games/ Firaxis Games/AP Images, p. 19 (top); © vilax/Shutterstock Images, p. 20; © Sony Computer Entertainment/AP Images, p. 21; © Richard Drew/AP Images, p. 23; © pressureUA/iStockphoto, p. 24; © Barone Firenze/Shutterstock Images, p. 25; © Casey Rodgers/AP Images for Xbox, p. 27; © Kevork Djansezian/AP Images, p. 28; Red Line Editorial, p. 29.

Front cover: © Junko Kimura/Getty Images.

Main body text set in Calvert MT Std Regular 11/16.
Typeface provided by Monotype Typography.

The Aftermath

Zed Books Titles on Conflict and Conflict Resolution

The hope that conflicts within societies might decrease markedly with the demise of the Cold War has been cruelly disappointed. Zed Books has published a number of titles which deal specifically with the diverse forms of modern conflict, their complex causes, and some of the ways in which we may realistically look forward to prevention, mediation and resolution.

Adedeji, A. (ed.), *Comprehending and Mastering African Conflicts: The Search for Sustainable Peace and Good Governance*

Allen, T. and J. Seaton (eds.), *The Media of Conflict: War Reporting and Representations of Ethnic Violence*

Cockburn, C., *The Space Between Us: Negotiating Gender and National Identities in Conflict*

Duffield, M., *Global Governance and the New Wars: The Merging of Development and Security*

Fisher, S. *et al.*, *Working with Conflict: Skills and Strategies for Action*

Jacobs, S., R. Jacobson and J. Marchbank (eds.), *States of Conflict: Gender, Violence and Resistance*

Koonings, K. and D. Kruijt (eds.), *Societies of Fear: The Legacy of Civil War, Violence and Terror in Latin America*

Macrae, J., *Aiding Recovery? The Crisis of Aid in Chronic Political Emergencies*

Moser, C. and F. Clark (eds.), *Victims, Perpetrators or Actors? Gender, Armed Conflict and Political Violence*

Pirotte, C., B. Husson and F. Grunewald (eds.), *Responding to Emergencies and Fostering Development - The Dilemmas of Humanitarian Aid*

Suliman, M. (ed.), *Ecology, Politics and Violent Conflict*

Turshen, M. and C. Twagiramariya (eds.), *What Women Do in Wartime: Gender and Conflict in Africa*

For full details of this list and Zed's other subject and general catalogues, please write to: The Marketing Department, Zed Books, 7 Cynthia Street, London N1 9JF, UK or email Sales@zedbooks.demon.co.uk

Visit our website at: http://www.zedbooks.demon.co.uk

The Aftermath

Women in Post-Conflict Transformation

EDITED BY

Sheila Meintjes, Anu Pillay and Meredeth Turshen

Zed Books
LONDON & NEW YORK

The Aftermath was first published in 2001 by
Zed Books Ltd, 7 Cynthia Street, London N1 9JF, UK and
Room 400, 175 Fifth Avenue, New York, NY 10010, USA

Cover design by Andrew Corbett
Designed and set in 10/13 pt Sabon
by Long House, Cumbria, UK
Printed and bound in Malaysia

Distributed in the USA exclusively by Palgrave, a division of
St Martin's Press, LLC,175 Fifth Avenue, New York, NY 10010

A catalogue record for this book
is available from the British Library ·

US CIP Data is available from the Library of Congress

ISBN   Hb 1 84277 066 7
         Pb 1 84277 067 5

Contents

Acknowledgements

Putting together a book that grew out of a series of multilingual conferences incurs many debts to the people and institutions who made the work both possible and such an enriching experience. We are very grateful to our funders – the Ford Foundation, the Royal Netherlands Embassy in South Africa, the International Development Research Center, the University of the Witwatersrand, and Rutgers University – for supporting our work and enabling us to meet each other. We thank the advisory boards in the United States and South Africa that guided us and the institutions that lent support: the West African Research Center in Dakar, the University of the Witwatersrand in Johannesburg, and Rutgers University in New Brunswick, NJ. We are grateful to the Committee on Health in Southern Africa (CHISA), to the organizing committees and conference planning staffs in Dakar and Johannesburg, as well as to the interpreters and translators who enabled us to communicate. The discussions that echo throughout this book were often inspiring, sometimes difficult, and in some cases painful.

We thank all of the participants for their generous contribution of time and energy, for sharing their experiences, exploring problems, and applying their knowledge to help answer the questions that were raised. The collective nature of this work is reflected in the alphabetical listing of our names. We are especially indebted to Jennifer Davis, who sat on the US Advisory Board, attended the conference in Johannesburg, and undertook the editing of the final manuscript. She joins us in thanking our authors for their cooperation and patience through many editorial changes. We thank Carol Barko for translating the chapters by Codou Bop and Myriam Merlet. We thank Louise Murray, our editor at Zed Books, for her encouragement of this project and the earlier book, *What Women Do in Wartime: Gender and Conflict in Africa*. We also thank Ousseina Alidou and Clotilde Twagiramariya for their contributions.

Sheila Meintjes, Anu Pillay and Meredeth Turshen

Notes on Contributors

Heike Becker completed her PhD thesis on the history of Namibian women's struggles during the nationalist liberation struggle and early postcolonial transformation at the University of Bremen (Germany) in 1993. From 1993 to 1997 she was a senior researcher with the Centre for Applied Social Sciences (CASS) at the University of Namibia. She has taught sociology, law, and communication studies at the University of Namibia and also worked as an independent researcher based in Windhoek. She is now a senior lecturer in the Department of Anthropology and Sociology of the University of the Western Cape, South Africa.

Codou Bop is a coordinator of GREFELS (Groupe de Recherche sur les Femmes et les Lois au Senegal). GREFELS is active in research on women and religion and leads protests and supports campaigns for women whose human rights are violated for reasons of religion. The Casamance chapter of GREFELS is a member of the Association of Senegalese Women for Peace in Casamance (where there has been a war for 18 years).

Malathi de Alwis is a senior research fellow at the International Centre for Ethnic Studies, Colombo, and at present is Visiting Assistant Professor of Anthropology at the New School for Social Research, New York. She received her PhD in Sociocultural Anthropology from the University of Chicago and is the co-editor, with Kumari Jayawardena, of *Embodied Violence: Communalising Women's Sexuality in South Asia* (Delhi: Kali for Women/London: Zed Books 1996). She has published many articles, which focus on feminist and peace movements in South Asia as well as on issues of gender, nationalism, militarism and humanitarianism, in various parts of the globe, in English and in translation. She is a founder member of the National Women's NGO Forum and the Women's Coalition for Peace, Sri Lanka, and a regular contributor to 'Cat's Eye', a feminist column on contemporary issues, in the *Island Newspaper*.

Sondra Hale is Adjunct Professor of Anthropology and Women's Studies at the University of California, Los Angeles (UCLA). Her research interests are gender politics, social movements and cultural studies; she has a special interest in North Africa and the Horn, with emphasis on Sudan, Eritrea and Egypt. She has carried out six years of fieldwork in Sudan and Egypt, and in 1994 and 1996 did research in Eritrea. Her book *Gender Politics in Sudan: Islamism, Socialism, and the State* was published in 1996. Articles by her have appeared in *Citizenship Studies* (1999); *Cairo Papers in Social Science* (1998); *South Asia Bulletin* (1994); *Reviews in Anthropology* (1998); *Feminist Economics* (1995); *Journal of African Studies* (1998); *The Muslim World* (1996); *Review of African Political Economy* (1992); and *Aljadid* (1999, 2000). Her essays have appeared in a number of collections – *Arab Women, Identity Politics and Women, Political Islam, Mixed Blessings, Frontline Feminisms,* and *Images of Enchantment.*

Okechukwu Ibeanu teaches political science at the University of Nigeria. He has published extensively on state-society relations, population displacement, and women in Nigeria. Among his recent publications are *Oil, Conflict and Security in Rural Nigeria: Issues in the Ogoni Crisis* (1997) and *Women Cooperatives and Power Redistribution in Rural Nigeria* (1996).

Rita Manchanda is programme executive in the South Asia Forum for Human Rights in Kathmandu, Nepal, and coordinator of its women and peace, and media and conflict programmes. Academically trained in International Relations at the Graduate School for International Studies, University of Geneva, she is a well-known journalist and writer on South Asian security and human rights issues. Among her many publications is an edited volume entitled *Women, War and Peace in South Asia: From Victimhood to Agency* (2001). She is the director of the research track of the November 2001 Colloquium on Women Waging Peace, a project of the Harvard University Kennedy School of Government.

Sheila Meintjes is Senior Lecturer in Political Studies and coordinator of the Gender Studies Programme in the Graduate School of the Humanities and Social Sciences, University of the Witwatersrand. She teaches African politics and feminist and gender studies and is engaged in research on women in electoral politics and gender-based violence. She is a member of the steering committee of the African Women's Anti-War Coalition, in charge of research.

Myriam Merlet is an economist who has been active in the Haitian women's movement since 1986 and has written many articles about the status of Haitian women. She is a member of ENFOFANM and responsible for its women's rights commission; she also coordinates the Women's Negotiating Committee (an umbrella for twenty-three groups) that works with the Haitian parliament and the executive branch of government on legal reform and programmes combating discrimination and violence against women.

Lepa Mladjenovic is a feminist councillor in the Autonomous Women's Center Against Sexual Violence, a women's NGO founded in 1993 during the war in Bosnia and Croatia. She is a co-founder and an activist of the Women in Black against War, a women's peace group in Belgrade founded to protest against the Serbian regime of Milosevic and its role in the wars in the former Yugoslavia. As a feminist lesbian activist in the lesbian rights group Labris, founded in 1995, she has written essays on lesbian existence. She has published articles on male violence against women, rape in war, feminist attitudes towards war, the role of women's solidarity in nation-states, the condition of lesbians in wartime, the role of feminist peace activists in wartime, and nationalism as a form of fascism.

Anu Pillay is a trained and experienced gender and development practitioner with a BA honours degree in Psychology and two years' MA training as a community psychologist. She completed a short course in participation and gender at the University of Wales Centre for Development Studies, Swansea. She is a co-founder and a board member of Masimanyane Women's Support Centre and board member of Tshwaranang Legal Advocacy to End Violence against Women. She consults on violence against women for the parliamentary women's caucus in South Africa, various NGOs, and Soul City Community Media. She was awarded the South Africa MaAfrika award for social contribution in 1996.

Tina Sideris has worked in the area of violence against women as an activist advocating against sexual violence and as a psychologist counselling women who survived violence in war and peace. She is a founding member of and still integrally involved in the Masisukumeni Women's Crisis Centre, which serves marginalised rural South African women.

Meredeth Turshen is Professor at the Edward J. Bloustein School of Planning and Public Policy, Rutgers University, where she has taught courses on gender, health, and human rights for more than ten years. She holds a DPhil. in comparative politics from the University of Sussex and specialises in public health policy. She has written three books, *The Political Ecology of Disease in Tanzania* (1984), *The Politics of Public Health* (1989), and *Privatizing Health Services in Africa* (1999), all published by Rutgers University Press, and edited four others, *Women and Health in Africa* (Africa World Press 1991), *Women's Lives and Public Policy: The International Experience* (Greenwood 1993), *What Women Do in Wartime: Gender and Conflict in Africa* (Zed Books 1998) and *African Women's Health* (Africa World Press 2000). She serves as chair of the Association of Concerned Africa Scholars, as treasurer of the Committee for Health in Southern Africa, and as contributing editor of the *Review of African Political Economy*.

Abbreviations

ANC African National Congress (South Africa)

CEDAW United Nations Convention on the Elimination of All Forms of Discrimination Against Women

ENFOFANM Organisation for the Defence of the Rights of Women (Haiti)

EPLF Eritrean People's Liberation Front

FIS Islamic Salvation Front (Algeria)

FRELIMO Mozambique Liberation Front

HAMADE Hagerawi Maheber Dekenstio Ertrawian – National Union of Women Eritreans (Tigrinya acronym)

IMF International Monetary Fund

JKLF Jammu and Kashmir Liberation Front (India)

JVP Janatha Vimukthi Peramuna (People's Liberation Front, Sri Lanka)

LRA Lord's Resistance Army (Uganda)

LTTE Liberation Tigers of Tamil Eelam (Sri Lanka)

MEP Mahajana Eksath Peramuna (Sri Lanka)

MK Umkhonto we Sizwe (the Spear of the Nation, South Africa)

MKM Khawateen Markaz (Kashmir)

MOSOP Movement for the Survival of Ogoni People

NATO North Atlantic Treaty Organisation

NGO nongovernmental organisation

NIF National Islamic Front (Sudan)

NMA Naga Mothers Association (India)

NRM National Resistance Movement (Uganda)

NSCN-IM Nationalist Socialist Council of Nagalim – Isak-Muivah faction (India)

NUEW National Union of Eritrean Women

NUEYS National Union of Eritrean Youth and Students

NYCOP National Youth Council of Ogoni People (Nigeria)

OMA Organisation of Angolan Women

OPFMD Organisation of Parents and Family Members of the Disappeared (Sri Lanka)

PFDJ People's Front for Democracy and Justice (Eritrea)

PLAN People's Liberation Army of Namibia

RENAMO Mozambican National Resistance

SADF South African Defence Force

SEWA Self-Employed Women's Association (India)

SIDA Swedish International Development Agency

SLFP Sri Lanka Freedom Party

SOFA Solidarité Fanm Ayisyen (Haitian Women's Solidarity)

SWAPO South West Africa People's Organisation

SWATF South West Africa Territorial Force

TRC Truth and Reconciliation Commission (South Africa)

UDM United Democratic Movement (South Africa)

UNDP United Nations Development Programme

UNHCR United Nations High Commissioner for Refugees

UNICEF United Nations Children's Fund

UNP United Nationalist Party (Sri Lanka)

UNRISD United Nations Research Institute for Social Development

UPF United People's Front (Nepal)

ZANU Zimbabwe African National Union

ZAPU Zimbabwe African People's Union

PART I

Overviews of the Themes

CHAPTER 1

There Is No Aftermath for Women

SHEILA MEINTJES, ANU PILLAY
and MEREDETH TURSHEN

We wondered what to call this book and how to refer to the period
that follows a ceasefire. The United Nations Research Institute for
Social Development (UNRISD) prefers the term 'war-torn societies' in
order to emphasise that 'the challenge of rebuilding societies after war
is much more complex and difficult than the task of putting an end to
fighting' (Stiefel 1999:5). The World Bank and several United Nations
specialised agencies have set up 'post-conflict' units; but some critics
argue persuasively, as does David Moore (2000:13), that

> the concept of 'post-conflict' [is] an excuse for the main development
> agencies and international powers to devote fewer resources to the amelio-
> ration of complex political emergencies in the third world and to allow
> structural adjustment policies to reign as usual, instead of the supposed
> dependency inducing tendencies of welfarist humanitarian assistance. To
> label war as peace is not only Orwellian, but also it justifies implementing
> shock therapy to create the market cure for war.

Our problem over the title was compounded by what we learned at
the workshop and conference on which this book is based. At the
workshop on 'West African Women in the Aftermath of War', held in
Dakar, Senegal, in December 1998, at the conference on 'The Aftermath: Women in Post-war Reconstruction', held in Johannesburg,
South Africa, 20–22 July 1999, and at the meeting of the African
Women's Anti-War Coalition that followed on 23 July 1999, we
learned that there is no aftermath for women (Meintjes 2000; Pillay
2000; Turshen 1999; Turshen and Alidou 2000). One participant
asked, 'How clear are the boundaries of these kinds of wars when

there's so much misery, violence and exploitation after the war?' (Malathi de Alwis, conference participant). Evidence confirms that the gender violence women experience in wartime increases when the fighting dies down (Goldblatt and Meintjes 1998; Ibeanu, this volume); and clearly there is no one aftermath because the scenarios following war are as various as the conflicts themselves (Turshen, this volume). Even within a single country, the aftermath of one war, for example the liberation struggle in Algeria, was different from that of another war, for example the Algerian civil conflict of the 1990s. Also, we wanted a title that would reflect what we have come to believe: the post-war period is too late for women to transform patri-archal gender relations.

One of our objectives in organising the conference on the after-math, which gathered together one hundred activist and academic participants from Africa, Asia, Europe, North America and the Caribbean and from national and international governmental and nongovernmental organisations, was to provide a new theoretical understanding of women's experiences in war-torn societies. Our point of departure was dissatisfaction with many of the recon-struction programmes, which are based on one of two approaches. Judging by the literature, agencies base their assistance on an assess-ment of either human needs or human rights. The needs-based approach to post-war socio-economic rehabilitation prioritises social and material needs, emphasising humanitarian assistance. The rights-based approach to post-war political reconstruction gives priority to political reorganisation – to human rights, justice and equality, elections, pluralism and participation – often defining human rights in the narrow sense of civil and political liberties to the neglect of economic and social rights. During the transition from war to peace, or from military dictatorship to democracy, the rhetoric of equality and rights tends to mask the reconstruction of patriarchal power, despite recent emphasis on women's human rights.

Although both rights and needs are important aspects of creating an environment for post-war reconstruction, neither is adequate, either alone or in combination, for the task of enabling women to realise substantive advancement. Neither approach recognises the real need women feel for social transformation rather than the recon-struction of the past. Many women desire to use the opportunities that arise in periods of conflict to remove traditional gender restrictions permanently (Becker, this volume). For them, as for us, true transformation encompasses a political economy open to women in ways that recognise their social and productive roles and contributions, as well as their desires as sexual beings. Equity and social justice are two aspects of this transformation, but it would be incomplete without recognising the particularity of women's sexuality and the way society has, in the past, shaped sexual mores to determine women's secondary status in civil society. Substantive equality means a fundamental shift towards the provision of specific rights related to women's gender roles, for example reproductive health rights, rights to further education and affirmative action.

Breaking Down the Category 'Women'

The first problem we confronted in the conferences was that of our identities: who were we and whom did we represent? No woman lives in the single dimension of her sex; we cannot assume that because we are all women we will make common cause. Gender is a social construction and to specify one's gender automatically entails questions about relations of race, class and political power, whilst war adds the dimensions of conquered and victor. Conference participants sidestepped this predicament and in their discussions concentrated on a narrower issue; they made clear by their example and by their reports that the women who live through war and conflict do not fall into a single group. Not only their experiences differ but also their connections to the conflict, and these experiences and connections determine their position in the aftermath (Bop, this volume).

Some women take up arms or enter soldiery behind the lines; their experience in the aftermath is linked to their training for war, the conditions of demobilisation, and the availability of services, especially for the disabled. Other women join organisations and take up new roles as mobilisers (for war or for peace) in their communities. Ogoni women were actively engaged in the struggle for greater local control of oil revenues and for the clean-up of pollution; as a result the Nigerian state targeted them specifically for violent reprisals (Ibeanu, this volume). Rita Manchanda (this volume) points to the ambivalence that feminists and peace activists display towards women militants and fighters; they tend to see them as used by patriarchal nationalist projects rather than as acting on their own. So some women undermine the new identity of others in the aftermath. Sondra Hale (this volume) points out that although Eritrean women fighters were indeed icons of liberated women, the pressure on former fighters to revert to traditional norms at the end of the war threatened to undo many of their gains.

The majority of women do not take up arms, and perhaps many 'do not identify with the objectives of the war, or feel alienated from the mechanisms of war, its apparent irrationality and its destructive consequences' (Sorenson 1998:11). These women also do not form an undifferentiated category. Women with access to wealth are able to leave when their safety is threatened; they may return after the war, relatively unscathed. Most women are too poor to emigrate; when they stay on alone, they assume tasks formerly assigned to men. Those whose men return will fare differently in the aftermath from those widowed by the war. Some women remain at home wishing for an early end to the conflict; afterwards they may want to return to what they perceive as the stability of pre-war arrangements. In some urban areas women may be relatively safe and have access to vital information and resources in wartime; for them the end of fighting will be different from the experience of women who found themselves in the cross-fire and had to hide or flee. In remote rural areas, some women were abandoned by their husbands, preyed upon by soldiers and rebels, or cut off from intelligence and food markets. In the aftermath they are the most deprived and destitute of all. Women who ran away to escape fighting and became internally displaced persons may have been sexually assaulted in the camps or abducted by rebels. This last happened to women and girls in Gulu who were kidnapped by Joseph Kony's Lord's Resistance Army in northern Uganda. The internally displaced do not have the benefit of refugee status given to those who cross international borders and come under the jurisdiction of the United Nations High Commission for Refugees (UNHCR). Repatriation is also not a uniform experience. In Rwanda the reception of women identified with the vanquished Hutu was not the same as that reserved for Tutsi returnees.

This list is not comprehensive and of course the duration of the war and the level of weapons technology employed are two more factors that condition women's experience of conflict and the aftermath. We hope this review indicates the great diversity of women in war-torn societies and shows how limiting the response of international agencies is when survivors are lumped together in one category.

Women's Wartime Gains and Potential for Post-war Transformation

Across these diverse groups of women in varied situations we noticed a common feature. Whereas most women experience loss in war, some unexpectedly make gains (Bop, this volume). It is a paradox that war offers opportunities for women to transform their lives in terms of their image of themselves, their behaviour towards men and towards their elders, and their ability to live independently. Again and again, we felt constrained to acknowledge the pain and suffering that women encounter:

> Women left behind whatever they had and ran for security. Sometimes they left their children behind or threw them into the river because they couldn't cope anymore. These women didn't have a wrap or blanket to cover their children. So in Angola we know only the losses of assets and lives. Still today there are women who have nothing to eat – they look for food in rubbish bins. (Faustina Naivele Chiungue, conference participant)

With some fear that our audience might think we were disparaging women's undeniably painful wartime losses, we decided to examine what women gain.

According to Manchanda (this volume), writing about the many conflicts raging across South Asia, 'conflict opens up intended and unintended spaces for empowering women, effecting structural social transformations and producing new social, economic and political realities that redefine gender and caste hierarchies'. She cites the emergence of Naga women as agents for peace in the fifty-year nationalist struggle in India's northeast, and she gives the examples of unarmed Naga women daring to protest against military rampages, entering into negotiations with the army to minimise the impact of violence, and managing community survival. Clearly women's wartime experiences, so frequently portrayed in terms of victimisation, offer the potential for social transformation. Equally clearly, transformation is not just about conditions or structures, but also about internal processes of consciousness, of creating words and language that will provide women with a sense of their own agency (Mladjenovic, this volume). In the wake of civil conflict, most people seem to crave stability. They are exhausted, yet face multiple tasks of rebuilding that demand tremendous energy. If war-torn societies are to bring about renewal and achieve a successful transition to peace, they must generate the necessary resources or become dependent on international aid. Women are key resources in the process of rebuilding society (Merlet, this volume). They have already shown their creative abilities in assuring their families' survival during wartime. Peace-builders are an important group because they give examples of how the seeds of transformation can grow. The question is, how can these grassroots groups be institutionalised to become forces for change in the aftermath? If they are institutionalised, are the terms of that process traditional or are they progressive and transformative?

Belief in the transformative potential of women's experiences is linked to recognition of both the historical specificity of wars, which differ from one country to another, and the particularities of many groups of women within war-torn societies. What kinds of survival strategies do women adopt when men become the targets of war and go into hiding or when men leave home to fight? Documenting what women do to survive in wartime is one way to make women's potential visible (Turshen and Twagiramariya 1998).

The Failure to Consolidate Wartime Gains

Why don't women realise their potential and sustain wartime gains in peacetime? Why and how is transformation rolled back? Women say they feel they are different during periods of conflict and that they act differently, but that society does not allow them to live differently in periods of reconstruction. Why? The historical record confirms that societies neither defend the spaces women create during struggle nor acknowledge the ingenious ways in which women bear new and additional responsibilities. As Manchanda (this volume) notes, women's activism in managing survival and community-level agency is predictably devalued as accidental activism and marginalised post-conflict, as politics become more structured and hierarchical.

Martina Belic, an invited speaker at the Johannesburg conference, said we are wrong to assume that the changes in women's wartime roles are dramatic. In reality – at least in the experience of the conflicts in former Yugoslavia – women were still fulfilling their usual caretaking roles, for the men who were fighting and for their families, as well as for other women who were victims of violence. Manchanda (this volume) has another interpretation: she believes the shifts in gender roles brought about by the upheaval attendant on conflict are dramatic, but that 'the impulse to women's social transformation and autonomy is circumscribed by the nationalist project, which constructs women as purveyors of the community's accepted and acceptable cultural identity'. She concludes that the return to peace is invariably conceptualised as a return to the gender status quo, irrespective of the nontraditional roles assumed by women during conflict. Malathi de Alwis (this volume) discusses yet another dimension of this issue: how Sri Lankan women use their roles as mothers to stage public protests and in so doing overturn simple generalisations about mothers being victimised or idealised.

The reasons women regress in the aftermath are various. It seems likely that many do not consciously internalise or conceptualise the changes in their roles; without a conscious translation, there can be no concerted effort to defend women's opportunities and gains in peacetime. If women do not transform their sense of themselves during conflict, they cannot defend themselves when, in the wake of war, men reassert their claims. Sometimes, even when women recognise changes in themselves, their perception is negative. One explanation of this negativity emerged at the International Tribunal on War Crimes Against Women held in Tokyo in December 2000, where it became clear that women blocked from testifying about their experience, women who were silenced and censored, could not experience long-term healing. One Chinese woman collapsed when she was prevented from showing her wounds to the audience at the tribunal. A Burundian woman collapsed when she described how her family had rejected her. The refusal to allow a trauma counsellor to help this woman uncover the moment of being overwhelmed amounted to a double silencing. The result was an unsatisfactory closure, the significance of which was a reassertion of shame and the idea that the telling was in itself unacceptable. At the same tribunal, the Dutch women who were held in Japanese concentration camps described how they had an opportunity to recount their experiences immediately after the Second World War. The Dutch people did not see them as transgressors and did not turn their stories into shameful projections that transmuted sexual torture into an attack on the honour of their menfolk. Rather, they were heroic survivors, praised, honoured, pitied, given sympathy and empathy. The reparations paid by the Japanese in compensation gave them recognition that was vital to their healing.

One variable at the heart of the failure to consolidate wartime gains is community. The collective strength of women and its opposite, isolation, whether geographic isolation or the lack of a framework for concerted action, was a dominant theme in our discussions. Refugee camps give some women an opportunity to work together and learn leadership skills, but this community may be lost and the momentum dissipated when women are repatriated and dispersed. Fighting together as soldiers also offers women camaraderie, which may be lost in demobilisation when fighters are dispersed. Women who mobilised civil society for national liberation – in Eritrea, in Mozambique's war against the Portuguese, in South Africa against apartheid, in Algeria against the French, to name a few liberation struggles – found large communities, sometimes extending beyond national borders, but activists found they could not sustain these support networks after the victory. Women who work for peace at the grassroots level, often at the peak of atrocities and instability, create a local sense of community, but they rarely reach national prominence. 'Women's activities in community or church groups ... are often labelled "volunteer", "charitable", or "social" even though they have a political impact' (Sorenson 1998:10).

For each group of women the changes experienced in wartime open the possibility of transformation. The question to ask in each context is: how is the seed of transformation planted, what causes it to grow or to lose its capacity to grow? We came to the view that the reconstruction phase is too late for women to assert themselves. The real opportunity for planting the seeds for transformation is during wartime, in conditions of conflict. This is why the African Women's Anti-War Coalition, the group that formed spontaneously during the

Dakar workshop and met after the Johannesburg conference, is so important: its strategy is to build upon and harness the transformative experiences of wartime, before reconstruction plans are fixed (Pillay 2000). The recognition of this timing makes strategically vital the reconception of conflicts and transitions as opportunities for gains to be made. During the upheavals of war women begin to move into new power relations; afterwards they risk becoming stuck and concentrating on their losses.

The Political Economy of Violence against Women

Violence is another of the variables that determine whether women will be able to consolidate wartime gains. Participants at both conferences spent a good deal of time analysing the nature of violence before, during and after war (Pillay, this volume). Some women believe that there is a continuum of violence in these three periods; others see wartime violence as a distinctly different phenomenon (Sideris, this volume, Chapter 9). Here we wish to draw attention to a subtext that runs through the three periods – the relation of violence against women to sexual control and the allocation of resources.

Many African and Asian societies distribute resources to women on the basis of women's purported 'virtue': 'good girls' – unmarried virgins, faithful wives, and celibate widows – qualify, whereas 'bad girls' – promiscuous women and women who were raped – don't. We interpret virtue in this context as a denial of women's sexuality. Underlying this denial is the rejection of women's autonomy. We say this because most women do not have access to resources in their own right; their fathers, husbands and sons control their access, and women's endowment depends on their relations with these men.

Wartime conditions – the absence of men, the penury of resources, and the violence against women – turn many good girls into bad girls. During war, women are caught up in the kinds of struggles over large and small assets that have dominated many of the recent African conflicts; in this strife the politically and militarily strong try to wrest assets from the weak. Rape figures importantly in the strategy of asset stripping by displacing populations from contested lands (Turshen 2000). Rapists strip women not only of their economic assets (food, clothing, jewellery, money and household furnishings) but also of their political assets, which are their virtue and their reputation. When women admit to rape by the 'enemy', they lose the respect and protection of their family and community. Yasmin Sooka, a human rights lawyer serving on the South African Truth and Reconciliation Commission and an invited speaker on the opening day of the Johannesburg conference, said it was 'imperative to do more work to deconstruct rape and sexual assault during times of conflict'. She spoke about 'honour' and noted that men regard the violation of women as a slight upon men's honour. Women who admit to having been raped besmirch the honour of their men. Many communities reject these women and throw them out; in this sense women have lost their lives and many feel they might as well be dead. Indeed, men often kill women who return with children born of rape, and women's suicide rates are high.

Another analysis sees this talk about honour as men's justification for killing or excluding women who were raped but not as an explanation of their behaviour in wartime when they are under military orders. In Marxist terms, honour is a superstructural explanation that remains in the realm of culture. At the base is what men stand to gain by systematic rape and the act of rejecting rape survivors' re-entry into the community. There is an interesting paradox not explained by the honour argument: on the one hand, communities will fight to protect their women, and families see rape as so awful that only the death of the rape victim can restore the family's honour. But on the other hand, rape was invisible in national and international courts and the law afforded little legal redress for this crime until very recently. What makes it possible to explain this widely observed double-faced attitude to rape is the recognition that patriarchal societies regard women as property and that the value of this property resides in women's productive and reproductive labour.

Many changes take place during war but they rarely have a lasting effect on the sexual division of labour. Some women return from war determined to maintain their newfound freedoms. They meet with a backlash against their attempts to redefine their rights. Violence intensifies because women have changed and are demanding auton-omy. Gender and generational conflicts over how to reorganise liveli-hoods in war-torn societies emerge and break women's resistance. In the aftermath, men use violence against women and women's fear of violence to reinforce their hold on women; they compel women to comply because they need to re-establish or preserve control over wealth and resources and, above all, over women's productive and reproductive labour. This control is the crux of the struggle over women's claims to equality and autonomy. Realizing that their access to resources depends on society's conviction that they are virtuous, women succumb to denying or leaving behind their wartime gains. The power to decide that women conform to sexual norms and thus deserve access to resources may reside in chiefs and clan heads, in such family members as husbands, mothers-in-law, and older brothers, or even in unrelated gangs of women (as happened in Europe after the Second World War when older women punished girls for having sexual relations with enemy soldiers).

The conservative backlash that takes place after war has its roots in the older generation's attempt to reassert control and re-establish 'traditions'. In material terms, tradition encodes the ways in which people organise their social existence, including production and reproduction. For the older generation, which depends on the young for survival in old age, it is imperative to re-establish the customary flow of wealth from young to old that obtained before the war. In the context of re-establishing livelihood, the older generation finds it particularly important to control young women. Their sexist view of women as commodities persists. Indeed, their view of sexuality is the first tradition they want to reconstruct, and they may use violence to do so.

Myths about Identity, Problems of Solidarity and Reconciliation

War brings many changes in the social construction of womanhood and manhood (Sideris, this volume, Chapter 4). In reaction to the fearsome dangers of battle and the unrelieved machismo of military life, men romanticise the mothers and wives they left at home; they construct stereotypes of femininity bearing little or no relation to the masculine roles that circumstances have forced on women. The clash between reality and the idealised vision of womanhood may be bitter in the aftermath, especially if women like and want to retain their new identities and men want to preserve the pre-war prerogatives of domination. Men may manipulate another, parallel, romanticisation – that of the male war hero – and use it to burden women with guilt; however hard women's lives were during the war, the myth maintains that there's no comparison with the hardships of battle. If a wife's subordination is a sign of respect for her husband's manhood, and if defeat has challenged that manhood, then men will reject empowered women and try to bury women's gains along with the dead.

The backlash against women's wartime identities is documented, yet we don't fully understand why gender roles revert in the aftermath. Why, for example, do women experience men as so powerful that they can't object to forced abortion or the abandonment of babies conceived in rape? Are men as transformed by wartime experiences as women are? Not all wars are about the kind of change that national wars of liberation propose, and not all national wars of liberation advocated the liberation of women (Bop, this volume). And in the aftermath of liberation wars, there is no systematic process of deconstructing racism or patriarchy – not even in South Africa (Meintjes, this volume). Most wars are about greed and do not require men to transform their relations with women. So the challenge for us is to deconstruct gender relations.

Men fighting wars that problematise identity may burden women with the cultural symbols of the religion/nation/ethnic group their leaders say is under attack, even as women are reaching out to build solidarity and construct peace across those very lines (Mladjenovic, this volume). In the aftermath, men returning with hatred for the 'enemy' may clash with women who have gained a new understanding of their community and a wish for reconciliation.

Whether men's fantasies or women's realities prevail depends on who controls the myths and the making of identities; the institutions that govern social and behavioural norms – the religious institutions, the schools, the different levels of the state – do not change. Who prevails also depends on what purposes the myths serve. Some are used to exclude categories of people from the material benefits of the new political dispensation. Reconstruction plans are usually blind to gender issues: men don't see the need for gender transformation and women are excluded from planning.

Power and Authority in the Aftermath

What is the role of religious institutions in the process of reconstruction? Does the way religious leaders treated women before and during the war have an impact on women's ability to transform their status in the aftermath? In Rwanda, a country dominated by the Roman Catholic Church, abortion remains illegal despite the desperation of many women who became pregnant after rape. In South Africa, the Dutch Reformed Church, which long found legitimating arguments for apartheid in the Bible, apologised to the Truth and Reconciliation Commission for its racial politics but continues to uphold its sexist views on women. In Algeria, under pressure from Islamic religious leaders, the government adopted laws based on the *sharia* to control women, over the vociferous objections of women who fought in the war for independence.

Religion is just one of the institutions that determine whether the old ways will be consolidated or new ideas will be diffused in the aftermath. Whether a conservative backlash develops depends in part on who is in control at the local level. Another determining institution is that of chieftainship. In parts of Mozambique, traditional chiefs are back in office and have the power and authority to settle disputes; they have legal power as well as control of the cultural symbols (Harrison 1996). They can define transgressive behaviour and decide who may obtain resources, such as land and water, as well as who has rights and who should be excluded from the community. Women depend upon the good will of chiefs, who have the power to define them as virtuous or undeserving.

The role of international agencies may be more significant than that of governments, especially if war has weakened the state to the point of total dependence on foreign aid. The impact of international intervention on women is felt at every level. Agencies that run refugee camps and insist on dispersing repatriated populations to their pre-war areas of origin may unwittingly undermine some of the gains women made in the camps. By creating a sense of community, women often established new identities and relationships in the camps and came to understand that women have human rights. Such new ideas are important in changing relations between women and men. Male refugees asked, why should women be protected in the camps since men beat up women before the war and would continue to do so afterwards? Some refugee camps provided an opportunity for men to learn different normative behaviours, a new vision easily lost if there are no social controls or incentives to sustain the changes in peacetime. The experience of transformation in the camps is a collective one, and many women believe that by remaining together they have a better chance of maintaining and building on their gains. At the Dakar conference in December 1998, women from Sierra Leone and Liberia demanded that they be allowed to stay in the new environments they had created. They understood that if they separated they risked facing the post-war backlash alone, and they feared the conservatism that is the hallmark of women's post-war experience.

Life in refugee camps can provide a model for women's leadership in the aftermath because many women become agents of change in the camps. To disperse them is to lose the power of transformation. Whilst we conceive of refugees as agents of change, it is important not to romanticise the experience. Not all camps provide opportunities for innovation. If women organised and created their own institutions in the Polisario camps, they were firmly under men's control in the Rwandan camps. How long people spend in camps and the attitudes of the host country and population toward refugees are also factors in whether the camp experience is positive or negative.

Outside forces are also important in establishing new rules for employment, trade, and property relations, all of which war destabilises. Of the three, property relations may be of greatest immediate importance to women because few hold deeds, and in many customary regimes, land use rights revert to a husband's family after his death. Widows are vulnerable to eviction, and in several countries women have organised for legal reforms to ensure their entitlements. But when external forces seize economic power from traditional authorities in the reconstruction of war-torn societies, the reforms they recommend may work against women. In the eyes of the World Bank (1998), 'post-conflict' African nations present international financial institutions with opportunities to create a 'market-friendly' environment; their primary advice is to universalise property rights. Preliminary data on the privatisation of land suggest that it seriously disadvantages women, who lose access to this prime agricultural resource (Gray and Kevane 1999; Turşhen 2001).

War also sweeps aside democratic mechanisms of accountability; governments at war give way to secrecy and use the national emergency as an excuse to suspend civil rights. Corruption follows this path, and the workings of government become less and less transparent to women because they so rarely hold office. Research is needed to establish whether a culture of corruption is especially liable to thrive where governments grant amnesty for war crimes. What is the relation between amnesty and impunity for violence, particularly violence against women?

Our Vision of a Transformed Society

Do women have a vision of the society they wish to live in after war and armed conflict? Many people say that since 1989 and the crisis of socialism, women and men have no ideal to strive for and the little vision that exists is contested. Societies focus in the aftermath on finding the truth about atrocities and on the reconciliation process; this diverts women from looking at the advances they made during war and distracts them from creating new blueprints. Because public rewards go to those who died, women's advances – the survival strategies that kept families alive and communities together – are erased from the historical record. In 1945, post-war European and American ideology emphasised motherhood and stressed the need for women to return to their domestic roles as wives and mothers. There were no medals or monuments to women who replaced men in the workforce during the Second World War, and no special acknowledgement of women partisans who fought in resistance movements.

Our vision is not equality with men but the full equity that would pertain in the context of new gender relations. What we want goes beyond equality to the transformation of social relations. We believe that women must acquire fair access to resources in their own right, and that the struggle in the reconstruction period is precisely over the terms of women's entitlements. Our desire is to describe the conditions that favour social transformation and to outline our vision of a society that respects women's autonomy and bodily integrity.

The studies presented in the second part of this book document women's struggles for transformed social relations in various post-conflict situations, in Haiti, the Balkans, Asia, and several African conflict zones. The common post-war pattern the world over has been the re-creation of patriarchal dominance in new forms, whereas these chapters corroborate women's belief in the necessity of challenging the old order and creating new democratic institutions. The authors document and analyse women's survival strategies and post-war activities, enabling us to identify the seeds of transformation and showing us the important role of solidarity with women in conflict zones. In the aftermath it becomes incumbent upon us all to develop conscious strategies that help women build on their activities and find ways of incorporating new gender relations in democratic societies.

CHAPTER 2

Women in Conflicts,
Their Gains and Their Losses

CODOU BOP

Africa is the continent most ravaged by wars in our time. Some wars have been fought over long periods, lasting, as in the case of Sudan, more than forty years. The bright lights of the media fall on a few, but many remain unknown and neglected. Wars of the poor, they use cheap but deadly arms such as land mines and light weapons, and their victims are counted in tens of millions.

Wars are the subject of numerous studies and conferences; their causes and their effects on regional and local economies and on populations are well known. Yet although the media repeatedly provide information that describes the tough conditions women endure to survive, particularly in refugee camps and on the roads of exile, they constantly ignore the actions women take as principal actors. The image conveyed, which endures in the onlooker's memory, is that of women as losers and victims. Such an image has serious consequences for a true awareness of the differential impact of conflicts on women and men and impedes the recognition of endogenous solutions that women propose.

Such a view explains the feeble actions taken to diminish the consequences of war for women, actions most often left to humanitarian aid organisations. The result is a continual marginalising of women, whose contribution researchers still largely ignore and whose influence official policies do not recognise.

It is widely accepted that women lose in wars, but important questions remain in need of answers. Are women always losers, and are they so collectively? Because they do not comprise a homogeneous group, collectively deprived of power, do those women who belong to ruling classes or ruling ethnic groups make gains? In what circumstances can women achieve gains, and what are the nature and the duration of their gains?

Although it is true that women are almost never the initiators of conflicts, are never the leaders of conflicts, and are rarely at the negotiation table, they have participated in all wars as actors. Thanks to the active role they have played in combat, either by inciting men to fight or, more frequently, by undertaking multiple tasks to support war, they have been able to register gains.

Social and Political Gains

The 1960s saw the majority of African nations peacefully attain independence. Others, such as the former Portuguese colonies (Angola, Cape Verde, Guinea-Bissau and Mozambique) and the countries under apartheid and white minority rule (Namibia, South Africa and Zimbabwe) waged long wars of independence, as did the settler colonies of Algeria and Kenya. Clearly there are great ideological, political and social differences between the wars of independence and the factional conflicts tearing Africa apart now. There is also a difference in the kind of society to be created, the nature of the commitment of combatants and the place given to women.

In colonised countries, people under the yoke of oppression developed a political consciousness that encouraged the most committed among them to organise in order to drive the coloniser out. Women, full-fledged members of society, were affected by the same processes of awareness. Some became involved in the organisations created, and, later, in the armed struggle for national liberation. Very few descriptions of the specific conditions of women soldiers are available. We know, however, that the majority of women participating in or supporting war played a secondary role, at the most an extension of their household work: providing fighters with fresh food, preparing meals and carrying supplies overland. But a relatively significant number of women became fighters, and among them, some, by virtue of their personality or their abilities, came to occupy important positions in the military hierarchy. In Africa, as everywhere in the world, the army, whether or not it is the liberation army, symbolises force and power. To become part of it means that one belongs to a dominant group. The sense of power that goes with belonging to a dominant group has led women fighters to transform the way they perceive themselves. It has contributed to changing their traditional identity as wives and mothers to that of fighters and liberators of their country. Yet acceptance of this new identity, whether and how long it lasts after peace returns, and its place during the process of national reconstruction, all represent particularly difficult challenges for women and for society to handle in the post-conflict period.

As struggles for social and economic liberation, the wars of independence brought at least the theoretical promise of change in the power relations between classes and the sexes. In Africa, most of the leaders of political parties in the avant-garde of independence wars drew to some extent upon Marxist-Leninist ideology with its credo of ending social inequality. In the parties of the avant-garde, as in the ranks of the armies of liberation, education and consciousness-raising about the inequalities of class and sex were part of the theoretical training of militants and combatants. The parties asked people to struggle against inequalities of class and sex in their daily practice. Just as training in the handling of weapons, in ideology and in theories of war were common practices, the avant-garde also encouraged sharing of household tasks, with the goal of introducing changes in the perception of roles and social status. Drawing on developments during the war in Uganda, Joan Kakwenzire confirms the possibility offered by the wars of liberation, of creating and accepting new roles for women and men. She notes that

> during the 30 years the war lasted, some women took an active part in the conflict either as combatants or in carrying out reconnaissance missions (espionage, logistical support). Furthermore, the roles of women in combat situations and in the home have dramatically changed and have had an impact on the relation between men and women. The multiple roles that women have taken on have engendered a new race of women. They have realised the potential of their own strength and this awareness has led some of them toward a more favourable socio-economic position. (Kakwenzire 1999)

Having opened the doors to public space – and hence to political space – to the committed, war first encouraged the emergence of citizen consciousness among a relatively large group of women and later strengthened their will to participate in decision making. In fact, wherever women have fought, arms in hand, with the support of men at their side, they have sought (clearly with unequal results) to promote the active participation of women in the political life of the country. In the initial years of independence, the leaders accepted a greater presence of women in new institutions and the creation of resources aimed at improving their living conditions. For example, Chungue notes that in Angola

> there is a percentage of women (although it does not satisfy us) in government. Women are asked for their opinion at important meetings. After independence, the women of Angola began to acquire skills they had previously not had and took positions they could not have held before. The OMA [Organisation of Angolan Women], which is the first organisation of women in the country, worked to influence the government in order to prove that women are capable of taking charge of important government functions. That took time but subsequently the government began to give work to women. (Faustina Naivele Chungue, conference participant)[1]

Becker notes the involvement of women in Namibian national affairs; she emphasises the changes occurring in the rural areas. According to Becker, Namibian women are making important advances in decision-making organs and in the traditional hierarchy in the rural areas of Owambo, in northern Namibia, which was an important centre in the war. In her view, the recent changes in women's participation in the structures of traditional authority are inextricably intertwined with the political changes that Namibia has experienced since the end of South African colonialism and the war. A new way of thinking about types of decision and how they are made has emerged in rural milieus since independence, particularly in Owambo, which widely consults on developments in the policy of the central government (Becker, this volume).

Finally, in societies where traditional religion, in which women play an important role, remains vital (for example, in Casamance in southern Senegal), women have strengthened their control as keepers of the fetishes believed to assure the protection of combatants. In this regard, the case of Alice Lakwena, a Ugandan priestess who was able to mobilise partisans and create an army that waged war against the regular army of Uganda for several years before she withdrew, is particularly interesting (Behrend 1991).

Examining other types of wars, notably wars between factions or ethnic wars, we see that gains obtained by women are less important, and that women are primarily in the position of victims rather than active subjects. Less involved than combatants, they focus their actions on their family or their clan. We have been able to see the emergence and strengthening of a certain female leadership within their midst, however, extending even to the national and regional levels.

The movement of populations, the scattering of families and the expansion of families headed by women have created situations where women had either to participate in decision making or to make decisions themselves. At the local level, women have sought to strengthen solidarity among themselves. Associations bringing together women of varied ethnic groups, enemies only yesterday, have come into being; similarly, women have formed prayer groups in drop-in centres. In these associations the women jointly undertake income-producing work, or seek to heal the physical, moral and psychological wounds of war.

At the national level, women have developed survival strategies and reconstruction plans for communities destroyed by war. They have engaged in lobbying belligerents to lay down their arms, and they organise consciousness-raising campaigns to help women become more fully integrated into the decision-making structures of the peace process in which they invest more and more energy. In face of the painful abuse of which they are victims, particularly the assaults on their bodily integrity, women have learned to unite, to organise in order to bring about a collective solution to their problems, and to ask for assistance or to request protection of their rights by appealing to international authorities. They have understood the importance of awareness and of the support that other women and volunteers outside their national territory can bring. Many have learned how to use the media and the internet to make their problems widely known and to exert pressure on governments or regional and international institutions. They have learned how to organise important campaigns, at the national, regional and international levels, to make demands for such goals as: an end to the use of land mines, the enforcement of treaties, an end to sexual violence, and recognition of specific acts of violence against women. The successes achieved are as yet limited, but women have obtained recognition of their right to bodily integrity and the judgement by the International Criminal Tribunal on Rwanda that crimes committed against women are crimes against humanity.

Economic Gains

No one contests the economic basis of most of the wars now taking place on the African continent. The conflicts offer countless opportunities to get rich to arms vendors, to the suppliers of troops, to the fighters themselves, and to their leaders. The role of diamonds and precious metals in conflicts in Liberia, Sierra Leone and the Democratic Republic of the Congo, and that of oil in Congo (Brazzaville) and in Angola, is evident. In this connection it appears that certain long and deadly civil wars fail to become the subject of news coverage, or of peace negotiations, precisely because the countries concerned have no oil or mineral wealth and their strategic position is not considered interesting by the great powers, in particular the United States.

Generally one of the belligerent groups controls the economic fortunes generated by war. It is easier for women to have access to the riches if they themselves belong to these groups. But since the principle of unequal access to resources also operates in wartime, women's level of wealth remains far below that of men. Moreover women never control the production or marketing of oil and minerals. Yet some women know very well how to seize the opportunities at hand in order to make significant economic gains during conflict. Analysing cases of women involved in the 1998 civil war in Congo (Brazzaville), Martine Galloy observes:

> the responsibility of reprovisioning the militia in power with fresh food was handed down to a woman on the select list. This operation, although it was an extension of domestic tasks, gave her access to the network that distributed payments of fees, permitting her to accumulate a real goldmine. On their end, the mothers and families of the militiamen profited from the war booty their sons reaped from the systematic pillage in force. (Galloy 2000)

But women were not content with these opportunities deriving from their traditional role. Some became famous for smuggling on a small scale, including contraband arms and precious stones. They also sold illegal drugs for their own consumption or for the needs of the camp they supported in the war. In Senegal, there have been many reported arrests of women partisans of the Movement of Democratic Forces of Casamance who agreed to sell cannabis in order to fund the rebellion.

As in the realm of politics, women have stepped out of their traditional roles to meet the economic demands of war. This movement between sex roles helped some women in sectors previously dominated by men and contributed to mitigating the prejudices preventing their advancement in economic and social spheres. In this regard, we have the example of changes in European countries during the Second World War, where women replaced men in factories and on farms, keeping their countries going by virtue of their productive work. In Niger, following the Tuareg rebellion, women had to face repression and displacement outside their traditional territory, as well as hunger and deprivation. According to Zara Mahamane (1999):

> They learned to unite and organise, to take initiatives by working together in NGOs (nongovernmental organizations) in cooperative partnerships for development. They devoted themselves to commercial ventures, to the hotel business and the craft industry. At present they are attempting to restore herds of livestock and are looking for ways to work with sponsors in order to learn new development techniques. They have learned to fight in order to live – the wait and see approach is over. (Mahamane 1999)

Gains with an economic base seem to last longer than political gains, probably because they raise fewer questions about the relations of power between the sexes in families and in communities.

The Loss of Identity

In Africa in general, the individual – man or woman – is tightly integrated into his or her clan, ethnic group and community. This integration is such that Western ethnologists have declared that in Africa the individual does not exist. Certainly colonisation, schooling and urbanisation have contributed to changing this situation and to the emergence of individualism in Africa. The family, the clan and the ethnic group still remain the cornerstones of society, however, and the reference points for individuals. Their break-up, as a result of armed conflicts, is a wrenching experience for the many refugees and displaced persons living in Africa, now numbering 7.4 million according to the United Nations High Commissioner for Refugees (UNHCR). The majority of refugees and displaced persons are women and children. Another consequence of the break-up of families and of communities is the disintegration, if not the end, of traditional inter-dependencies that permitted the poorest to survive. This disintegration exacerbates the precariousness of women's living conditions.

Exile also has its hazards: flight to a foreign country, death of close relations or separation from them and from one's community, and surviving in camps with strangers for indeterminable periods of time. Such events deprive individuals of all their points of reference, familial, clan and national. Women are particularly affected.

In countries where religious fundamentalism is rampant, especially in Muslim countries such as Algeria, Iran and Afghanistan, women experience another kind of identity loss that must be taken into consideration. Forced to wear the *hijab* (veil) or the *chador* (enveloping cloak) or else face punishment that can go as far as death, women find themselves constrained to adopt an identity, known as 'Islamic', which, in its attempt to make them invisible, to deprive them of their mobility and to relegate them to the private sphere, denies them their identity as subject and citizen.

Loss of Bodily Integrity

Assault on the bodily integrity of women, of adolescents and of little girls is a central and universal fact of all wars. Despite the absence of statistics in Africa, where many counties do not yet permit complete and detailed reporting on this issue, accounts given by victims provide some idea of the extent of their violence. Gang rapes, countless sexual abuses, mutilation of limbs, forced marriages, forced sexual relations and pregnancies, forced labour, and summary executions were phenomena in all the clashes that have torn Africa apart.

In Rwanda in 1999, the Association of Widows of the Genocide, Agahozo, conducted a study on the kinds of violence suffered by women (AVEGA 1999). This study, based on a sample of 1,125 women living in the prefectures of Kigali, Butare and Kibundo, revealed that 74.5 per cent had experienced sexual violence such as rape perpetrated by individuals or groups of men, incidents of forced incest (for example, rape of one's own child or parent), the cutting of genitalia, the insertion of cutting or piercing objects in the vagina, and rape by one or more men infected with the AIDS virus. Galloy reports the testimony of an old woman in Congo (Brazzaville) raped by her own son, a militiaman forced to commit this act by his comrades. 'My son no longer dares to look at me. It isn't his fault, it's the Ninjas who made him rape me. They fired on me so that I'd obey' (Galloy 2000).

Adding to Women's Responsibilities

Wars are characterised by extensive mortality. Women are killed, lose their children, a husband or family members. The high mortality rate of men in wars, the displacements and migrations bring profound changes in families. One of the most significant is the formation of households headed by women who assume all responsibility for the household's upkeep. In Rwanda for example, '34 per cent of the households today are headed by women who, in most cases, have lost all (or almost all) their children and must take care of countless orphans left by close relatives or distant dead relatives' (Mukamulisa and Mukarubuha 2000). The high rate of dependency characteristic of this type of family adds greatly to women's vulnerability.

In addition to the growing number and size of households headed by women, the absence of men has serious repercussions on the capacity of women who remain in the village to gain access to resources. Men usually negotiate arrangements relating to access to land and work and, in their absence, women may lose both. Even when women have access to land, the lack of a male workforce has a very negative impact on the level of agricultural production, and hence on the availability of food.

The prejudicial assumption that only men are heads of families further weakens the households from which they are absent. This is true of all locations, whether urban or rural, and including refugee camps. Furthermore, most often, in the absence of men, official statistics count only households that are headed *de jure* by women, that is by widows or divorcees, ignoring those that are run *de facto* by women because their husbands have gone to war or have migrated.

The distributors of aid (food, tents, land, etcetera) may marginalise families headed *de facto* by women, who may therefore find themselves in the most extreme destitution.

The precarious living conditions of women who head families force them to develop individual strategies for survival that are not without risk, such as prostitution or smuggling. In some cases, women agree to marry nationals of countries of refuge for the sole purpose of surviving. The women call this kind of marriage a 'marriage of hunger'.

Economic Losses

Wars are one of the causes of the economic underdevelopment of the African continent. Wars contribute to the unravelling of the economic fabric at the local and national level, the flight of investment capital and human resources, the breaking up of local and national business, and unemployment. The extensive use of national economic resources to modernise armies, purchase arms and pay militiamen is a serious obstacle to developing social sectors such as education, health or job creation. At the end of the war, the national economy is so depleted that the new authorities have no alternative but to apply to international monetary institutions for loans, which are granted with so many conditions attached that they only serve to intensify poverty.

It is now widely recognised that wars and structural adjustment policies do not impact equally on women and men. In addition to their lack of competitiveness due to their weaker schooling and training, women's unequal access to resources, the impact of war and adjustment policies all heighten their vulnerability. In Burundi, for example, at the end of the conflict,

> almost one million people live in conditions that cannot be more inhuman and they are threatened by all kinds of illnesses and by acute malnutrition. In this environment of extreme poverty aggravated by ruinous hostilities, there is a new category of persons, the disaster victims born of events: women represent 54 per cent of the total number. (Ntwarante and Ndacasinyaba 2000)

At the end of the war, on returning to their community in the rural area, women may lose already established property rights because they have become widows or because their land is given to a demobilised combatant. Since women are the main producers of subsistence foodstuffs consumed by the family, this situation may lead to cases of famine. In the cities, salaried women may lose their jobs because the state or their former employer is no longer able to pay salaries. A woman may also lose her job because the state or the employer has decided to give priority to hiring men, justifying this choice in terms of the need to pacify men, who are quicker to show their anger or to make trouble. In such cases the women often turn to the crowded informal sector, an area already open to women in the past. The lack of capital and the presence of competition become insurmountable obstacles to their success.

At the end of the conflict, the new government generally declares a formal demobilisation accompanied by the surrender of arms and distribution of aid or land. Men are most often the beneficiaries of these measures while women combatants find demobilisation and the return to civilian life lead mostly to alienation and poverty. According to Jeanette Eno,

no one ever raised the question of reintegration in Sierra Leone. Female ex-combatants had intended to return to their homes. But in many cases, these women and their families could not return. The fact is that while they were doing their combat training along with the boys, the girls had also committed rapes, torture and murder and had taken drugs. Viewed in terms of traditional values, they had broken sacred laws and were considered impure. Besides, how would they earn their living? The young women who returned to their community were confronted by situations of extreme poverty and social degradation. (Eno 2000)

This account of the female ex-combatants in Sierra Leone could also apply to the Eritrean women described by Sondra Hale, who notes that

a great number of demobilised combatants were women. Among them, most came from rural areas. They had changed so much that it was impossible for many of them to return to their village. Of the 12,000 demobilised women combatants, half had divorced, a status that could have .very negative consequences since their children could abandon them. They did not have much money, no work and little or no education, especially the rural women. Not only could they find themselves unable to return to their village, but they could also find themselves 'unmarriageable'. (Hale 1999)

Women in Niger faced similar problems. Mahamane (1999) observes: 'After the conflict, the men who have survived receive compensation. But women, the sisters, the mothers and grandmothers of the dead, what compensation have they had?'

The question of reintegrating women into their community of origin at the end of a war is an important one. Unfortunately, it has not received much attention from researchers and decision makers. If economic reintegration is important, social and psychological reintegration is crucial. In many African communities, for example, the murderer of an individual is obliged to offer a burial place for the remains in order for the soul of the deceased to rest in peace. If this obligation is not fulfilled, the assassin becomes unclean and can be cleansed of the stain only by carrying out particular ceremonies and by offering very costly compensation to the family of the deceased. The unclean individual can carry out these ceremonies with family support. But families discriminate between men and women in this regard: they are more likely to help men than women. In situations like this, persuaded that they are unclean, and rejected by their families and their clan, a large number of women ex-combatants decide to stay in the cities where, lacking work, they engage in prostitution.

Women's Loss of Leadership

Women's loss of rights to exercise leadership on the political and social levels, rights won in periods of conflict, is the most extreme and most longlasting of their losses. In post-war periods, especially in countries where the situation is unclear and neither war nor peace prevails, authorities rarely give concrete expression to any hope of changing relations of power in favour of the socially subordinate. This was the case in Europe at the end of the Second World War; it has been the case following independence wars in Africa and elsewhere, and it has also been the case after factional wars.

No systematic analysis has yet explained why African women have lost the leadership positions they had previously won. One of the reasons could be that women themselves need to admit that their own interests as a group – meaning the struggle against inequalities between the sexes and against patriarchal ideology – take second place to the struggle for national liberation. In this regard it is interesting to recall the Maoist concept of principal and secondary contradictions, which influenced many African groups and political parties that claimed this idea as their authority. According to this concept the principal contradiction is between the country and the foreign invader; all other antagonisms, including inequalities between men and women, are 'contradictions within the people' which, because they can be resolved more easily, may be put off to a more or less distant future. Women members of the groups and parties who accepted this system of ideas and practices may have committed a historical error by agreeing to give second place in their strategies to transforming social relations between the sexes; but perhaps they also erred in their assessment of the political and social situation of their country.

During the war, at its end and at the time of peace negotiations, authorities mainly emphasise issues relating to the conflict itself and to the sharing of power between the belligerents. Gender issues are virtually ignored. It should be no surprise that women encounter enormous difficulties as soon as reconstruction begins and that it is so hard for them to gain access to land and to property, to repeal an outmoded family code (personal law), or to win representation in decision-making spheres. Thus, despite their participation in the armed struggle, there are few women among the elected representatives in many African parliaments – fewer than 10 per cent in Angola, 18.1 per cent in Namibia, and 14 per cent in Zimbabwe.

The 'satellite' status of women's organisations inside the ruling parties illustrates the marginalisation of the issue of equality between the sexes. For decades, in fact, the parties in power have incorporated women's organisations. Their lack of autonomy has contributed to the absence of a political and ideological vision – focused on the specific interests of women – whose objective would be to transform gender relations. Women's loss of the rights they won on the battle-field, notably equality with men, is also mirrored inside families. Hale interviewed Eritrean former women combatants who recognised that

> society, men and women, continue to use tradition, religion and custom to prevent women from freeing themselves. Superficially, society accepts the [progressive] ideas, but underneath it does not accept equality. In

order to change our relatives, our society, we must change their ideas. When we try to explain this to them, they don't easily accept. When they saw us fighting against the enemy, they could accept that. Today, they tell us repeatedly that we must marry, have children, stay at home and take care of our children. (Hale 1999)

Losses in Education

In periods of conflict, women and girls often lose access to education. At the end of the war, many young people find themselves with no education or training and with little chance of finding work. As Chungue emphasised,

> the biggest difficulty is formal education. The girls have more problems than the boys. Some marry because it's the only way to survive. Many young people, from eighteen to twenty years old, have not had any access to education since 1975. Other young people, having completely lost their roots, stay in the cities. We do our best to educate them. But it's hard to start at twenty ... some young people are too traumatised to be able to learn. (Chungue, conference participant)

In Casamance, one of the most fertile regions of Senegal, a conflict begun in 1982 between the Movement of Democratic Forces of Casamance and the government has displaced rural people. The war has destroyed villages; land mines made cultivation impossible and were a cause of mass migration. Many people fled to the towns, where poverty has become a new problem for the women, and where children are not attending school.

Conflict can have unintended, contradictory effects, however. According to Manchanda (see her chapter in this volume), the Maoist insurgency in Nepal has affected school attendance in surprising ways. Parents are sending sons to study in Kathmandu, the capital, fearing the influence of Maoists and the sweeps of government militia who regard boys as obvious suspects. The number of girls studying in village schools has increased dramatically. Whereas few girls used to attend classes, they now make up 50 per cent of all students in some village schools. Under the influence of the Maoists, girls are learning an ideology that promotes women's liberation, in contrast to the traditional hierarchical structures of exclusion and sequestration that bind Nepali women.

Losses in Health

Women run serious health risks during conflict. The most common concern physical handicaps and disabilities caused by the explosion of land mines buried in farmlands or in roads, the effects of which can last for years after the end of the conflict.

Mental health problems, relatively seldom taken into consideration, are equally important during conflict. They are caused by the traumas suffered after physical or sexual violence or by economic difficulties. Health workers rarely recognise them and rarely make the mentally ill the object of psychological, material or appropriate legal assistance.

The precarious nature of women's living conditions, especially the living conditions of those women who are heads of families, may lead them into practices that put their health, and even their lives, at risk. Prostitution, with no possibility of negotiating the use of a condom, can multiply the risks of HIV infection. A study of the acts of violence suffered by women in Rwanda indicates that 66.7 per cent of the women surveyed have AIDS (AVEGA 1999).

In other respects, by virtue of their reproductive role women are traditionally the guardians of the health of family members. The increase in the numbers of handicapped people, of invalids, and of the sick that results from conflict adds to women's responsibilities and has a negative impact on their own health.

Conclusion

It is clear that the type of conflict, demographic changes, and membership of a particular class or ethnic group all have profound influences on the gains and the losses of women in periods of armed conflict. This analysis of various situations has shown the fragility of women's gains compared to the acuteness of their losses. The absence of a political perspective for transforming relations between the sexes may explain the precariousness of the rights women achieve. In fact, when they engage in the struggles described, women rarely seek to challenge the patriarchal practices and ideology that are the basis for inequality between the sexes. Reinforcing the changes in social roles that came about as a result of the conflict could be a first step. But the most important is to build – before, during and at the end of the conflict – a strong women's movement, one that bears a plan to transform gender relations, one that is linked to civil society, one that is ready to struggle to strengthen democracy and to respect the human, economic and political rights of women.

Note

1. The comments cited in this chapter were made in July 1999 at the Johannesburg conference on 'The Aftermath: Women in Post-War Reconstruction', in discussions held in the workshop on women's gains and losses, which was chaired by Codou Bop, interim co-ordinator of the African Women's Anti-War Coalition. Participants included: Faustina Naivele Chungue, Association of Rural Women (Farming Women), Angola; Jennifer Davis, executive director, the Africa Fund, New York, USA; Charlotte Lindsey, International Committee of the Red Cross, Geneva, Switzerland; Malathi de Alwis, Senior Research Fellow, International Centre for Ethnic Studies, Colombo, Sri Lanka; Margaret Ling, Zed Books, London, UK; Ancil Adrian-Paul, International Alert, London, UK.

CHAPTER 3

Violence against Women in the Aftermath

ANU PILLAY

Women have come together all over the world, in different countries and at different times, to discuss the issue that plagues them everywhere – violence against women. Their exchanges have given birth to extensive descriptions of violence in peacetime, during war and afterwards. Indeed a veritable lexicon of violence against women has emerged as women talk to one another. Women at a workshop in Dakar, in December 1998, talked of explicit violence, implicit violence, violence in public, institutional violence, economic violence, and violence in the home. They reported that violence during war escalated into the most atrocious and heinous acts of brutality and torture and intensified in the aftermath of conflict. Mass rapes became gang rapes, mass murders turned into serial killings. Legitimating violence as a means to end conflict effectively legitimised the use of violence to resolve conflict in the home. Women in all these gatherings asked the same questions: What can we do to protect ourselves in the conflict and in the aftermath? How can we prevent violence against women? How can we help society heal from this trauma?

Papers presented at the 1999 conference on 'The Aftermath: Women in Post-war Reconstruction' held in Johannesburg confirmed that violence against women has reached unprecedented heights globally. Worse than ever before, it seemed still to be worsening – in prevalence, intensity and form. Despite the formal gains made, the national laws promulgated, the international focus represented by United Nations activities such as the 1995 Fourth World Conference

35

on Women in Beijing and the establishment of the Convention on the Elimination of All Forms of Discrimination Against Women (CEDAW), the documents written, the testimonies given all over the world, violence persists – with a frightening tenacity. We witness it with a growing sense of horror.

The world stands by and watches as girl babies are raped to death, daughters are sold into prostitution by their parents for food, wives are blinded with acid and disfigured for life – the list goes on and so do the questions. Why is it happening, how can we stop it, what should we do about it?

Yasmin Sooka, President of the Human Rights Committee of the Truth and Reconciliation Commission (TRC) in South Africa and one of the keynote speakers at the Johannesburg conference, made this statement:

> Gender-based crimes are not taken seriously enough by the state. In peacetime we note the ineptitude with which the state, the police and the judicial system deal with crimes against women. No attempt has been made to deal effectively, efficiently and humanely with women victims of crime. Instead women are revictimised by the system.

Lona James Lowilla, working with the United Nations Children's Fund (UNICEF) in southern Sudan, pointed out in her presentation that before the Sudanese civil war, the violence against women that existed – such as arranged marriages, bartering of women, and wife inheritance – was closely related to the prevailing culture. Violence escalated during the war, with multiplying cases of rape of women. Sooka quoted Indai Lourdes Sajor (1998:2), editor of a book produced by the Asian Centre for Women's Human Rights:

> Violence against women in armed conflict situations is one of the most heinous violations of human rights in terms of its scale, the nature of the atrocities and the number of persons affected. Yet history hardly recorded war crimes committed against women.... One of the most powerful reasons for this denial is [that] violations perpetrated against women are not viewed as being important.

A clear pattern emerged from presentations made by conference keynote speakers on the issue of violence against women. Violence against women happens in peacetime, is intensified during wartime, and continues unabated in the aftermath. We are faced with a societal scourge that marches on inexorably without pause and without remorse.

Efforts to eradicate this deeply embedded pattern have resulted in greater awareness of the problem, with more women talking to yet more women. Further, women's rights are now spoken of as human rights, yet still the violence does not stop. Where do the roots lie and what will it take to exterminate this horror? Nothing short of total eradication will work; we heard from many women that the slightest latitude towards violence during peacetime results in horrific atrocities during war, and the violence continues for decades.

We had gathered at the Johannesburg conference to ask the following questions, to find some answers or at least create forums where answers can emerge.[1] How can post-conflict transition be used to move beyond the reconstruction of pre-war gender relations to real social transformation? The transitional period towards democracy opens the space for women's voices to be heard. Why then does violence appear to increase in this period? Women made gains during war, why are they not sustained in the aftermath? What do we need to do to move beyond the rights-based approach, which focuses on legal reforms, and the needs-based approach, which highlights the social conditions that give rise to violence against women? Is it possible that women could shift towards seeing themselves as proactive creators of their own realities?

Participants in the first thematic workshop used the presentations by Myriam Merlet from ENFOFANM (Organisation for the Defence of the Rights of Women, Haiti) and Marionne Benoit from the National Coalition for Haitian Rights as a framework to explore these questions. Conference planners asked that we use a gender analysis to understand not only social and personal violence in the aftermath of conflict, but also the economic violence of military budgets that deprive women of education and health services; and the cultural violence that uses religion, tradition and custom to deprive women both of new identities and new symbolic meanings forged in wartime, and of the security that makes creative life possible. We were asked to explain recurrent cycles of political violence in order to inform policies that would be formulated later.

An Analysis of the Experiences

Merlet and Benoit highlighted the phenomenon of the feminisation of poverty. They said that as socio-economic mechanisms collapse, communities face critical backlogs in the provision of water, sanitation, schools and access to health care for women and children, leading to high mortality rates. Although women are often responsible for their families as breadwinners and single parents, they are confined to the subsistence level of the informal sector or to low-paid work within factories. Although Haiti is not a country at war, they argued that violence on many fronts produced a very similar situation to war, framing a context that was familiar to most participants. The fragmentation of society, deterioration of family structures, economic decline and the resulting feminisation of poverty shape the context within which Haitian women seek to build peace and create a new order.

> Alongside the violence perpetrated against the individual, there is economic and political violence. Haitian women find themselves in the position of being the market's shock absorbers. They are both producers and consumers of goods ... domestic production by Haitian women basically keeps the population alive. But this production is not valued and is even hidden. It is not spoken about. (Merlet, conference presentation)

This analysis suggests that control exercised over women is linked to control of their labour. The approach shifts from the traditional view that violence against women is located in the male psyche and draws attention to an interesting materialist viewpoint – the political economy of this phenomenon.

'In the context of civil war, combatants use rape strategically in order to acquire women's assets' (Turshen 2000). In her analysis of the political economy of violence against women during armed conflict in Uganda, Meredeth Turshen argues that in Uganda, as in many civil wars, both government and rebel forces used violence systematically to strip women of their economic and political assets. Women, she says, are not only constructed as property in which the assets available for transfer are women's productive and reproductive labour, but are also targeted for their property, which is often livestock and land for the army.

These arguments led the group to consider two intense questions: Can male domination persist if women's contributions are economically recognised, valued and remunerated? and Is there an aftermath for women?

Although women are particularly vulnerable during wars and amidst the consequent destruction of social, cultural and communal institutions, the public and particularly the media's concentration on women as victims of organised violence almost completely ignores their role as accomplices in a negative sense or as activists and comrades in a positive sense. This biased image has negative effects on women in the post-war reconstruction phase. Their experiences during war, their perceptions and experiences of family and society and their relative distance from the realm of power should confer specific competence on them as conflict managers and peace brokers, but they are marginalised because this role does not fit into the picture of victimisation (Swiss Peace Foundation 1998). Yet women are also perpetrators: 'We had a case ... where a woman was assisting guys to hijack another woman.... She was an accomplice, making it easy for the men to kidnap the women'. (Mmatshilo Motsei, conference participant)

What Underlies Violence against Women?

This question generated many comments, views and further questions from participants. Men believe they have to dominate women to feel unambiguously male. The notorious gang rape and stabbing of Valencia Farmer, a young girl in the western Cape, South Africa, was cited as an example. She was raped as part of a gang initiation ritual to establish male power and honour: 'you are not a man until you rape a woman'. Cultures with that ideal demonstrate high violence against women. Participants believed that power relationships between men and women are the root of violence. The patriarchal structure of society enables men to use and abuse their power. Another comment indicated that our binary construction of sexuality does not allow flexibility. Gender stereotyping ensures that women remain outside of policy and decision making.

The workshop discussants drew on the work and experiences of participants as we grappled with the underlying causes of violence against women and debated its elements. Four emerged as the most powerful forces involved: inequality of power, social acceptance of violence, the construction of masculinity, and economic power.

Inequality of power
Many women described how this inequality exposed them to gender-specific violence. Unequal power relations between men and women are manifested in social practice and in beliefs and values that promote male superiority and female inferiority. Gender is stereotyped into rigid, binary roles of male as protector and female as nurturer with the objectification of the female as 'property'. Thus women are 'owned' by men and their violation by the 'enemy' is a violation of male posses-sion. When situations pose threats to male superiority or domination, extremely violent forms of reassertion and control emerge (Pillay and Bop 1999). Lona Lowilla spoke of how men raped young girls in the Sudan: if the men could not penetrate a girl, they would break a bottle and force it into the girl's vagina.[2] Women and girls were silent about this, she said. They were ashamed and kept what had happened to themselves.

Social acceptance of violence
Violence against women is socially sanctioned as a form of discipline in peacetime and legitimises the use of violence during war and afterwards. Many women reported that even though violence *per se* was not condoned in their societies, women expected to be 'disciplined' by their husbands or brothers for any misdemeanour. This allows marauding soldiers in wartime to extend the idea of discipline through acts of uncontrolled violence and degradation that discipline the women and all who are connected to them. The seeds of violence can also be noted in the behaviour of agents of socialisation, like clergy who legitimise the oppression of women in some form or another. A woman seeking assistance from the clergy is often reminded of her duty towards her spouse and of her obligation to ensure that the marriage works so that the children are cared for adequately. In many countries women are legally minors, or agents of socialisation still regard them as minors.

'This is much more serious than genocide in the camps', Marie

Immaculée Ingabire of Rwanda asserted. 'We knew that [the genocide] would end one day, but now this is normal life.... The witchdoctor tells a man to rape a four-year-old to get rid of a spell, and people with a sexually transmitted disease (STD) are told to rape a virgin. This is a plague that threatens our continent and, indeed, our whole world' (Ingabire, conference participant).

The construction of masculinity
Peer group pressure plays an enormous role in wartime rape, as it does in peacetime gang assaults. Men who refuse to participate are regarded as 'chicken' and not man enough. They dare not refuse. Those who do not participate will still not condemn those acts. 'The men who rape and violate women count on other men's solidarity; they expect men [who do not participate] to keep quiet. This is what is missing, the positive male role models who will stand next to women to address the issue of violence in society and violence against women' (Swiss Peace Foundation 1995). Mmatshilo Motsei of ADAPT in Johannesburg emphasised that 'men violate women because they can'. She talked of redefining masculinity and the role that all members of society play in the process. 'When we talk of changing institutions, we must remember that we are part of the institutions. We must also talk about ourselves; how we change as mothers and look at the role of the family in reinforcing violence' (Motsei, conference participant).

An important question that provoked considerable debate was the function performed by the aggressive model of masculinity. 'How does it serve men to uphold this model?', participants asked. Discussants asked whether in South Africa, the macho masculine model served to protect men from racial abuse. Women felt that this may be a common perception amongst men, but that in reality socio-economic power was decisive in who could abuse whom.

Ingabire's input on war violence, violence in the refugee camps, the transition after the genocide and the violence in Rwanda today underscored the lack of seriousness with which male policy makers view the issue: 'After the genocide, they categorised the criminals and put the rapists in the fourth category. The women are not dead, they said. We [the women] protested and brought Kigali to a standstill for them to put the rapists in category one' (Ingabire, conference participant).

Economic power

Economic power often determines a woman's responses to violence, and a woman's lack of economic power is mainly expressed through her remaining in an abusive and dangerous situation. The construction of masculinity, which puts pressure on men to provide for their families financially, means that men perceive high levels of male unemployment as emasculating, and this results in violence against women. Economics plays a significant role in shaping the macro context of unequal power relations based on race, class, sex, gender, age and so forth. Overcrowding, bad street lighting and other dangerous conditions in periurban areas place women in lower socio-economic levels of society at risk of violence. 'Women's work' is largely unrecognised, undervalued and under- if not totally unpaid. Male domination is in serious trouble if women are recognised for their work and contributions to society. Control over women equals control over reproductive labour and the more than half of productive labour that women provide (Braam and Webster 2000).

Violence against women is a system in itself and has to be seen in its entirety. It permeates every facet of society and is expressed socially, economically, politically, culturally and professionally. Looking at the multiple manifestations of violence, we recognised that there is no aftermath for women. Violence continues throughout because the underlying causes remain intact. Although the focus on rape during war brought these crimes to international attention, rape is not the only atrocious situation. The implicit violence highlighted by the Dakar workshop is far more insidious and pervasive. Women are left alone with their children and are forced to struggle for their survival. They suffer all kinds of hardship and have to struggle to meet their basic needs. Frances Spencer of the Johannesburg Trauma Clinic reported that in her study of Somali refugees she found:

> They had come close to death, had witnessed the death of family members and been forcibly separated from their families.... They had no sustainable income, lack[ed] accommodation and [there was] over-crowding.... They could not provide for their children in terms of food, clothing and schooling. (Spencer, conference participant)

Police and the military harass women; governments and the media verbally abuse and disrespect women; governments and religious leaders have denied women abortion in cases of systematic rape; families reject women if they become pregnant through rape, and looters dispossess women. The overwhelming pervasiveness of violence against women points to collusion among societal forces that could well be described as a conspiracy to maintain the low status of women in society in order to lessen the perceived threat that one can only assume women must pose to men economically, socially and politically.

What Do Men Lack that Makes Them Inflict Violence on Women?

The discussion on the underlying causes of violence against women led the group to question how fathers could turn on their daughters and wives, and sons on their mothers and sisters. What is happening in society that allows men to perpetrate terrible crimes against women, especially the women of their own families? Why do women's bodies become the battleground, the tool, and the weapon of war and violence? What happens that allows a sexual organ to be used as a weapon in war in order systematically to murder and maim women?

'Except during genocide when there is an ethnic link, violence against women is violence without distinction,' Ingabire pointed out. She asked, 'What do they want from us?' Lynette Hlongwane suggested the question be turned around to move the locus of responsibility away from its traditional place with women; she asked, 'What do they lack?' Others agreed that it was essential not to ask the question in a way that once again victimises women.

The discussion also examined the psychosocial makeup of the male psyche as participants tried to understand the violations from the intrapsychic perspective. 'Men are not independent beings, the male identity cannot stand by itself.' In socialising men to repress all that is feminine within them, society also requires men to repress and oppress all that is feminine outside of them. As long as society values aggressiveness and violence as manly traits and encourages men to beat each other up, we will not eradicate violence against women. In order for men to carry out atrocities against women, they need a psychological construct that reduces women to property and objectifies women as the 'other'. It is this perception of 'otherness' that allows men to carry out the most heinous acts of violence.

Emerging Themes

Three powerful themes emerged from this discussion, directed toward developing a strategy to deal with violence against women. The first is the need to perceive violence against women as a whole system and, as Merlet pointed out, to recognise that 'women must inhabit all sites of the struggle'. Eradication can only be achieved if every factor obstructing women is challenged and set aside. The second major theme is the importance of dealing with the material conditions and economic base of violence against women. Women's sexuality is controlled in order to control their vital reproductive and productive labour without which male domination cannot survive. Women must therefore overturn the economic imbalances and strive in this arena to gain equality. Third, women stressed the need to align the women's movement against violence with a powerful, positive male alternative to the current macho masculine models. The deconstruction of masculinity and masculine images of security is imperative. We must resocialise our society to accept and celebrate both the masculine and feminine in everything and to break down systematically the brutal images that are used to perpetuate the idea of manhood. Just as the war against racism needed people from all races to give it power and credibility, so does the gender war needs powerful, positive males who exemplify both the masculine and the feminine in themselves and who will stand alongside women in the struggle for enduring peace.

Conclusion

Conflict, war and shifting social orders provide women with opportunities to break out of stereotypes and stifling societal patterns. Social patterns are profoundly upset at such moments, presenting new possibilities. If women seize these opportunities, transformation is possible. The challenge is to protect the seeds of transformation sown during the upheaval and to use them to grow the transformation in the transitional period of reconstruction. We believe this is the way out. The transition from war to peace, from autocracy to democracy, from one social order to another, opens the way for sustainable and real transformation of gender relations.

Notes

1. The participants gathered for this discussion were women from a rich diversity of background, culture and experience who immediately agreed that the issue of violence against women cut across every single boundary. They were Marionne Benoit, Movement for the Support of Victims of Violence, National Coalition for Haitian Rights, Haiti; Rubeina Desai-Duarte from the Nissa Institute for Women's Development, South Africa; Henda Lucia Ducados, Gender and Development, USAID/Angola; Lynette Hlongwane, Gender Advisor to the UN, Pretoria, South Africa; Marie-Imaculée Ingabire, a journalist from the Women's Media Association, Kigali, Rwanda; Lona James Lowilla working with UNICEF in southern Sudan; Myriam Merlet, Organisation de Défense des Droits des Femmes, ENFOFANM, Haiti; Asha Moodley, *Agenda* magazine, Durban, South Africa; Veronica Matsepo Mukasa, African Gender Institute, Cape Town, South Africa; and Frances Spencer, representing the Centre for the Study of Violence and Reconciliation, Johannesburg, South Africa. Anu Pillay, specialist and activist on gender-based violence in South Africa and interim coordinator of the African Women's Anti-War Coalition, chaired the session.

2. The practice of infibulation is widespread in Sudan (editors' note).

CHAPTER 4

Problems of Identity,
Solidarity and Reconciliation

TINA SIDERIS

Conventional wisdom portrays war as a state in which soldiers and military institutions are the primary targets of battle and the principal participants in conflict. Actual war experiences contest this conception. A different picture of war emerges, in which homes and families constitute the battlefield while gender, race, ethnicity and class define the targets of attack. This picture shows how ordinary people are embroiled in warfare. It depicts brutal violence inflicted on civilian populations, property plundered, infrastructure demolished, and social and cultural relationships assaulted – a process of overall social destruction.

If gender, race, ethnicity and class define the targets of attack then the experience of war is specified by social background and identity. For example, women suffer the general brutality inflicted by violent conflict, yet they also suffer particular attacks whose form is defined by distinct notions of female sexuality. Massive social conflict and repression can also shape social identities in significant ways. Military discourse defines specific criteria of masculinity. Ethnic and religious ideologies propagated by warring parties establish what it means to be Croatian, Bosnian, Hutu, Tutsi, Muslim or Christian. In the social chaos produced by war, women, to ensure survival, may take on roles previously reserved for men. As they do this, their sense of what it means to be a woman shifts in subtle ways.

Similarly the psychosocial damage done by war and political repression is specified by social background and identity. For example, dislocation and the attendant loss of social belonging caused by war affect men and women differently (Sideris 1999; De Wolf 1995; McCallin 1991). Because the damage has socio-political roots, the nature of the trauma is constituted in the interaction of the individual with society, mediated by institutions, social groups and other individuals (Martin-Baro 1989:18). This, according to Martin-Baro, must be understood with reference to the general dehumanisation of social relations produced by war, which establishes a framework for structural, group and interpersonal relations according to which the 'Other' is negated.

What are the implications of the identities shaped by war for social transformation in the aftermath? What is women's potential to help resolve social and political divisions created by massive social conflict? What are women's experiences of achieving solidarity across ethnic, religious and class barriers, of acknowledging the Other? Do truth commissions or war tribunals effect reconciliation and how are women involved in these processes? What healing strategies are appropriate post-conflict? These are some of the questions that were asked at the fourth thematic working group of the Aftermath Conference held in Johannesburg in July 1999.

Shireen Hassim, a political scientist at the University of the Witwatersrand, led the workshop. Her work has explored women and nationalism particularly amongst women in KwaZulu Natal in South Africa, where political conflict between the Inkatha Freedom Party and the African National Congress (ANC) deteriorated into low-grade civil war during the 1980s and 1990s. Papers from Lepa Mladjenovic of Women in Black in Belgrade and Martina Belic from B.a.B.e. (Be active, Be emancipated), Zagreb, provided the framework for workshop discussion; both have worked as feminist peace activists. As visa restrictions prevented Mladjenovic from attending the conference, Belic read her paper and message of solidarity. Workshop participants brought to the discussion a rich diversity of knowledge derived from their work and personal experiences.[1]

Multiple and Shifting Identities – Socially Constructed, Contextually Based

In intense discussion, members of the workshop shaped a conception of 'identity' that implies contingency, agency and fluidity. Among many insightful observations the following typify key elements of the exchanges:

> 'Identities are constructed out of the way society sees us and out of hate and fear of other things.'
> 'Being a woman is not necessarily something that causes us to be peace activists.'
> 'Identities can bring us privileges and of course disadvantages.'
> 'To look at the question of identity we need to look at it in specific contexts.'
> 'War impacts on the identity of women and men.'
> 'There are layers of oppression and discrimination in women's lives.'
> 'Both in war and peace the stigma that is attached to women as victims of violence remains with them forever.'

Participants did not define 'identity', but a review of the discussion suggests reference to self-representation and the subjective experience of personhood. Also avoided were debates that distinguish 'identity' from subject formation and ideas of 'subjectivity' and 'subject positions' current in feminist post-structuralist thought.[2] It will become clear however that the discussants rejected notions of a singular and fixed identity into which people are socialised and to which they are tied lifelong.

Lynne Cawood, presenting her research results, traced layers of oppression and violence in black South African women's lives under apartheid. Starting in the family, women were discriminated against as girl children in ways that for some included sexual abuse. Violence and discrimination dominated their adult lives. Institutionalised racial discrimination and structural violence based on racial categories determined their experience of the social world. Poverty and job reservation policies forced the large majority of employed black women into domestic work, where white women oppressed them. Many black women also continued to experience violence in intimate relationships. Women who joined the struggle for national liberation reported exploitation by male comrades, detention and torture in the hands of male and female state operatives, and rape and sexual abuse by members of the state security forces.

Cawood's presentation locates the experience of women in a particular historical context and shows how patriarchy intersected with a particular form of racial oppression and class division to structure the experiences of black women under apartheid. Although she did not discuss the differences in the experience of white women, her work suggests that race and class created hierarchical divisions between white and black women that added another dimension to black's women's repression.

Thus South African women emerge from apartheid with a subjective sense of womanhood that is constituted by differing experiences of gender, race and class relations. In this sense subjectivity is socially constructed under specific conditions. Under apartheid in South Africa there was not a single category 'women'. Race and class positioned women differently, informing particular social practices and material conditions and producing specific restrictions and rewards.[3] Notably, however, while there may have been various experiences of being a woman (and a man) under apartheid, the difference between men and women is consistently specified by relations of subordination. In Cawood's paper this is indicated by the discrimination inflicted on black women who joined the struggle for liberation by their male counterparts.

Cawood's presentation raised two important questions. Is the experience and threat of sexual violence a consistent feature in the construction of women's subjective experience of themselves as women and as women in relation to men – their gender identity? Lillian Kimani argued strongly that sexual violence constitutes a core element in women's understanding of themselves and serves to construct them as victims.

> Both in war and peace the stigma that is attached to women as victims of violence remains with them forever and it is passed on from one woman to another. From the time you are born your mother tells you that as a woman you are not safe. You know that you are vulnerable because you were born a woman. I was born during the civil war in my country [Kenya] in the 1950s and I can imagine how my mother tried to protect her baby during the war. They used to hide in the bush. Although I did not know the war situation, I know that fear. My mother has transmitted it to me psychologically. (Lillian Kimani, conference participant)

The second and related question, Can women transcend the weight of the oppression? is reflected in the above view. Many women construe themselves and are socially constructed as passive victims of their circumstances. In the context of war and political repression this construction is usually associated with traditional notions of women as nurturers and peacemakers, the innocent victims of war. Essentially this is a question of agency. Do women, who in a real sense are victims of subordination and violent control, resist these circumstances? In other words, in addition to being subjects of oppression, are women also the subjects of their histories, able to engage in conscious social action? A related question that emerges is, Does being a woman necessarily exclude violent social practices?

History is filled with evidence of women as individuals, in groups and in social movements who struggle to resist their subordination, even in war. Sharing with workshop members work I had done on the war experiences of Mozambican women, I reported that women construed themselves as both victims of brutal atrocities and survivors who actively tried to find ways to protect themselves and their dependants. Indeed women may even draw on the more conservative notions of gender to help them to resist in wartime. For example Mozambican women identified mothering as a fundamental source of resilience. They attributed the actions they took to save and protect others to the fact that they are mothers. These women reframed the burdens inherent in nurturing roles as sources of resilience. Because they took on roles perceived as the preserve of males, in effect becoming providers, their consciousness of themselves shifted to include a sense of strength and capacity.

The workshop discussion provided an account of the complexity of identity formation, particularly gender identity. Reflections of participants on their work and personal experiences located gender identity in time and space, described it as constituted in multiple intersections with race, class, and ethnicity, and as shifting. In essence, deliberation on what massive social conflict does to men and women confirmed the relativity of gender identity. Examples drawn from South Africa, Rwanda, and the former Yugoslavia provided ample evidence of women perpetrating violence.

Martina Belic's opening presentation referred more directly to the dimension of agency in identity formation.

Being a woman or having gender identity is not necessarily something that causes us to be peace activists or to resolve conflicts. Some women form their war identities on the other side of the war. At some points there were small numbers of women who were feminists and peace activists and were opposed to the war. But I realised that there was the same number on the other side, right-wing women who were warmongers. Of course most women remained in between the two sides. (Belic, conference participant)

The view that gender identity is socially constructed and that there are a variety of ways of being a woman or a man within particular historical situations raises the further question, Do individuals choose their social positions? Of course we are all aware of the material conditions, social discourses and ideologies that set the limits of the possibilities and constraints for the construction of different forms of identity. But workshop participants sought explanations for Belic's observation that in war some women select the identity of peace activists and others select the identity of agents of war.

Ria Convents argued that feminist consciousness is a resource for women to resist violence: 'I think how you get an identity is how much help you get from feminists'. This echoes themes laid out by Mladjenovic in her opening address to the conference. She pointed out that the work of activists fighting hatred and nationalism in the former states of Yugoslavia was made easier by the fact that feminist networking pre-existed the war. Mladjenovic identified several factors as assuming particular importance once the war began, including the following: that solidarity became the political and personal aim of feminist anti-war activists; that feminist anti-war activists made sure to create as many opportunities as possible to meet each other; that feminist politics means that we take care of ourselves (one's national group) in wartime as much as the 'Other' (the national group across the front line) (Mladjenovic 1999).

The twists and shifts in gender roles and identities produced by the conditions of war also apply to men. Sideris pointed out that the male-dominated arena of war could do two things to the identity of manhood or masculinity. On the one hand, men who have been unable to protect their wives, daughters and dependants or who cannot provide for their families because of the social destruction in war feel their manhood eroded. On the other hand there are men who have a militarised and aggressive sense of manhood. In a peace situation these are the only two options that men see available to them.

The question arises of what resources are available for men to resist violence and construct more positive identities. Paradoxically, although war is a male-dominated arena, men's identity might emerge from conflict even more damaged than women's. Many women gain strength from the experience of war because they and their children have survived. Women can then reconstruct their lives with their children and many feel they can do this without men as heads of households. In my view, men feel threatened by this survival and so retreat into trying to reassert their manhood in the only area where this seems possible – in intimate relationships.

Ordinary men often don't find a positive role to play in reconstruction, especially when war has destroyed the economy. I am not arguing that economic empowerment of men and women will be sufficient to combat violence, but I do contend that states in post-conflict periods do not pay enough attention to masculinity and the threats it has suffered. Society does not offer men an alternative sense of manhood or masculinity. Participants noted that post-conflict combatants are generally demobilised rather than demilitarised. Many men have neither the skills nor the opportunities to play a positive role in reconstruction in the aftermath. Workshop participants reflected on cases of male ex-combatants involved in criminal activities, depression in men, increased rates of suicide amongst men post-war, and the expression of their anger and frustration in the domestic sphere.

The immense social and material demands created by war can produce subtle but critical shifts in gender identity. This does not mean that war creates new gender identities. There are consistent and shared dimensions of gender identity that endure through time and space. In particular, relations of subordination specify the difference between men and women, and the experiences and threats of sexual violence play a central role in constituting the subjective experience of what it is to be a woman. Yet if identity is mutable and contains agency, there is hope. Hope is reflected in the conscious social action women have taken to transcend oppression and violence, and such action is integrally linked to social organisation and political consciousness.

Women Crossing Political and Social Divisions

Feminist consciousness and feminist social practices are identified as a crucial resource in the fight against violence, hatred and nationalism in the former Yugoslavia. Elsewhere there is greater reservation about the ease with which women can cross social divisions. The differences are linked to distinct histories of oppression and division. For example, race and class relations were such under apartheid in South Africa that black women experienced the vast majority of white women as contained in the category of oppressors. They saw white women as privileged by virtue of belonging to this group. This specification of difference between black and white women by inequality in power has left unresolved feelings of mistrust. Lillian Kimani describes this dynamic well:

> It is very difficult for us in South Africa to talk about black and white women. There are efforts for women to speak in one voice, they all agree on many issues relating to violence against women. But it will take time to develop trust between the two because there was exploitation of one by the other and there was violation of one by the other, especially on an economic level. And that has created mistrust.

Lynne Cawood argues that even in formal political structures historical divisions linger: 'I think in the present day in our political structures there is a lot of distrust and difficulty. Racism is perceived and in many ways still exists. So we need to find a way of working with those processes because they can be very difficult for women involved in those structures'.

The power of racist ideologies and the social and economic practices they informed under apartheid is reflected in the strength of the struggle for *national* liberation to which the struggle for the liberation of women was subordinated. Research suggests that women's activism was directed predominantly in support of national liberation. Where women did raise feminist issues these did not find ready support within the liberation movement (Horn 1991; Hassim 1991; Malibongwe Collection 1990). Thus there has not been a strong feminist consciousness or feminist social movement in South Africa even amongst activists, let alone across racial divides. Added to these factors is the current reality that after transition the large majority of black women remains economically vulnerable whereas most white women continue to occupy positions of privilege. These conditions operate against joint social and political action though there are issues, such as sexual violence, that could unite women.

In contrast, Alice Ngezhayo described the powerful capacity of women to cross ethnic and religious divides in a particular area of Burundi and bemoaned the lack of acknowledgement accorded to their reconciliation and reconstruction achievements.

In Bujumbura with the ethnic killings, there was a lot of violence being committed. Suddenly areas that had been occupied by the Hutu ended up with camps and everyone was in the same big group and all sorts of violence was perpetrated against them. The Tutsi women could see what was happening inside the camps and they tried to be helpful to the Hutu and show some solidarity. Because of this the Hutu women decided they might as well return to the areas they lived in before. They decided if they were going to die and to be treated so badly they might as well go home. The Tutsi women came in to help them and they started their agricultural activities and sending kids to school and so on. And the men started to realise that the women had gone back to try and live their lives as they had done in the past. The women were at home, the areas started being rebuilt and the women started rebuilding houses. Because of this exchange a type of solidarity developed in those areas between Hutu and Tutsi women. They realised their efforts had brought positive benefits. Unfortunately the government did not see these efforts as positive. The government is still asking what women's role was and of what use they have been. So the government is saying Burundi women aren't of much use. So now they feel they have got to go in another direction and take positive action. I am saying that even in Burundi no matter how much women do and how much reconstruction they take part in, their efforts are never seen to match those of men. It also shows that as women we can develop useful exchanges inside a country and at an international level. (Alice Ngezhayo, conference participant, translation from French)

It is not unusual for women to receive little recognition for the crucial role they play in reconstruction and reconciliation in the aftermath. This was a strong point made repeatedly in the workshop discussion, and also emerged as a common theme in the conference as a whole. Ironically, one of the ways in which women have received recognition has been in the form of violent threats opposing their anti-war activism. Martina Belic argued that this is a natural reaction to powerful women in society because they constitute a threat. Discussants frequently revisited the critical issue of power in gender relations. Even where war effects a fundamental shift in gender relations and gender identity amongst combatants, in the aftermath the inequality in power that specifies the difference between men and women remains resistant to transformation.

Responding to Alice Ngezhayo and referring to Sondra Hale's opening-day address on post-revolutionary life for women of the Eritrean People's Liberation Front, Penny Plowman commented on the overwhelming nature of the problem:

> I'm struck that in Burundi you have gone through so much in terms of breaking down barriers, but then you explained that there is an expectation that the government will accept and support you. And this is very interesting. In the example presented yesterday about Eritrea, women had been taken into the bunkers as equals and they expected that when they came out society would accept them and their new ideas, as if society had similarly changed its ideas. So it shows that there needs to be a space for things to change. It is so complex, coming into a hostile environment, and there can be a backlash against those women. It is overwhelming. (Penny Plowman, conference participant)

Addressing the role of changes in formal political structures, I argued that these do not necessarily challenge the inequality of power that maintains relations between men and women. For example in South Africa, although increasing numbers of women have taken up positions in the political decision-making structures, and although the constitution protects the rights of women, it has nevertheless been difficult to transform those relations of power that sustain violence against women.

This argument contests the rights-based approach to inequities in gender relations. However in societies emerging from repressive governance with a history of gross human rights violations, it is dangerous to dismiss the significance of legal and constitutional rights. Beth Goldblatt argued for the importance of creating a state that enforces and looks after people's rights at every level. 'I think there is a case to be made for developing a human rights framework for reconstruction, to build into the society a rights framework and culture so that people understand that what happened should not happen again' (Goldblatt, conference participant).

While legal and constitutional rights are significant, it may be more realistic, particularly in periods of transition, to expect civil society organisations to ensure that the state carries out its responsibility to implement and protect legal and human rights. Fatou Dieng Thiam emphasised this point. It seems to indicate the need for stronger women's organisations in the aftermath.

Work with feminist networks suggests the important role support and solidarity amongst women can play in challenging gender inequities, both within and across borders. Women can use solidarity networks to achieve such key goals as: raising women's consciousness about the fundamental inequalities that exist in gender relations; ensuring recognition of the part that women play in reconstruction and reconciliation; and campaigning for women to have a more prominent role in the decision-making structures and processes that shape transitions. Successful solidarity movements require strength at grassroots level, and they need to guard against what Shireen Hassim has described as the differential sources of power that can develop in networks: 'Even in that process we have to recognise the differential sources of power in networks like that. They can be very helpful but there is also a politics around them, and the terms on which those networks operate have to be negotiated.'

Women's potential and will to resolve social and political divisions must be located in context. They are contingent on the particular history of violence and oppression women have experienced, the specific circumstances they find themselves in during war, and the conditions that face them in the aftermath. To reiterate the point made by Martina Belic, the fact that one is a woman does not necessarily make one a 'conflict resolutionist'.

Yet women do play a pivotal role in the reconstruction of society in the aftermath by virtue of their unique relationship to domestic institutions. It is a paradox that the very institutions that play such a crucial role in the continuity of society embody the relations of power that perpetuate the subordination and vulnerability of women. These power relations display a disturbing resistance to change that can be difficult to understand.

Truth Commissions, Tribunals and Healing in the Aftermath

I'm worried that we are generalising about women in the aftermath. I think we need to look at the way things are different for women. For example here [in South Africa], some women have become affluent, are members of parliament and are successful. They have been acknowledged and that is part of their healing. They are seen as spokespersons for women in liberation. Then there are activist women who were lower down the ranks but who to some extent have been acknowledged. But then every single black person in this country suffered under apartheid, and for the ordinary person the experience is that they have not been recognised. There are a myriad of things that made up the experiences of being black in this country, and there has been no acknowledgement of their suffering. How can they heal?

(Goldblatt, conference participant)

In situations of political repression and war, extreme trauma results not only from interdependent, discrete acts of repression – torture, assassination, rape and mutilation that are frequently coupled with social and cultural destruction, but also from the disruption of social arrangements, activities and institutions that give people a sense of belonging and meaning. In addition, women face underlying structural violence – the chronic violation of dignity through deprivation of basic human rights in daily life. The all-encompassing nature of the violence and repression results in individual psychic injury and collective social traumatisation (Sideris 1998). How can individuals and societies heal when this happens?

A rich discussion on individual and social healing and a deep reflection on truth commissions produced a view emphasising the necessity of multifaceted approaches to healing in the aftermath. Participants identified the need for healing strategies that address individual psychic injury, community fragmentation, socio-cultural destruction and socio-political transformation, without proposing a false separation between the individual and the social.

Beth Goldblatt opened the discussion with a presentation on women and the Truth and Reconciliation Commission (TRC). She pointed out that the commission was not accessible to most women for a range of reasons. Only three special hearings were held for women; many women felt uncomfortable about exposing experiences of violence, particularly sexual violation, in public forums; some women felt they had dealt with the past and did not want to open up old wounds; others confronted a sense that submitting the violations they had experienced at the hands of comrades felt like a political betrayal.

Participants acknowledged the political benefits of the TRC process, which created a public arena where the past could be exposed, debated and contained. But many argued that it had limited value for individuals; some even examined the negative consequences it may have produced. Lillian Kimani suggested some negative effects on individuals: she said that the TRC process has not dealt with the pain and suffering that still remain for many people. She argued that it is the support of social movements rather than political drive that ultimately assists people to break the silence. Kimani contrasted the political process of the TRC with reconciliation in communities at very basic levels, especially where conflict has severed people from each other.

A point about women not participating in the TRC hearings – to what extent do you think the TRC was politically driven and so played a role in preventing many people, not just women, from speaking out? Like with the Holocaust it took a social movement to bring it out. In Kenya with the Mau Mau, it took thirty years for the Kikuyu to talk about this war, which had affected social arrangements. The Anglican Church stressed reconciliation with your neighbours, although many of your neighbours had been involved in the massacres. There was reconciliation from the community; it worked. It is different to the approach found in South Africa, which used the TRC. Also with the TRC the cases became a major international drama and you became another victim in the process of the hearing. Journalists followed people after their testimony, and it became a bit too much. Many black South Africans have resented the whole political drama of the TRC. It is the government that has gained credibility from the TRC. The TRC has only dealt with the surface. We have not dealt with the pain and suffering yet in South Africa. (Kimani, conference participant)

Reflecting on the truth commission in Chile, which held closed hearings, Angelica Pino Davis identified the lack of support provided to individuals who testify as a major failing of truth commissions. In her view people are left feeling that they expose themselves and get nothing back. These views suggest that truth commissions have inherent limitations for psychosocial healing. At a minimum, if we accept their political benefit and in some situations necessity, it is important to build in mechanisms that provide real and effective support for the individuals who come forward and whose testimony is so crucial for the truth commissions.

Healing requires reconciliation and reconstruction within communities at a grassroots level. It is at this level that women are most often involved, although their efforts and the value of this kind of reconciliation are usually neither recognised nor acknowledged. Hence campaigns for the recognition of women's social and economic roles are not only aimed at achieving gender equity but also attest to the crucial part that their social activities play in reconciliation and reconstruction.

Martina Belic warned against an idealised view of reconciliation defined in terms of social mixing across racial, ethnic and religious boundaries. She pointed out that in the states of former Yugoslavia 1 million marriages across ethnic and religious boundaries ended in divorce in the face of the war and the ideologies that informed it. In her view, material reconstruction that goes beyond rebuilding houses, churches and schools to rebuild the economy is necessary for reconciliation. 'How are people going to reconcile if they are struggling to survive?' she asked.

Individual and social healing, which requires reconciliation in the sense of mending social divisions and coming to terms with the past, can take several generations. At the same time, participants agreed that perpetrators of violence should be held accountable. Okechukwu Ibeanu argued that, although aggressors who testified to their crimes at the TRC may have facilitated acknowledgement of responsibility, many perpetrators did not present themselves. Should charges be brought against them, he asked? If not, would impunity encourage a lack of moral accountability in society? How can anger be resolved without retribution and justice? In the workshop discussion, as in the wider society, these remain unresolved, perhaps irresolvable, questions.

Healing mechanisms must be appropriate to specific social contexts, and existing cultural coping systems should be respected. No single healing process can be prescribed. Strategies to address individual psychic damage could include support, psychotherapy, reconstruction of memories through testimony and documentation, culturally specific healing mechanisms such as indigenous purification ceremonies, religious ceremonies, collective mourning, and compensation. Many speakers stressed the necessity for governments to assume responsibility for providing such services or the resources to support culturally specific practices. Social healing and social transformation – including real economic reconstruction, the implementation and enforcement of legal and human rights, reconciliation at grassroots level, and democratic political processes – facilitate individual healing.

Conclusion

Social context – the specific political, economic and socio-cultural conditions in which people live at particular historical moments – is crucial for understanding identity, gender identity and the way in which massive social conflict impacts on the experience of what it is to be a man or a woman. This is not to suggest that people are passive victims of their circumstances. Men and women are agents who reflect on the world and act accordingly, but their social worlds frame their actions. If social context mediates the experience of repressive social forces, then responses in the aftermath – reconstruction, reconciliation and healing – must also be firmly located in context. Although an analysis of social context reveals differences in the experience of repression and its outcomes, this does not mean that these experiences are always noncomparable events. For example, although gender-based violence may differ in form and incidence, it is a shared feature of many societies. This experience can be a unifying factor for women. In this sense gender may elicit greater similarity in the experiences of women from different social contexts than between men and women in the same context.

Yet, in my view, context can affect the way sexual violence is perceived. The political content of rape is more visible in war. Society tends to label peacetime rape as private and generally explains it in terms of dysfunctional relations and attitudes between men and women. This separates violent sexual relations, and the construction of masculinity and femininity, from an analysis of power relations. Deprived of such an analysis the task of transforming these social relations becomes more difficult. The workshop identified strategies to challenge the social relations of power that perpetuate sexual violence. These include: enforcing constitutional and legal rights; transforming justice systems; increasing the presence and profile of women in political decision-making structures; ensuring economic empowerment of women and men; supporting grassroots women's networks as well as national, regional and international solidarity; and addressing social constructions of masculinity.

Notes

1. Participants from South Africa included: Lynne Cawood, a psychologist whose research with women has examined the psychological impact of gender violence perpetrated by the South African state under apartheid; Beth Goldblatt, a legal researcher who examined the South African Truth and Reconciliation Commission (TRC) with reference to women and argued for special women's hearings of the TRC; Shireen Hassim, a political scientist at the University of the Witwatersrand; Tina Sideris, a psychologist who conducted research with and counselled Mozambican women refugees and who still works with marginalised rural women survivors of rape and domestic violence. Participants had come too from other parts of Africa, and from further afield. Ria Convents is a feminist lawyer in Belgium, where, she argued, there is no war in the conventional sense but there is a gender war between men and women. Alice Ngezhayo, from the Burundi Centre for Women, is engaged with rural and intellectual women in promoting the return of peace. Fatou Dieng Thiam, based in Switzerland at Femmes Africa Solidarité, deals with conflict resolution and management. Okechukwu Ibeanu, a political science lecturer, worked with Ogoni people during the crisis in Nigeria. Lillian Kimani, a consultant on violence and trauma from Kenya, has worked in southern Sudan, Rwanda, Guinea and South Africa. Angelica Pino Davis, from Chile, is currently based at the South African organisation Nissa Institute for Women's Development. Penny Plowman, a consultant and researcher on women and development, was involved in producing a video of the conference.

2. As an overview of the fourth thematic workshop at the Aftermath Conference, this chapter seeks to stay close to the views reflected in the discussion. I used inverted commas in the first instance to indicate that participants did not define the concept 'identity'.

3. Workshop participants did not engage in debates about whether ideologies or discourses construct subjectivity. Feminist post-structuralist analysis has been useful for suggesting the range of discourses that constitute human subjects but, most important, for pointing out with reference to gender that in any particular context there is not one gender system but a range of gender discourses, which can be contradictory or competing. Thus

engendered subjects are constituted in many ways, not only by gender, race, class and ethnic discourses but also by intraculturally varied gender discourses.
4. These questions have important implications for the issue of sexual violence. If, in the transition to democracy, men who raped receive immunity from prosecution and therefore from punishment on political grounds, could this be interpreted as licence to perpetrate sexual violence as long as there are socially sanctioned reasons? And who determines these reasons?

CHAPTER 5

War and Post-War
Shifts in Gender Relations

SHEILA MEINTJES

Ordinary people in everyday life define war as a male preserve. They
see men as the warriors and defenders of the nation, whereas women
are the auxiliaries; they provide logistical support or, in the domestic
realm, keep the home fires burning as the wives and mothers of
soldiers. In war zones, communities live in the crossfire of military
confrontation and, in these life-threatening situations in contested
territory, women and children are potential victims. Feminist
historians and social scientists have challenged this conventional
picture to create a more complex understanding of war. They have
shown that gender roles in wartime are more varied and that women
as well as men play significant combat roles. This does not mean that
women have not been victims. War disrupts the continuities of life in
drastic ways. Mortar bombs and other firepower kill, injure and
destroy women, their communities and the infrastructure of their
lives.

Women warriors exist in the classical myth of the Amazons, in the
ancient aristocratic women fighters of Britain's warrior Queen
Boadicea and in the pre-colonial female regiments of Dahomey, West
Africa (Ehrenreich 1997: 126). Women have been camp followers for
centuries, provisioning armies with food supplies. In modern wars,
women have played important roles on the war front in intelligence
gathering, communication and transport, in addition to providing
nursing services. In conventional wars, military leaders have restricted
women's combat roles, but even this is changing as some armies draw

women into combat regiments. The evidence of women's active roles in supporting and conducting war is abundant. In the thirty years of revolutionary wars in Africa from the 1960s to the 1990s, women soldiers fought in the bunkers with men. In the Eritrean (see Chapter 8), Zimbabwean and South African liberation wars, to name a few, women took up arms to fight for independence.

As women and men are drawn into war, the relations between them inevitably shift. Women become soldiers, labourers for the war effort, national political actors, refugees, and survivors of violence, assuming roles previously reserved for men. It is in these role changes, as war draws ordinary women and men into fighting, that opportunities emerge to forge new social relationships and identities, including those of gender. The nature of change varies from one war zone to another, and the ability to sustain new social relationships and identities depends upon the way in which the transition from war to peace occurs.

This chapter explores some of the dynamics of change in gender relations in the shifting contexts of war and its aftermath. My objective is to identify the context and factors that enable a move towards women's equality and development during the ravages of war and afterwards. I also seek to identify why and how oppressive patterns of subordination and violence against women endure from one period to the next. The discussion that follows engages with the relationship between the political economy, the state and gender relations, in order to understand how post-war reconstruction can either impede or enhance the positive transformation of gender relations. These issues formed the backdrop of the discussions that took place at the Aftermath Conference.[1] Although none of the questions asked there is easily answered, this chapter sets out the parameters of the debates and the tentative conclusions we reached.

The discussion draws upon a wide range of examples from Eritrea, Mozambique, Rwanda, South Africa and Zimbabwe in order to evaluate the gendered consequences of war and the different outcomes. We conclude that, although women do gain from the shifts in gender relations during war, they may lose their wartime gains in the cusp, that period between war and peace. Thus the transition from war to peace emerges as a critical moment in the shifting terrain of gender power.

How War Mobilises Women

There are a number of general, and perhaps obvious, points to make about the changing context of war and the post-war period. First, the political economy of war mobilises society for the war effort to produce food, clothing, munitions and other war material. This mobilisation includes men and women in different ways: men (and some women) as soldiers, and women (and some men) as farmers and factory workers; women also provide support services, either in the home or in the military. Second, government often suspends the rule of law and replaces it with martial law, which enables new forms of control over people, ostensibly for purposes of security. Out of these changes in military, economic and political structures arise unique opportunities to redefine power relations between men and women. The questions we ask are: Why are these opportunities not sustained in the aftermath of war? Why and how do women lose the chances for change that war offers? We discuss these questions in relation to two specific situations: women mobilised to fight in liberation armies, and women who seek safety in refugee camps.

Gender relations in liberation armies

One common element of wartime in virtually all twentieth-century examples is that war provides women with employment and, some-times, educational opportunities. Armies trained women not simply in the use of arms, although this was certainly a central aspect of all training in the military, but also in logistical and administrative areas. Logistics required a thorough knowledge of topography as well as basic engineering skills. Communications required understanding of complex signal operations, including the way radios and telephones worked. In Eritrea and in Zimbabwe during the 1970s the liberation armies attracted women because they provided employment, but training conditions were very different in the two wars.

In Eritrea, men and women were trained together and lived side by side in the bunkers. Privacy was a luxury in those circumstances, but alongside this integration came strict rules against sexual harassment and violence. The equality experienced between women and men in the Eritrean struggle, despite some unevenness, opened up new and transformative experiences. Although the entry of women into the liberation army occurred later than men's entry, and women enlisted in a male-dominated and hierarchical world, comradeship pervaded the relationship among soldiers in the bunkers.

The equality between Eritrean women and men fighters contrasts with the experiences of women in the Zimbabwe liberation war. Whereas the Eritrean army treated women with rough equality, the two Zimbabwean independence movements, the Zimbabwe African National Union (ZANU) and the Zimbabwe African People's Union (ZAPU), trained women separately and housed them in separate barracks. In Zimbabwe, moving accounts by former women combatants stress the grim conditions under which they were absorbed into the guerrilla armies. Many of the women interviewed twenty years after the end of the Zimbabwean war admitted that ZANU and ZAPU fighters had abducted them.

> We were at the bus stop at Filabusi waiting for buses. It was quite late and some strange men approached us and asked where we were going. We told them that we were going to school. They said that nobody was going to school to learn while they were living in the bush suffering. They ordered us to leave our luggage there and go with them. (Musengezi and McCartney 2000:15)

Many women who independently chose to join the liberation armies and crossed over into Mozambique described the interrogation and abuse that accompanied being admitted into the liberation armies. Commanders first interrogated new recruits, then admitted them to refugee camps, and only then chose them for military training. This is the reminiscence of Nancy Saungweme about her experience in the Zimbabwean war:

> We underwent interrogation before we were allowed to go to the main camp at Dorai. We were blindfolded so that we could not see the way we came and who was with us. They were trying to stop us from escaping, I think. Some comrades ran away from the harsh conditions....
>
> I was accused of being a spy for the Rhodesian Government. I was young, beautiful, educated, and a teacher, I was told. I had no cause to leave Zimbabwe. Some of the comrades seemed to find it hard to believe that some of us who had passed O-levels and held jobs could forgo all to fight a war. I was beaten; my buttocks hurt. Sometimes I wished I were dead....

Sometimes people who were said to be spies were paraded before us. They would be beaten in public while we watched; about one hundred lashes on their buttocks with sjamboks or sticks.... While some people suffered beatings, others died from disease. Our hair was full of lice. Jigger flies ate away the flesh between our toes. To me that was the war. (Musengezi and McCartney 2000:48)

Fear and hopelessness led many of those in the camps to escape reality by smoking *mudzepe*, which, like hemp or *dagga*, induced a state of intoxication. Yet thousands of young women and men left Zimbabwe for training in Mozambique. Once training began, the situation changed for the better for recruits. Trained in sections and platoons, women found a new identity for themselves. The army provided military uniforms and trained the women with the men. The women learned guerrilla tactics and, above all, became very strong and fit. Nancy Saungweme described the effects: 'After two months of training I stopped menstruating and so did the other women. We were just like men. We were pleased because we thought it was macho. We wanted to be identified as fighters, as men' (Musengezi 2000:48).

In the aftermath, when the soldiers returned to civilian life, ex-combatants faced many difficulties. Although they had learned new skills, women found it very hard to get a job after the war. (This may be why some former soldiers romanticised life in the military.) In Eritrea as in Zimbabwe, the most negative consequence was unemployment. Those who had entered the liberation army with little education returned to a life of hardship and few opportunities.

Refugees
If the integration of women into armies represents an obvious shift in gender roles, the life of women in refugee camps reveals interesting possibilities for transformation. In 1999, there were 3.1 million refugees and an estimated 11 million internally displaced persons in Africa (US Committee for Refugees 2000). Women and children account for 80 per cent of refugees in most camps. The United Nations High Commissioner for Refugees (UNHCR) and nongovernmental organisations (NGOs) can provide some food, shelter and counselling services to help people deal with their losses. But resources are constantly in short supply, and refugees often begin to develop new productive enterprises that include producing food. Women take on

new and additional responsibilities in the camps, creating networks of survival and drawing on inner, untapped resources to carve out new arenas of independence. Some women emerge with a new sense of their own capabilities and strength.

According to Heywote Hailemeskal of UNHCR, refugees arrive in camp with few material possessions, but their cultural baggage may be intact. Camp life alters men's and women's roles and responsibilities, creating an artificial situation. By providing relief assistance, humanitarian workers take away men's role as protectors, and this may leave them with a sense of impotence and frustration. Some people feel the need to hold on to traditional views and conservative ways. Women may embrace traditional practices such as female genital mutilation and abandon modern practices such as family planning. There may be clashes between conservatives and progressives.

Yet many women experience the camp as an opportunity to live free from subservient traditions; this freedom can lead to transformation. Manchanda (see Chapter 7) mentions that Tamil women fleeing conflict in Sri Lanka found that the spatial exigencies of camp life produced an erosion of the caste hierarchies and pollution practices that had previously so limited their mobility. In Rwanda after the conflict, women made up an estimated 55 per cent of the population and headed 33 per cent of families. Traditionally, women had no right to own land, and widows returning from refugee camps could not reoccupy their homes; yet tradition also dictated that women were not responsible for building houses. UNHCR tried to address these issues by organising not only training projects to teach women the skills they needed to build shelters, but also a land rights conference to bring about new legislation to implement change.

We can thus understand refugees in a new way, as agents of change. With nothing to lose, refugees living on the margins are often engaged in a process of transformation. Their task becomes one of reinventing the institutions of social life in order to survive. In the post-war period, however, the gains made by refugees in developing new social capital are at risk. This is because refugees are usually repatriated. In this process, they lose the new networks, social relationships and resources developed in the refugee camps. It is not surprising that refugees do not always wish to return 'home', for return means the destruction of their newfound world.

Military Demobilisation and Political Remobilisation

There are important questions to ask about how genuine the commitment of political movements is to gender equity. Gender sensitivity was well and good in the bunkers but if their commitment is genuine, the new government needs to carry changes through into the post-war period when demobilised soldiers are reintegrated into social and economic life. Carrying through this commitment to gender equity is not a simple matter because the priorities of war are different from those of post-war reconstruction. Although the rhetoric and ideology of gender equity presuppose gender transformation, the immediate need for skills, and the lack of resources to develop new ones, pose particular practical problems for new states.

Men find employment more quickly than women in skilled or semi-skilled work. Such work may or may not have any relation to the skills learned in the military. Women face the usual obstacles to employment in fields conventionally dominated by men. Although liberation armies were integrated, the market-driven productive enterprises of societies in the process of economic reconstruction may or may not be. Job market segregation presents the first practical hurdle that alters the possibilities for women's employment and often blocks what had appeared to be a transformative process.

In South Africa, high levels of unemployment accompanied the dismantling of structural apartheid in an international context of globalisation and economic marginalisation. At a formal level, and in terms of the institutionalisation of policies to further the interests of women, it is instructive to compare South Africa's transition with that of Mozambique, Eritrea and Rwanda. From at least the 1950s, South African women were at the forefront of protest and organisation against apartheid. The key to their successful mobilisation and sustained political action resides in two significant phenomena. The first is that, since the Second World War, the black working-class population has experienced high rates of urbanisation. The second is the high level of worker, women and youth mobilisation and, reaching beyond these groups, the organisation of civil society to include the establishment of professional and business organisations as well as community organisations known as civics. From at least the 1960s, in spite of the repression of the apartheid state, mobilisation and politicisation continued.

Women in townships, in the suburbs and in rural areas organised around their particular needs and interests. They established organisations, whether as women or in their communities, that often transcended the racial categories and ethnic divisions the apartheid state had forced upon them. Women gained a sense of their right to full equality from this separate organisational culture during the thirty-year struggle. Because South Africans demanded equality – not simply civil and political rights, but also socio-economic rights and redress – women had an opportunity to push for an expansive notion of equal rights in the transition. And it was the existence of vibrant women's organisations inside the country that ensured the reflection of women's interests in the new constitution.

Similar levels of civil society organisation and political remobilisation were not present in many of the societies that emerged from war. Not fully developed in the discussion at the workshop about Eritrea, for instance, was how the gendered nature of the political movement and its leadership, or the syncretic nature of the different Marxist ideologies and social practices of the movement, shaped women's participation in the struggle. There was no organised movement to remobilise women in the aftermath to act or lobby in terms of women's interests and needs. The national debate excluded a woman's agenda. Military demobilisation deprived women of the gains they made during the war.

The Long-term Effects of Wartime Changes

Economic, social, political and demographic changes during wartime have lasting effects on the age structure of populations, the proportion and geographic distribution of men and women, and the responsibilities of citizens, especially women. Shifting battle fronts create refugees; firepower, food shortages and epidemics sicken and kill both soldiers and civilians; the number of widows grows, as does the number of children orphaned. In the long run, these changes affect gender relations.

Economic changes

In Mozambique, for example, the decade-long liberation struggle profoundly altered the geographical distribution of its population. More than 1 million people moved into Maputo, the capital, during the war against Portugal. This influx created a huge demand for infrastructure that could not be met because civil war quickly interrupted reconstruction and put the economy back on a war footing.

During the liberation war, FRELIMO (Mozambique Liberation Front) developed new ways of living in the zones it had liberated from Portuguese rule. A combination of state farms and farming cooperatives provided women with at least an ideology of socialist equality. Workshop participant Sonya Nhantumbo, a researcher from Eduardo Mondlane University, described what happened in different phases of the transformation after 1975 as shown in a study carried out in the village of Mitelene in Manhiça District, near Maputo. The farmers in these communities formed cooperative structures that were of a political nature, based on Marxist principles. They divided profits on egalitarian lines. From 1975 to 1980, these cooperatives produced food and exported some of it. But the civil war against RENAMO (Mozambican National Resistance), which lasted from 1976 to 1992, disrupted this system. During the conflict RENAMO targeted the cooperatives, forcing the farmers to abandon their agricultural lands and flee to urban or periurban areas.

Many of the associations belonged to women. This was a new development, for traditionally communities allocated land to men even though women farmed it – women did not have the right to own land but had rights of access to land in order to produce food for their families. In fact the 1976 constitution did not protect private property; not until the new constitution of 1990 did private property owners have a legal defence. After 1990, these associations fought for full rights of ownership. Some NGOs supported their endeavours by providing agricultural extension education and training to potential women farmers. Because many of the old cooperatives were in infertile regions, new associations emerged to try to claim fertile land elsewhere.

Nhantumbo argued that one of the main problems with reconstruction in the rural areas was that the government often allocated farms to non-farmers. The intellectual elite in Maputo – those with economic and political power – acquired the land the farmers had left after 1976. Moreover, independent women farmers faced problems of availability of accessible markets to sell their products. As in most post-war societies, educated Mozambican women and women with political influence and status found paths to economic independence and political power. But for poor, uneducated women, the transition to democracy and post-war reconstruction did not necessarily translate into improved access to resources, let alone transformation. The experience of Mozambican women points to a key question: is it possible to speak of democracy or equal citizenship in these new developmental states when women do not have economic or social independence? We must see the integration of women into the process of change and the economy as an important variable in explaining the reconstitution of gender relations in either a transformative or a conservative direction in the aftermath of war.

Social changes
In some countries – in Eritrea and Rwanda, for instance – women have seemed to abandon in the post-conflict era many of the social changes they had won and social roles they had assumed during the war. In the aftermath of the Eritrean liberation war, women were apparently unsuccessful in consolidating the social gains they made during the conflict. The state introduced an electoral quota at local level, and as a result women hold between 23 and 30 per cent of all local government seats, but women were not so successful at the national level.

One of the most significant reasons for this retrogression is that the reconstruction of societal relations entailed the reassertion of restrictive family values. Women became the bedrock of constructing the peace through their roles as mothers and caregivers of the nation. Despite progressive rhetoric, social policy in emergent democracies and post-war societies in reconstruction takes for granted that women will be the caregivers – not equal partners or, more significantly, not equal citizens. The focus on economic reconstruction provides an opportunity to redefine women's roles in terms of family responsibilities or, by extension, to identify women as those most able to assume social responsibility for education and welfare.

Emphasis on the family, though, does not always lead to a closing of opportunities for women. In South Africa, the rhetoric of motherhood was closely linked with the struggle for family life in the context of the apartheid migrant labour system. One of the first acts of the new South African government was to promulgate free health care for mothers and for children under six years of age, acknowledging the right to motherhood as well as the right to health. Women had played a significant role in the anti-apartheid struggle, militantly reacting to and organising against restrictions that kept families apart and against the establishment of a racially and sexually segregated labour market. In the first post-apartheid decade, South Africa began dismantling the racialised basis of society. In the transition, women were well organised and vocal, inserting their demands for gender equality (in which women and men receive the same treatment) and equity (fair equivalents for women and men) during the negotiations (Albertyn 1994; Meintjes 1998).

Political changes

The presence of women in government has been significant in Eritrea in the post-war period, partly as a result of the strategies adopted by the National Union of Eritrean Women (NUEW), which held workshops to encourage women to run for office in elections and brought strong pressure to bear on prominent women to become candidates. The women's lobby encouraged women's unions at the local level. The Eritrean People's Liberation Front set a quota at local levels, so women did well in the local elections, winning 23 to 30 per cent of the seats. Women did not do as well at the national level. A lobby pushed for 50 per cent of ministerial posts to be held by women, but only one powerful woman found a place, as the Minister of Women. Several ministries did employ women 'in powerful positions. The NUEW strategy did not include women ex-combatants. Women fighters were not educated and their skill was fighting, not politics.

The participation of women in public politics may have contradictory effects, however. In the post-war period in Mozambique, although the government appointed women to key posts, the result was not the feminisation of public policy but rather the masculinisation of these women, who were cut off from the women's movement. Because of the masculinisation of women's leadership, the government did not attend to women's needs. Nhantumbo gave the example of a district in which the local authority president was a woman who placed emphasis on women's rights. During the local elections, the party used the issues of land rights and sanitation to mobilise women. The land issue appealed to women in the provinces, where they had limited access to agricultural land near roads and markets and therefore could not sell their produce. But after the elections, the politicians forgot these issues and changes did not take place. Instead, the party relegated women to activities regarded as appropriate to women. Nhantumbo suggested that it is important to focus on strategies for integrating women's needs following the mobilisation of women into representative positions. Part of the problem might be the lack of mechanisms for women's organisations to retain the accountability of women politicians (Nhantumbo, conference participant).

Mozambique has eschewed a specific focus on women in the establishment of its structures of governance. The Ministry of Social Affairs deals with women's and children's affairs. In parliament, a Commission for Social Affairs encompasses women's problems. This lack of designated responsibility has meant a loss of focus on the problems of violence against women and young children. Nhantumbo observed that only the NGOs focused on these problems, but in order to function they are dependent upon foreign donors for funding. Foreign donors often dictate an NGO's agenda, weakening the independence and potential for development within organisations. Instead of programmatic action, most NGOs (including one run by Graça Machel) have changed their focus to research and education.

Gender mainstreaming (the incorporation of gender concerns into activities to deal effectively with the obstacles that women face) is a possible mechanism for ensuring that gender transformation benefits women. The process has unfolded differently in various post-war situations. South Africa has gone some way towards mainstreaming, but it is not a panacea. The gender machinery set up in the post-apartheid era did not take the lead in policy formulation. Instead, a combination of civil society organisations and individual activists, both within the parliament and outside, made the difference in gender-sensitive policy making (Albertyn et al. 1999).

The Women's National Coalition formed in South Africa in the early 1990s reached across political allegiances in civil society, specifically to ensure that women's substantive issues found their way on to the national political agenda. Although disagreements often surfaced, the overall objective was to include effective equality in the constitution as a fundamental principle. Agreement on this aspect of the women's agenda unified the Women's National Coalition and created bonds among women that transcended political differences. The ongoing national civic networks were significant for advocacy around many gender policy issues, enabling women in parliament and civil society to work together to ensure that policies and legislation really met women's needs. Activism of this nature requires the organisation of many groups in order to maintain links, a task that is not always easy, because many organisations themselves are fluid and in transformation. It is not an embedded process.

Although the South African government and constitution have highlighted gender equality, practical and normative problems remain. Masemanyane, a women's NGO, participated in a research project to evaluate women in politics. Women politicians expressed concern about men dominating politics. ANC women parliamentarians complained of the ANC caucus ignoring them even when the chief whip noted their wish to speak. Moreover, when women tried to meet together, they were unable to do so because rooms were unavailable. Other problems included the difficulty for working mothers of attending evening meetings and the blocking by bureaucrats of some women's acquisition of computers.

In South Africa, the new democratic framework, and especially the protection of civil and human rights embedded in the new constitution, did contribute to creating the conditions for gender equity. But neither the Commission for Gender Equality, nor the Office on the Status of Women, which controls structures in government such as the gender desks, initiated the development of gender equity policy. Rather, well-placed individual feminists in parliament, in partnership with lobbies and organisations in civil society, pushed women's equality and equity issues. In the formulation of policy around such issues as violence against women, maintenance payments, reproductive rights and customary law in South Africa, activists were also involved in drawing up legislation through their participation in the South African Law Commission. Amongst those actively involved were not only feminist legal experts, but also violence counsellors, for example. This was an important strategy in fostering a new relationship between civil society and government. Involvement of women's organisations in policy making provided a challenge to society's traditional views about the capacity of women for governance and decision making. The interventions also shifted the boundaries of policing, which conventionally eschewed interfering in the private realm, to create new institutional mechanisms to deal with violence against women. It was understood that even judges were part of the problem. Gender mainstreaming challenged the way society conceived of policy making, the law and its agencies, including the courts and the police.

Conclusion

Why are gender shifts so fragile, and is the reversal of gender shifts inevitable? Are women complicit in restructuring patriarchal power in the process of post-war reconstruction, or do they struggle against patriarchal reconstruction? The answers to these questions are complex, because in the period immediately following the cessation of hostilities, it is the male political leaders who meet to broker peace. This is the moment at which women should be participating in the structuring of the new order, yet this is the precisely the moment at which women are not present. Unless women are organised in the period preceding negotiations and are prepared to push a woman's agenda in the context of the peace-making process and the power brokering, there is a danger that the men in power will sideline the needs and interests of women, in both practical and strategic terms. Thus it is important, as the above examples have shown, that women follow up the changes wrought during wartime by means of an organised force, whether this is in the form of a coalition or some other organisational structure.

Note

1. I chaired the workshop on shifts in gender relations. Participants included Marguerite Coly Keny, Fédération des Associations Féminines du Sénégal, Ziguinchor, Casamance, Senegal; Patricia Ellis, Women's Foreign Policy Group, Washington, DC, USA; Cathy Feingold, Ford Foundation, New York, NY, USA; Doreen Foster, Masimanyane Women's Support Centre, East London, South Africa; Lloys Frates, USA; Sondra Hale, Department of Anthropology, University of California, Los Angeles, CA, USA; Heywote Hailemeskal, Office of the UN High Commissioner for Refugees, Addis Ababa, Ethiopia; Jean Munro, Peacebuilding and Reconstruction Program Initiative, International Development Research Centre, Ottawa,

Canada; Bernedette Muthien, Quaker Peace Centre, University of the Western Cape, Cape Town, South Africa; Sonya Nhantumbo, University of Eduardo Mondlane, Mozambique; Gael Neke, University of the Witwatersrand, Johannesburg, South Africa; Maureen Ringo, South Africa.

CHAPTER 6

Engendering Relations
of State to Society
in the Aftermath

MEREDETH TURSHEN

Most African women live under more than one 'state' in the sense that they live under more than one set of laws, and that fact complicates any discussion of women in relation to the state. In the aftermath of war and armed conflict, many women want to reopen the question of their status, and if they have fought in a liberation war, they may have high expectations of improving their condition. At least two legal regimes govern women's lives simultaneously: the statutory regime of the nation-state and the customary regime of their natal household or clan. When women marry into a society ruled by a different set of customary laws, they are subject to yet a third regime. Sometimes it is clear which laws take precedence, but that clarity may not be honoured in practice or even in court, especially in the areas of personal law (matrimonial regimes, for example) that most affect women. Men's interests dominate both statutory and customary systems, which are patriarchal. Of the two, women have found it harder to change customary regimes; the reasons for this are complex, not the least important factor being the legacy of colonial rule in the nineteenth and twentieth centuries.

Colonial officials subsidised African men in order to increase men's productivity, generate more revenue from wage labour and cash-crop agriculture, and spur capital accumulation, all in the interest of supporting the state (Parpart and Staudt 1989:11–12). Subsidies took the form of access to resources (land titles, credit and extension services, for example) and ascendance in state institutions. Some analysts hold that male elders allied themselves with colonial rulers to secure their control over women through customary law (Martin Charnock, cited in Parpart and Staudt 1989:7). As colonial rulers extracted wealth, they compensated African men by aiding and abetting their control of women. The refusal to recognise the cash value of women's work enabled men to acquire the wealth that subsidised colonial capital accumulation. And by entrenching gender hierarchy, the state was able to lower the cost of reproducing labour (Parpart and Staudt 1989:6).

One enduring question for feminists is why even those liberation movements that espoused equality failed to deliver the promised emancipation to women once they took power as the legitimate government. Nada Ali attributes the failure to deal with women's issues after independence in Algeria to France's use of women's liberation as a way to construct Algerian society as backward.[1] Algerian women are more likely to attribute their setbacks to the military regime that assumed power after 1965 and successfully suppressed all opposition until 1988. Sondra Hale (see Chapter 8) says that after liberation the Eritrean People's Liberation Front (EPLF) failed to pay attention to the constraints of traditional processes that Eritrean women encountered on their return to family life and that this failure amounted to the abandonment of certain social gains that EPLF women had experienced in the bunkers. 'Among these gains were free social relations with men, relaxed social customs and habits – including dress and hairstyles – the lack of social pressure toward marriage and childbearing, the collapse of the conventional gender division of labour, and the like.'

Two basic questions are of utmost concern to this discussion. Does the consolidation of women's wartime gains depend on the state (for example, legal reform, social spending) or on women's organisations and movements (for example, the ongoing mobilisation of women)? Do the difficulties women encounter post-war stem from 'traditional' attitudes towards women (and men's expectations of women's place in the culture) or from the problems of reconciling the very different sets of behaviour that prevail in the bunkers and in civilian society? The questions arise because, far from disappearing in the postcolonial period, the contradictions of customary and statutory regimes remain unresolved. One reason is that many states emerge from war weakened, in the sense that they are narrowly based, resource-poor and unwilling or unable to meet the needs of their diverse populations. The World Bank and international donors often recommend that such governments decentralise, a strategy that exacerbates these contradictions. In the aftermath of civil wars that are fought by identity groups, an environment of decentralised, weakened government fosters the re-emergence of local customs. Lepa Mladjenovic says that violence creates identities (see Chapter 11). In Africa, a process of 'retraditionalisation' reinvents latent ethnic identities.

Tradition

Chapters in this volume by Codou Bop, Tina Sideris and Sheila Meintjes (chapters 2, 4 and 5) show how patriarchal gender relations undergo important changes during conflict. In the absence of men, women take some painful steps forward: they begin to transform traditional gender roles as they assume men's former tasks; they gain access to public spaces previously denied them; some even achieve a degree of economic independence. Under the harsh conditions of civil conflict, women do demonstrate an ability to transform their lives. In changing women's gender roles, war provides opportunities for some women to emerge as leaders. Yasmin Sooka, a human rights lawyer who chairs the Human Rights Committee of the South African Truth and Reconciliation Commission (TRC), Judge Albie Sachs of South Africa's Constitutional Court, and Thandi Modise all describe African National Congress (ANC) comrades who broke out of old moulds during the anti-apartheid struggles.

If this is so, why do negotiators exclude women from decisions on the shape of the peace and from activities to reconstruct society that follow the signing of treaties? A variety of answers emerge: some women want to maintain their new freedoms (for example, Eritrean fighters) and participate in decision making in public forums, whereas others collude in the reversion to the old status quo (the role of mothers-in-law in Eritrea; see Chapter 8). Women's expectations in the aftermath differ according to their experiences and engagement in the conflict: for example, some women were themselves combatants, or had sustained male combatants; many were refugees and internally displaced; others remained in their homes in urban or rural areas. Some women return from war exhausted, thinking, 'Let me now just use this peace to gather my family and to try to get more bread on the table, some better shelter'. Other women come back with very different ideas, developed because they were combatants or because they were in exile mobilising women, or because they were actively engaged in war support work. They say, 'Let me continue the transformation of society for which I have been fighting.' Not only expectations determine participation in the aftermath, but also rules about who can speak with authority: Thandi Modise notes that tensions exist between 'insiders' who remained in South Africa during the struggle and people who returned from exile. In some cases men's expectations were radically different from women's: some men wanted only the comforts of a home and a woman to cook, clean and bear children. This image raised the issue of post-war return to 'normalcy'.

Heike Becker (see Chapter 14) considered the picture of women going back and picking up the pieces and asked, 'How do we see normality, does the return to normality automatically mean it is the same as before the war?' Kate Lifanda thought some women just wanted normalcy, meaning society as it was before the war: 'parents trying to send children to school; husbands trying to be with their wives; parents trying to marry off their children; people acting the way they have always acted within their culture and tradition'. She questioned how much culture and traditions changed in wartime. When the war stops, when 'things go back to normal, people go back to what they know, to what they are comfortable with, to what they identify with, which is the traditional society that very often is not advantageous to women.' Nada Ali agreed that a return to pre-war normality would not favour women because male leaders had defined what is normal. Artemisa Franco concluded, 'I don't think we will reach consensus on what is considered normalcy. The normalcy [Mozambican] people cherished, women especially, was the end of the war ... [but] the culture and the spiritual aspect [of society] had been broken.'

Clearly each war is different, and war is as uneven as development; not all parts of a country are affected equally or in the same ways. Many societies do not survive war intact. In the West African Workshop on Women in the Aftermath of War held in Dakar in December 1998, women from Liberia said, 'If only those [traditional] structures had survived, we could use them to our advantage, but they have been destroyed.' And women from Sierra Leone said, 'Nothing of the old structure exists; there isn't anything to go back to which will give you that [traditional] identity.' Kate Lifanda thought that the aftermath, as a transition stage, is an ideal time to review constitutions and laws to ensure that international instruments such as CEDAW (the UN Convention on the Elimination of All Forms of Discrimination Against Women) can be integrated into national legislation. She wanted legal institutions that would protect everybody, particularly the most vulnerable. She also outlined the need for strengthened national institutions, so that existing laws could be enforced, 'because if the laws and institutions are weak, what is the point of reporting on violence? There is no point.'

In discussing the effect of changed gender roles on women's participation in reconstruction, one must take account of the variety of state formations emerging from war in Africa, which range from military regimes to pluralist democracies, and from strong to weak to no state at all. The re-emergence of customary practices is not confined to any one type of regime. Even in democratic and socialist states that adopted egalitarian statutory laws in the period after the liberation war, tradition now prevails. The Zimbabwe Supreme Court ruled 5–0 in 1999 that tradition overrides both the constitution and the 1982 Majority Age Act in a case brought by a daughter evicted from her father's estate by her half-brother. Citing the deep roots of patriarchy in Africa, the judges said that the nature of African society relegates women to a lesser status, especially in the home. A woman should not be considered an adult within the family, only a 'junior male'. Justice Simbarashe Muchechetere said the Majority Age Act, which affirmed that women over eighteen years old could not be treated as minors, had been interpreted too widely and had given women rights they never had under customary law. Because it is a full-bench decision by the Supreme Court, there is no appeal (Tucker 1999).

Heike Becker (Chapter 14) notes that debates in Namibia about the Married Persons' Equality Act turned on the commands of both African tradition and Christianity, according to which, opponents argued, women and men could never be equal. This act, which parliament adopted in May 1996 despite broad opposition from men, did away with the husband's automatic marital power and position as head of the family. Becker found a widespread perception in Namibia that women's rights and African tradition, particularly customary laws and political-judicial institutions, are eternal foes.

Yasmin Sooka, stressing the long-term impact of war, says that violence has an endemic effect on society. 'Violence, which manifested itself formerly in political life, has had a spill-over effect and it now manifests itself in crime.' In tracing the conversion of political violence to crime, Sooka notes that 'one of the legacies of apartheid has been the erosion of family life and values.' At the same time she suggests that the traditional gender construct of South African society still prevails and that the majority of men still regard women as commodities to be used by them: 'The deeply patriarchal nature of our society has meant that women more than ever are the subject of violence and sexual abuse.' These observations raise an important contradiction: war erodes some traditional values but not sexist beliefs, which (not coincidentally) were of most use to the state – whether colonial, apartheid or postcolonial.

In some societies in which women have borne the brunt of wartime violence, women are joining men in bringing back certain customs. Movements that reassert the power of tradition to heal, purify and hold communities together have arisen in several countries. Not all of the practices are positive: some are violent and some target women. The Holy Spirit Movement of Alice Lakwena in northern Uganda started as a cult of affliction centred on the healing of individual soldiers and infertile women. In August 1986 Lakwena organised the Holy Spirit Movement Forces to wage war against the government, witches and impure soldiers, using a complex initiation and purification ritual in which she freed the Holy Spirit soldiers from witchcraft and evil spirits (Behrend 1991). Similarly, in Mozambique, communities are using ceremonies to cleanse and purify people returning to areas affected by the war, to venerate ancestral spirits, and to appease the spirits of dead soldiers (Honwana 1997). In the Mozambican province of Mutarara, the spirits of dead soldiers seem always to afflict women, who pay heavily to rid the community of their persecutors (Robert Marlin, personal communication).

In rural areas of Owambo, Becker found Namibian women seeking new traditions that incorporate new values and more long-standing cultural elements. Rural Owambo women are taking up abstract constitutional notions of gender equality to change their lives for the better. They are becoming visible in local public forums and are redefining the gendered traditional politics of the colonial past, despite disempowering experiences of increasing violence, female poverty and social disintegration. Perhaps this provides a model for resolving the contradictions of old customary and new statutory laws that women in other countries could consider.

Sex and the State

In the aftermath of conflict, men attempt in three ways to reassert their control over women, which slipped from their grasp during wartime. First, they escalate social violence, both at home and in public: personal violation of women increases in the aftermath, sometimes at higher rates (and younger ages) than before (see Chapter 3). As in the past, men rely on state and customary regimes to condone this abuse. Men control women by controlling women's sexuality, and in the family they hide behind the pretext that this is the private sphere, a pretext protected by the state and custom. Unless women challenge social norms about rape and sexual abuse, unless they force change in both customary and statutory law and practice, this alliance between men and legal regimes will continue to oppress them and erode their wartime gains.

Second, men reassert control through political violence: in the aftermath of conflict, men overlook women, discount women's powers to resolve conflict, underuse women's ability to mobilise communities for reconstruction, and even remove women from leadership positions. More, men co-opt women and women's organisations to serve their political parties and ends. Thandi Modise relates how, in South Africa just before the 1994 elections, the Inkatha Freedom Party's Women's League and the ANC Women's League were coming together. This rapprochement was suspended because of the elections. 'So women retreated and there was more violence and rape,' highlighting the tension that can run within women's organisations over where loyalties lie and whether women organise along party lines (ANC/Inkatha/UDM) in an 'us versus them' way. Artemisa Franco agrees that women are tied to their party's agenda. 'In Mozambique now we have one of the highest percentages of women in the parliament, 28 per cent. But are those women taking women's perspectives to the legislative table?'

Third, men reassert control through economic violence against women. Empirical data show deterioration in the material status of women after wars (for example, increasing poverty, loss of assets, and loss of access to land), as well as demographic changes (for example, more widows, more women-headed single households, fewer men, more polygamous marriages and rising birth rates); we know these changes have deleterious economic consequences for women. Yet in the face of this evidence, most states fail to compensate women for their losses during conflict, fail to compensate women fighters, and fail to demobilise girl soldiers and reunite them with their families in the same way as boy soldiers.

United Nations Secretary-General Kofi Annan wants warring parties in Africa held accountable for their actions. He recommends that combatants be held financially liable to their victims under international law when civilians are made the deliberate target of aggression, and he wants international legal machinery to be developed to facilitate efforts to find, attach and seize the assets of transgressing parties and their leaders (UN 1998:12). Julie Shaw notes that companies, businesses and arms traders profit heavily from war. In addition to the arms trade there is the drug trade and sex trafficking. Many rebel movements finance their wars by running drugs for arms. In Algeria, for example, the FIS (the Islamic Salvation Front) was heavily involved in running arms and drugs; now it is controlled by an external 'mafia' that will be hard to dislodge (Claudine Chaulet, personal communication).

What is the relation of the war-torn state to the economy – the national economy, the parallel economy and the global economy? How does the war economy transform states beyond the militarisation of the economy? What place would war-torn states find in the global economy? What are women's roles in the war economy and what could they be in the aftermath? These are some of the many questions needing research.

In this context it is misleading to suggest that 'women are *never* central to state power' (Parpart and Staudt 1989:5). One should not confuse or conflate women's lack of political participation in public office and institutions with women's contributions of productive and reproductive labour on which the state depends. In this sense, I would argue, women are *always* central to state power, even when they are invisible in state formation, occupy political and leadership positions in symbolic numbers only, and receive no remuneration for their labour. States institutionalise men's control of women's productive and reproductive labour in part by institutionalising men's control of women's sexuality (Parpart and Staudt 1989:4), and the role of social violence in maintaining this control is widely documented (Carrillo 1991).

Women in Government

Thandi Modise cites an exceptional example of the difficulties of developing policies and strategies to influence the process of achieving democratic representation of women's interests in the aftermath. South Africa has adopted some important structures to listen to women on the ground: the office on the status of women, the commission for gender equality, and the proposed women's charter. Modise attributes these successes to women fighters who said, 'We were next to you in the bush; we'll be next to you in the government.' Women forced the ANC to adopt a one-third-quota system (which works for and against women). But although women occupy high positions in the military structures (the current deputy minister of defence is a woman), they have not been involved in diplomatic relations: no women flew with the peacemakers when South Africa became involved in the Congo; and when a South Africa delegation went to Rwanda, women had to fly there by their own means.

> Clearly women have an important role to play and we must stop shutting ourselves out of the processes. As we usually don't want war, we stay out of these situations. The ANC Women's League says we must be there. We can do a lot of critical things. We can say that the peacekeeping force must include women and people who understand the country's culture. Women in this situation could monitor the incidence of violence against women, rape, etc. (Thandi Modise, conference participant)

Letty Chiwara asks how women can counterbalance men's power-house of resources and their ability to mobilise. She wonders whether women are as willing as men to use dirty tricks to get what they want.

(Some of us thought of Indira Gandhi and Margaret Thatcher and answered, yes!) Chiwara raises an important question: how can we mobilise women to vote for women? The United Nations Development Programme (UNDP) funded a project on women in decision making to try to put women into local authority positions in Zimbabwe. It didn't work because women at community level wouldn't vote for women who were being proposed for these positions. Nada Ali explains that some women might not vote for another woman because of her politics. She wouldn't vote for a woman who thought that women's human rights should not conflict with religious beliefs and patriarchal traditions. On the other hand, the evidence suggests that women are voting for women: according to Becker (see Chapter 14) some 40 per cent of all members of Namibian city, town and village councils are currently women, and almost a quarter of the members of the National Assembly (the first house of parliament) are women. The situation is similar in Eritrea: women represent 22 per cent of the national parliament and women's representation at the regional level exceeds the quota set aside for women (see Chapter 8).

Strong states emerged from the liberation struggles in South Africa and Zimbabwe. More typical, in the aftermath of violence, is a weakened state with few resources or, as in the case of Somalia, no state at all. What chances do women have to transform gender relations in these circumstances? What are women's experiences in civil society?

Women in Nongovernmental Organisations

Because so many African women are excluded from formal politics, their public participation often occurs in women's civil society organisations, which have flourished since 1990. Women's reliance on nongovernmental organising emerges strongly in every country. Artemisa Franco notes that in Mozambique, where administration of the law is weakening, civil society organised itself to come to the aid of the vulnerable: many NGOs are doing legal aid for vulnerable people because the legal framework is weak. She points out that sometimes governments fail to communicate with civil society organisations, and some civil society organisations regard government as hostile, especially when their views aren't accepted and integrated in state policies. She faults state policy makers for failing to consult the people on their needs and expectations: 'They only come out during elections.'

There is a tendency not to define society and to assume that society is coterminous with civil society. On reflection, this assumption is questionable: the state and the family are part of society, but usually civil society occupies the space in between. Also, each actor defines civil society in a different way, according to his or her own agenda. Then, too, people have a tendency to recognise only positive examples of civics. Nada Ali is acutely aware of how the National Islamic Front (NIF) regime in Sudan mobilises women: 'the NIF ... succeeded in attracting female members in the urban areas who subscribed to the NIF's construction of women as markers of Islam.' As a result, women were physically absent in post-1985 formal politics, and the various frameworks aiming at reconstituting Sudan were gendered as male. She concludes that, in some cases, the line between state and civil society is thin, and not all women's civil society organisations deal with women's problems (Ali 1999).

We are critical of the role of NGOs in neoliberal policies, which assign to charities the work of providing services formerly offered by the state. African liberation movements believed in nation-building and strong states. This is why Teboho Mpondo thinks that South African women are waiting for the state to deliver. But today international donors postulate privatisation and recommend downsizing the state except for the military, which is needed to control popular opposition to austerity policies. At the West African Workshop on Women in the Aftermath of War, women from Sierra Leone and Liberia said, 'When we look back at the liberation movements, they all had great expectations.' But today women aren't waiting, as they know that states offer nothing. Nada Ali says that because there is a contradiction between religious organisations and women's human rights in the Sudan, religious organisations with patriarchal traditions should not be the sole source of services for women. This issue arose in Rwanda in 1994 when Catholic medical missions refused to provide abortions to women who had been raped, and now society bears the problem of unwanted or abandoned children.

Lina Zedriga describes an experience from Uganda, where the World Bank is testing the policy of privatisation.

As a civil society organisation we first documented the impact of structural adjustment programmes on the rural women. We made a case study of the extreme north [of the country] (the revelations of that report are terrible) and presented it in a silent demonstration to the World Bank in Uganda. This silent demonstration forced the government to recognise women's organisations, and we now have three seats in the economic policy unit, which is the highest level of planning. Our goal is to influence government decisions regarding IMF [International Monetary Fund] and World Bank privatisation plans and structural adjustment programmes. The lesson we learned is that we must document the impact of these policies; we must have our facts, so that when we call our governments to task, they will listen.

Women in Peace Negotiations

Formal peace negotiations among representatives of warring parties serve to define basic power relations and to identify priorities for immediate post-war political activity (Sorenson 1998). In most cases negotiators excluded women from high-level parleys, which society considers male domains and which employ discourses and practices that are closer to men's reality than to women's. Women also lack direct influence in identifying the priorities for reconstruction that are usually part of a peace agreement. One notable exception is Somalia: Somali women received an invitation to participate in an early peace conference in Mogadishu. Later, many clans forced the rejection of a recommendation that all regional representations to the Transitional National Council should include at least one woman; this was because they would not accept being represented by a woman (Jama, cited in Sorenson 1998).

Women most often find ways to work for peace and reconciliation through their strength in grassroots organisations. Frequently they initiate their activities at the peak of atrocities and instability. Women from all walks of life participate in this informal peace-building work, but their activities are often disparaged as 'volunteer', 'charitable' or 'social', even when they have a political impact (Ferris, cited by Sorenson 1998). Though positioned on the margins, grassroots organisations show their ability to mobilise large numbers of women and to translate individual grievances into legitimate social concerns (see chapters 7 and 13). They constantly challenge authorities and other members of society with demands for peace, non-discrimination, accountability, recognition of human rights, etcetera. Many women work to build a new culture of peace at the local level by organising peace education and community-based reconciliation and social reconstruction activities (Sorenson 1998).

Men disparage women's peace activities as only a natural extension of their nurturing and caring domestic roles as wives and mothers (see chapters 7 and 13), despite women's well-documented participation in wars as combatants. (Angola, Chad, Eritrea, Kenya, Liberia, Mozambique, Namibia, South Africa and Uganda all had female fighters, and some Rwandan women participated in the genocide.) Agnès Allafi speaks movingly about her experience as a fighter in Chad and of women's work for peace: 'We celebrated the Week of the Women and the International Day for Women from 1 to 8 March 2000; our theme was women and a culture of peace.'

Women and women's organisations (including refugees and women living in exile) are now demanding representation in peace negotiations. They recognise the necessity of identifying all stakeholders – internal and external, public and behind-the-scenes – and naming what each stands to gain from peace, if women are to participate effectively in the peace process. Women and women's organisations are also aware of the political economy of war, the vested interests that profit from and work to sustain chaotic conditions. Angela Raven-Roberts suggests that in reality there are several tables at peace negotiations – one on the constitution, one on legal reforms, etcetera – and that each table should be gendered and involve women. In order to be heard, women need to be higher up in the various structures – within movements, armies, political parties and opposition groups – and they need to be organised. This means enabling women to sit at the peace table, to represent women and to discuss the issues that must be put on the table. For this they need capacity training at all levels, as well as a sense of how to use this training process to foster mobilisation and dialogue regarding representation and change. Women need links with other organisations to know what is happening in other countries.

Women's wish to be included in peace negotiations is more than a simple demand for a proportional numeric representation. Based on the belief that institutions governed by men are unlikely to reflect women's specific interests and views, the demand reflects women's increasing awareness of the potential for transformation and reform in periods immediately preceding and following peace. The aftermath is too late. Efforts should be made to integrate women's important work at the grassroots level into the main exercise of building peace (Sorenson 1998).

Demobilisation and Demilitarisation

The reintegration of demobilised combatants is a costly and complex process that is crucial to peace-building. An estimated 1 million combatants and militia are eligible for demobilisation in Africa. The tendency has been to focus on the reintegration of demobilised soldiers, refugees and internally displaced persons; more recently persons marked and marginalised by torture, disability, widowhood, etcetera are subjects of concern. The issue of integration is relevant to all members of society because the social, economic and political composition of every war-torn society inevitably undergoes profound changes (Sorenson 1998). From a gender and family perspective, integration often means dealing with disintegration. 'Newly gained economic freedom and independence, long years of separation and exposure to new social environments and attitudes, new perceptions of the role of the family and its members, and forced migration in search of employment, all contribute to continued dismantling of existing social institutions and the establishment of new ones' (Sorenson 1998:ix). Social integration is about defining new, guiding, social values and establishing corresponding relationships and institutions based on many factors, including kinship, social and economic interests, and shared experiences and circumstances (Sorenson 1998).

Demobilisation in militarised governments that came to power through warfare is filled with extreme contradictions. And given the long duration of many civil wars in Africa, the deep penetration of the military in civil society means that demobilisation has to be a much more profound process than the decommissioning of soldiers. Artemisa Franco suggests that both demobilisation and reintegration are needed.

One of the failures of demobilisation in Mozambique is that ex-combatants have nothing to do. During the war they didn't acquire skills or have job training. The only skill they have is how to handle a gun and kill. The success of demobilisation must be judged by reintegration. Otherwise, at the first call, men will remobilise; they still have their guns somewhere. In some provinces when they are hungry, they stop cars on the road and they shoot, stealing whatever they can. When women demobilise they work in the informal sector, the black market and border trade with South Africa. But men often don't find their feet in any kind of business and become criminals, recruited by gangs, the mafia and drug dealers across southern Africa. (Franco, conference participant)

Lina Zedriga supports demobilisation but notes the vicious cycle caused by the ongoing wars in northern and western Uganda. The government demobilised a large percentage of the army and gave the soldiers a very good package including corrugated iron sheets and money to build local housing. But the government then recruited these demobilised soldiers to fight rebels in the north and west and later sent them to Congo.

We need to intervene in such circumstances to say, hey, this is wrong! Some of those demobilised soldiers who were recruited and sent to the north were then abducted by the rebels and are now fighting against the government. So this is the scenario in Uganda. It is very absurd. It is very sad. (Zedriga, conference participant)

She suggests that there is a need for a mechanism to monitor demobilised soldiers, so that we could take action in cases of abduction or recruitment. She wants to hold governments accountable and calls for transparency between the state and society.

Kate Lifanda urges the creation of a culture of nonviolence and recommends peace education for all, at all stages, in schools, in government, wherever, so that people will understand the need to have peace rather than violence as a culture. With peace education, people must be informed of their rights. 'If you don't know your rights you can't have access. If the institution is not there, you can't go to the institution and be protected. If the constitution doesn't have it, where do you even begin?'

Reconciliation and Reparations

Many current African conflicts are civil wars in which the legitimacy of the state is contested, and many women suffer at the hands of both state and non-state actors. The issue of reconciliation, therefore, has especial salience for women. In some instances the former state is defeated and dissolved (as was the case in Uganda after the NRM (National Resistance Movement) fought its way to power in 1986), but in others the new style of conflict resolution dictates power sharing by the former warring parties (as in Mozambique and Sierra Leone). At the West African Workshop on Women in the Aftermath of War, women from Sierra Leone talked of the impossibility of returning to villages that were now governed by the very men who had raped them. Amnesty has a different meaning for men than for women; it leaves women feeling vulnerable to further attacks, particularly when the attacker was a former neighbour, a common situation in civil wars.

Yasmin Sooka talks about reconciliation and reparations, a theme repeated by others. South Africans established the Truth and Reconciliation Commission (TRC) at a time when the world was engaged in major debates around the questions of amnesty and whether truth commissions could deal effectively with accountability and truth seeking. Sooka thinks we have come a long way since then, and now the successful South African model is available to other countries. But she acknowledges that the South African debates, like the world debates, were not gendered. The TRC was weak on extracting the truth about women and on giving them just compensation.[2] 'If one examines the statistics of who made statements to the Commission, more than 55 per cent were women. Invariably they talked about the experiences of their menfolk, their children, and loved ones' (Sooka 1999). Women did not talk about themselves.

Many women gave testimony on the trauma experienced over the loss of home and possessions, either at the hands of police with their bulldozers or through the deliberate violence of an attack that drove them out. South African women have shared the experiences of forced migration and displacement with women in other parts of the world, including the experiences of being housed in *ad hoc* shelters, relocating to other countries and staying in refugee camps. In Alexandra and the East Rand of South Africa, one of the first tasks of the new provincial government was to ensure that people were able to reclaim their old homes in the townships. The loss of a home and dear possessions, often the only visible means of security for the family, causes trauma that cannot be underestimated: some women never recover.

Lina Zedriga discusses legal structures to deal with the aftermath of war. She notes that, in addition to the South African Truth and Reconciliation Commission, other truth commissions had convened in Africa – in Chad and Uganda. She wonders how effective and gender-balanced they were in their administration: 'Do they have something in place for the women complainants or victims? What redress is there?' She notes that truth commissions meet mostly in capital cities; she recommends that these institutions move to the areas where most affected women live, so that the commissions can have an impact on the ground. She relates her experience at a workshop for women living in camps in Gulu, a war-torn area of northern Uganda.[3] 'They were so bitter at the state. Their houses were burned, they were raped, their husbands were killed, and their sons were abducted. They feel they lost a lot and must be paid, they must be compensated or the rebels must be arrested and brought to justice.'

Conclusion

War, as we all know, has destabilising effects on states, on ethnic communities, on families and on individual women and men. The aftermath is both an opportunity for women to transform political relations and a dangerous situation in which weakened states fail to give women the security or resources they need for reconstruction. Constitutional and economic issues play a part in the work of integrating gender into post-war reconstruction strategies and policy. Women need to demand new structures and services to ensure their access to land and to public services; they need to consider how structures and services might be shaped to contribute to a lasting peace. Apparently more than social pressures are needed to overcome customary barriers to women's access to land: legal reforms are necessary. Nor can faith-based charities provide the public services all women need: state resources are necessary to reach the entire population equitably. Conflict creates new problems of social dislocation and cultural disorientation, for which local communities are best suited to finding solutions; international material aid and technical advice are essential to rebuilding societies but should be subordinate to local institutions so as not to become a barrier to creative local problem solving. Given the extraordinary diversity of aftermath experiences, divergent thinking is necessary in addressing both the process of democratic representation of women's interests and the social transformation of gender relations in state and society.

It is essential to ensure the representation of women and women's organisations at every stage of any peace negotiation processes. Yet the systematic use of violence suppresses women at every stage and as a result men exclude women from decision making in public forums, from the political processes leading up to conflict, from the decisions and actions that occur during conflict and from decisions on the shape of the peace and of activities to reconstruct society that follow the signing of treaties. If women are to transform decision-making processes, we need more research to understand better the profound changes in gender (and generational) relations during conflict and the pressures on men and women to reverse or conserve those changes in the aftermath.

No clear cut-off day marks the end of conflict and the beginning of post-conflict, as many processes continue long after wars end. Post-conflict demilitarisation of society is important in establishing a culture of peace, and all women, including those living in exile and refugee camps, have a special role and contribution to make in building the peace processes.

Notes

1. The comments cited in this chapter were made in discussions held in the workshop on relations of state and society in the aftermath that took place at the conference on 'The Aftermath: Women in Post-Conflict Transformation', held in Johannesburg on 20–22 July 1999. I chaired the workshop. Participants included: Nada Mustafa Ali, Sudan Women's Alliance, London, UK; Agnès Allafi, Ministère de l'Action Sociale, N'Djaména, Chad; Heike Becker, University of Namibia, Windhoek; Letty Chiwara, national programme officer, UNIFEM, Harare, Zimbabwe; Patricia Ellis, Women's Foreign Policy Group, Washington, DC, USA; Artemisa Franco, secretary-general, Association of Human Rights and Development, Maputo, Mozambique; Kate Lifanda-Freeman, UNICEF,

Abidjan, Côte d'Ivoire; Teboho Mpondo, student at the University of the Witwatersrand, Johannesburg, South Africa; Angela Raven-Roberts, Tufts University, Boston, MA, USA; Julie Shaw, director, Urgent Action Fund for Women's Human Rights, Fairfax, CA, USA; Frances Spencer, Trauma Clinic, Centre for the Study of Violence and Reconciliation, Johannesburg, South Africa; and Lina Zedriga, National Association of Women Judges, Kampala, Uganda.

2. Goldblatt and Meintjes (1998) give a full account of how the TRC came to consider gender, as well as a detailed analysis of women's struggles under apartheid.

3. The Lord's Resistance Army, led by Joseph Kony, has been attacking northern Uganda and abducting children since the early 1990s. The government has established camps for the displaced, but they afford little protection from the LRA, which raids them for supplies.

PART II

Contemporary Experiences

CHAPTER 7

Ambivalent Gains
in South Asian Conflicts

RITA MANCHANDA

The dominant image of women in the iconography of war is that of the eternal victim, passive and without agency, an outsider to the battlefront. Women are visible as the overwhelming victims, direct and indirect, of violent conflict. Violence consists of rape and the trauma of displacement, disappearances, torture and killings, as well as the gendered politics of body searches at checkpoints. In the aftermath of war, women are victims of the fallout in domestic and societal violence of predatory masculinities and misogyny fostered in conflict. Peace researchers with a feminist consciousness are interrogating this dominant discourse of victimhood to make visible the complexity and multiplicity of women's experiences of conflict (Lorentzen and Turpin 1998).

In the bubbling cauldron of South Asian conflicts, moving beyond the passivity and powerlessness of victimhood, women have forged survival strategies, mobilised resistance and entered into negotiations of power with the security forces, the administration and the courts. Women have formed mothers' fronts and coalitions for peace, women have become guerrillas and soldiers, and women have emerged as agents of social change, conflict resolution and transformation. In this chapter I argue that, in addition to inflicting traumatic loss and destitution, conflict opens up intended and unintended spaces for empowering women, effecting structural social transformations and producing new social, economic and political realities that redefine gender and caste hierarchies (Das 1995).

There is a need to integrate into the dominant discourse of women's experience of loss in conflict, the parallel and more problematic subtext of gains – processes that open up ambivalent spaces for women's agency through loss (McKay 1998; Sharoni 1998). The gains discourse tends to make peace researchers uncomfortable. They are sceptical of the possibility of protracted conflict effecting desirable structural transformations in the context of the entrenched social hierarchies and inequalities of gender and caste that exist in South Asia. The lack of a critical analysis to determine the processes of change wrought in conflict limits the sustainability of these gains after the conflict ends and indeed adds to the burden of guilt of women who are assuming new roles without appropriate cultural frameworks to legitimise them (Rajasingham-Senanayke 2001).

Moreover, these processes are crucial to understanding the potential and obstacles in strengthening women's peace-building efforts in post-conflict situations. For, as politics becomes more structured and hierarchical, politicians predictably devalue as 'accidental activism' women's agency and activism in managing survival at the community level, and they marginalise women after the conflict is over. Women participated in the mass political mobilisation of nationalist anti-colonial struggles in India and Bangladesh and in revolutionary peasant movements in the 1940s in Tebhaga and Telegana in India. Despite this historical record, societies force women back into the kitchen after the conflict ends (Kannabiran and Lalitha 1987). This central paradox also characterises postcolonial ethnic, nationalist/community struggles in Kashmir and India's Northeast region and the Tamil conflict in Sri Lanka. It is precisely at the time of dramatic shifts in gender roles brought about by the societal upheaval attendant on conflict that the nationalist project circumscribes the impulse to women's social transformation and autonomy; this project constructs women as purveyors of the community's accepted and acceptable cultural identity (Jayawardene 1987; Chatterjee 1987). Women's role in maintaining cultural identity may explain why society invariably conceptualises the return to peace as a return to the previous gender status quo, irrespective of the nontraditional roles women assume during conflict.

In problematising the dual 'loss and gains' discourses, South Asia offers a study in contrasts. At one end is Afghan women's experience of absolute loss in two decades of conflict; at the other end is the emergence of Naga women's agency for peace in fifty years of nationalist struggle in India's Northeast. In the middle is the dark area of empowerment through arms, namely the woman militant, epitomised by the armed virgin of the Liberation Tigers of Tamil Eelam (LTTE) and the Maoist women guerrillas in Nepal's People's War. Feminist discourses deal with the problem area of the woman militant by locating her as a 'cog in the wheel' in patriarchal nationalist projects, as, for instance, LTTE women (Coomaraswamy 1997). To thus deny women militants agency is to deny the complex evolutionary processes of change in protracted conflicts. As we plot the transformative experience of women from relative invisibility to visible protagonism in the public sphere, in revolutionary struggles such as Nepal's People's War, it is evident that although the ideology provided the space for expansion of women's rights, women joining the movement have also shaped that ideology and restructured their roles.

One crucial variable is the nature of the conflict, ranging from nationalist conflicts as in Nagaland and Kashmir in India, to 'ethnic' conflict as in Sri Lanka, to the revolutionary Maoist People's War in Nepal. Generally in South Asian conflicts, the male leadership in both nationalist and revolutionary struggles finds it necessary to support the mobilisation of women in both combatant and noncombatant roles. But this is an essentially instrumental relationship with women's activism, rarely involving any programmatic engagement with the women's question. Historically, an analysis of women's experiences in the anti-colonial and revolutionary struggles of South Asia – for example, the 1940s peasant struggles in Tebhaga, West Bengal, and Telegana, Andhra Pradesh, India – shows that society thrust leading women activists back into the home in the aftermath (Custers 1987). As we will see in this chapter, women mobilised in the struggle are conscious that the struggle for democratic rights and justice should also mean rights and justice for women. They willingly postpone an engagement with the women's question so as not to divide the struggle. But once the peace process begins, transforming the conflict, negotiators marginalise the mobilised women and devalue their activism.

The notion of 'aftermath', especially from the perspective of women who experience a continuum of violence from the battlefield to the home, is problematic (Cockburn 2001). Women's insights into the structural inequalities that often lie at the heart of conflict show how conflict and peace are part of an integral process, so that peace settlements that do not address issues of justice are only a pause in a strategic engagement with the conflict (Samaddar 1999).

Conflicts produce unintended structural changes, and it may be that these changes have a greater impact on the expanding space available for women's agency than did the women who were mobilised and empowered in the struggle. Confronted by the institutional terror of the security forces and armed groups, men joined militias, were killed, imprisoned or retreated indoors, leaving women, literally and metaphorically, to organise family survival and become the bulwark of the social survival of the community. In the midst of their trauma of loss and devastation, women created new meanings and new realities that challenged the status quo. Ultimately it may be women's myriad quiet and invisible mutinies that succeed in contesting the pressure to return to reconstructed traditional roles in the aftermath.

Two factors reinforce the importance of understanding the transformative potential of change that South Asian conflicts foster. The first is the abysmal status of women in the region, which ranks at the bottom of the global gender development index. Aftermath reconstruction and rehabilitation policies at national and international levels must strengthen conflict-induced processes that change oppressive, exclusionary social structures, sanctioned by religions, that limit women's mobility and degrade their value. The second is the dire need to tap women's perspectives on the possibility of non-aggressive ways of negotiating the reconstruction of conflict-prone identities in South Asia. My assumptions are that women's experiences of violence are gendered and that the praxis of conflict negotiations is also gendered; women have the potential to emerge as agents of nonviolent ways of dealing with conflict and building peace. Conflict situations bring into focus women's activism in the informal space of politics, but politicians must conceptualise these new empowering changes if they are to translate this activism into political authority and enable women to affect formal political structures in the aftermath.

Society must build solidarity networks at the local, national and international levels to make sure that the space opened up does not close even before there is a realisation that it existed. Humanitarian and development discourses need to recognise and shore up these empowering changes. Development organisations need to strengthen culturally enabling frameworks, which legitimise new empowering roles and new realities, especially as the ideological frameworks of nationalist and ethnic struggles tend to configure women as purveyors of tradition and community identity.

This chapter focuses on four ongoing and protracted conflicts in South Asia. As readers from outside the region are likely to be unfamiliar with the nature of these conflicts, it is necessary briefly to contextualise each of the struggles, which are sites of women managing survival and negotiating conflict. Field research on women negotiating conflict and building peace in South Asia, a participatory research project of the South Asia Forum for Human Rights, provides the framework for analysis (Manchanda 2001b). The emphasis is on the dualistic nature of the changes wrought by protracted conflict, where because of the loss itself, some ambivalent spaces for women's agency become possible. I also look briefly at the social impact of women becoming militants and the limits of the militant women's empowerment in patriarchal ultranationalist projects and revolutionary struggles.

Kashmir: Domestic 'Accidental' Activism

The Kashmir dispute has been on the United Nations (UN) Security Council agenda since 1947, when India and Pakistan emerged as independent states following a bloody partition of the British colonial territory. Competing claims on the Muslim-majority territory of the erstwhile princely fiefdom of Jammu and Kashmir have led to full-scale wars between India and Pakistan and a continuing low-intensity war. Two fifths of the territory is in Pakistan and the rest is in India. Both sides committed themselves to holding a plebiscite to enable people to exercise their right of self-determination. Neither has done so. Pakistan maintains the fig leaf of separateness in Pakistan-held Kashmir, the most underdeveloped part of Pakistan. In Indian-held Jammu and Kashmir, India has steadily eroded constitutional guarantees of autonomy that the territory negotiated on accession – guarantees that were sacrificed at the altar of New Delhi's territorial and ideological security. Successive rigged elections were catalytic in sparking a popular pro-freedom, pro-separatist upsurge, which in 1990 morphed into an armed struggle that the Indian state has savagely repressed.

Eleven years of ongoing conflict have militarised Kashmir, brutalised Kashmiri society and transformed its tradition of liberal (Sufi) Islam to politicised fundamental Islam. The soldier-to-population ratio is 1:7. Official figures admit 34,000 people have been killed, although pro-separatist political leaders claim 70,000 have died. The daily experience in the border districts and the rural areas continues to be one of unabated terror and insecurity, although the intensity of the violence since it peaked in 1993–95 has abated somewhat in the towns. Women are direct and indirect victims of violence by the state's security forces and the militants. Kashmiri women have been displaced and widowed; they have lost bread-winners and loved ones; they have been denied access to maternity facilities and education; and they are direct victims of 'crackdowns', abduction, rape, torture and murder. The trauma of loss and the daily experience of terror and insecurity have produced a high incidence of post-traumatic syndrome (PTS) cases. Records of the government mental hospital in Srinagar show a sharp rise in PTS cases from 1,700 in 1990 to 17,000 in 1993 and 30,000 in 1998, and most are women. The narratives of Kashmiri women in the conflict are not only of passive victimhood but also of agency, manifested in the form of domestic activism of ordinary women and the political mobilisation of women in the struggle.

The struggle's populist demands created the social sanction for Kashmiri women to come out into public space. In the first popular phase of the Kashmiri struggle, 1989–90, women were visible everywhere – massed in front of the nightly processions to the mosque raising the cry of 'aazadi' (freedom) and demonstrating outside the UN office in Srinagar. Coming out of their homes and neighbour-hood, and marching alongside the men, were empowering experiences for Kashmiri Muslim women. Women seized the democratic space for popular protest. They would march to the UN office, often shielding the men, braving lathi (cane) blows and tear gas. Reports of excesses by the security forces would see them rush out to protest. When security forces picked up a boy, women from the neighbourhood would go to the security bunker, agitate and secure his release.

Women's political activism was most visible during this spontaneous phase of popular struggle. Popular participation, if it was structured at all, found some organisational articulation through the Dukhtarane Millat (Daughters of the Faith, a fundamentalist organisation) and the Muslim Khawateen Markaz (Council of Muslim Women) associated with the Jammu and Kashmir Liberation Front (JKLF). Anjum Zamrood Habib, general secretary of the now largely defunct Muslim Khawateen Markaz (MKM), recalls, 'We would visit jailed militants, take them shoes, a shirt, pyjama, cigarettes and collect funds to bail them out.' Habib adds, 'We did go for training in the use of guns, but we never used them.' Hundreds of women in the veiled *burqa* brigade of the Dukhtarane Millat would demonstrate publicly against excesses by the security forces. Dukhtarane Millat also ran a blood bank.

The ideologues massaging the populist groundswell encouraged and even manipulated women's participation. They used women to enforce a people's (militants') curfew; to act as guards blocking access by security forces; to serve as couriers; and to be the propaganda front line challenging human rights violations by the security forces. However, as the Kashmir conflict became both more militarised and more masculinised, it undervalued and marginalised women's contributions. After ten years of violent conflict, the once highly visible women political activists of the Dukhtarane Millat and the MKM had virtually disappeared.

Kashmiri women's domestic activism has been more enduring than their political activism and has had a continuing structural impact; it has opened up space to rework gendered family and societal relations. In protracted conflicts like that in Kashmir, where the cultural space for women in the public sphere is extremely restricted, women's political mobilisation takes the form of domestic activism. Ordinary women forged survival strategies for their families and communities in their daily lives. The political action of ordinary women arises from their everyday reality, from the concern they affirm for the safety of their family, and from the sustenance they give to their community (Neugebauer 1998; Sharoni 1998). Situations of struggle politicise women's daily activities and the management of survival, from their reproductive to their nurturing roles. The structural implications of this domestic activism in effecting desirable changes in gender relations must be conceptualised if it is to reinforce the possibility of securing the ambivalent gains of conflict.

During protracted curfews in Srinagar, Kashmir, which lasted for months, hundreds of ordinary women initiated informal food supply networks at the community level. This act was a politicisation of women's primary roles as nurturers. As men retreated from the public space and went underground in the face of massive state repression, housewives stepped outside the cultural framework of the family to make the rounds of detention centres and torture cells looking for the disappeared and to negotiate with the institutional power structures of the 'enemy', the army, administration and the courts. The upheaval of conflict undermined the cultural controls that otherwise restrict women's movement in the very conservative societies of South Asia and opened up spaces for women's domestic activism. However, it also produced a backlash, manifest in the veiling of Kashmiri women.

Violent conflict blurred the divide between the private sphere of the family and the public sphere of men and politics, as women used their traditional invisibility in the public sphere to create the space for their activism. Put another way, the public sphere entered the private sphere as the management of survival became politicised. Indeed the political mobilisation of the domestic sphere challenged the dichotomy between the domestic sphere and the public sphere of politics. Managing survival demanded that ordinary women develop the habit of listening to the news, reading or having newspapers read to them, and staying connected to an informal grapevine.

Mishra Basheer, a government schoolteacher from Sopore in Kashmir, explained how women managed.

> We had to find out about strikes and curfews. We needed to know when there was a crackdown or where there was an explosion or crossfire. Our children, our men were out there. We had to be alert about what the militants were saying about wearing *burqas* or who was being accused of being an informer. When we women met, what we talked about were crackdowns, custodial deaths, disappearances and the new diktats of the militants.

An extension of the 'stretched roles' of women as mothers and primary care givers led to the founding of the Association of the

Parents of the Disappeared in Kashmir. The organisation grew out of Parveen Ahangar's untiring personal search for her missing son and became a democratic mobilisation around motherhood for justice. At a time when both the security forces and the militants threaten the space for democratic protest, the association is one of the only voices demanding justice, at great personal risk. It politicises women's traditional motherist role by taking the private act of mourning into the public space. Such action by women in defence of their men is socially accepted as a legitimate extension of women's traditional roles. Within the structure of armed patriarchy, it is precisely as women that they have the right to access powerful men and can move them to compassion. But it also carried these ordinary women into the public sphere of negotiations with the powerful security forces and the administration for the rescue and safety of their families. It turned Parveen Ahangar, an illiterate housewife, into a political agent and a key mobilising figure in the revival of civil society political activism for peace in Kashmir.

Backlash: Veiling Kashmiri Women

At the same time, armed conflict also reinforces sexist roles. It militarises manliness, makes a macho-misogynist of the soldier/militant and masculinises the struggle (Enloe 1998). Emasculated by a powerful armed enemy, men hit back by reasserting control over women. At one level, the campaign to veil Kashmiri Muslim women reflects the reassertion of male control over their 'own' women. More critically, the compulsory veiling of women seems to be integral to defining a politicised Islamic national identity, as has been the experience in Sudan, Iran or Afghanistan. The graphic representation of women's subordination as symbolised by the veil exposes the gendered nature of the process of constructing a nationalist identity (Wilford and Miller 1998).

The *burqa* had not been part of the cultural ethos of Kashmiri identity, which was shaped by the liberal traditions of Sufi Islam. But the Kashmiri insurgency politicised Islam, fostered a fundamentalist Islamicised Kashmiri identity and pressured women, who embodied the community's identity, to wear the veil. To understand why Kashmiri women accepted that their primary identity was that of belonging to a community whose marker for women was the veil, which disadvantaged them, it is necessary to look at the manner in which a beleaguered community constructs the discourse of identity. It uses issues of sexual harassment and mass rape to foster alienation and hostility against the 'Other' and to push women to accept this version of their community identity. More women are wearing a veil now than before the insurgency, though many shed the *burqa* once the pressure eased. Indeed there was an active oppositional politics to the veiling campaign, which alienated many women from the movement.

The Naga People's Struggle: Women of Peace and Militant Women

India's Northeast region is a heterogeneous mosaic of indigenous communities that are different from the majority of the heartland's Aryan-Dravidian peoples. Over 200 groups with distinct community-based identities constitute the population of this region, which is carved up into seven states that divide communities along internal and international borders. Issues of regional deprivation, assimilationist policies and self-determination of oppressed nationalities have made the region a cauldron of intersecting conflicts. The Naga people's armed struggle for independence against the Indian state is the longest-running internal conflict in post-independence India. The Naga reject the authority of the Indian state, laying claim to a distinct historical, political and cultural national identity that dates back to pre-colonial times. The Naga put forward their claim to independence at the time Britain transferred power to India. Their struggle took a particularly violent turn in the 1970s when India deployed the army and suspended fundamental rights in Nagaland and the adjacent Naga areas of Manipur state. Arbitrary arrests, extrajudicial killings, disappearances, rape, torture, arson and regrouping into collective camps leading to economic dislocation and famine affected every family. Interfactional feuds among the Naga and between the Naga and the Kuki have further intensified the violence.

In 1997 the dominant armed Naga group, the Nationalist Socialist Council of Nagalim Isak-Muivah faction (NSCN-IM), entered into a ceasefire agreement with the Indian government as part of a peace process. Although the ceasefire was extended in July 2000, the armed group has threatened to withdraw, alleging bad faith on the part of the Indian government. The traditional Naga Council of Elders, the church and myriad women's organisations in the region have mobilised in support of the ceasefire and the peace process. In September 2000, as the peace process came under increasing strain, the president of the Naga Mothers Association (NMA), Neidonuo Angami, and the president of the Naga Women's Union of Manipur, Dr Gina Shangkham, put pressure on the Indian government and the armed groups to abide by the ceasefire and find a political solution. Faced with a crisis caused by the arrest in Bangkok of a top Naga militant leader who was en route to peace talks in Geneva, concerned civil society mobilised in support of the peace process, to ensure that it was not jeopardised. The presence in Bangkok of the president of the NMA, alongside the Naga Council of Elders, as a legitimate and integral part of the democratic mobilisation for peace, symbolises the changes in Naga society, which now accepts women in public space as a result of fifty years of struggle.

Among the different Naga tribes, relatively egalitarian structures give women more space for autonomy than do the caste-ridden patri-archal Hindu and Muslim societies of mainstream India. However, neither traditional nor nontraditional institutions accept a decision-making role for women. There are no women in the Ho, the Naga Council of Elders that makes community decisions, but the societal upheaval attendant on conflict has propelled women to enter negotiations to minimise the impact of violence and manage community survival. In Nagaland and adjoining Manipur, women have organised to protect the men from army roundups, they have campaigned for justice for women raped by security forces and have worked across the conflict divide to appeal for an end to bloodshed.

Only unarmed women dare to protest. In July 1997 after the NSCN-IM ambushed the Assam Rifles, this paramilitary force of the central government went on a rampage in the Naga town of Ukhrul in Manipur state. They rounded up and beat the men, including school-teachers, and terrorised the town. A women's group, the Tangkhul Shanao Long, took the initiative to open up a dialogue with the army and persuaded them to release forty civilians. In an effort to instil confidence among the people, the women appealed to the shopkeepers to open their shops and they encouraged the return of people who had fled.

The NMA has come to represent women of peace in South Asia. In 1994–95, when killings by the security forces and internecine violence between rival factions reached a peak, the NMA launched a campaign: 'Shed no more blood.' They appealed for an end to the killings in a pamphlet that said: 'The assassinated man may be a husband, a father, a son or a brother. His whole family is shattered by his violent liquidation no matter what reasons his liquidators choose to give for snuffing out his life.'

In a symbolic gesture to reject violence, irrespective of who the perpetrator was, the NMA persisted in dignifying all victims by covering each body with a shroud (Goswami and Dutta 1999). Women's peace teams walked to remote areas appealing to rival factions to stop the violence. Once the ceasefire was declared, NMA activists trekked to the headquarters of the NSCN Kaphlang faction in Myanmar to persuade the leader to accept the ceasefire. This is in keeping with the old Naga tradition of women peacemakers (*phukh-relia*) during war. Recently, the NMA and the Naga Women's Union of Manipur appealed to Indian Prime Minister Vajpayee and Isak Swu, chairman of the NSCN, to heed their cry for peace and to sustain the peace process.

The NMA peace initiative turns on the moral authority of the mother and the socially sanctioned space available within the Naga tradition for women's peace activism. The political space also suggests the possibility that women can constitute a group to mobilise around peace issues across the conflict divide. It is precisely as mothers that women have this space to appeal to the powerful and move them to compassion and shame. The NMA initiative, which represents the use of motherhood for women's political mobilisation, also reveals its limitations. Naga women still do not sit in the village council of elders where formal political decisions are made. However, the men recognise their presence in the informal dynamics of the peace process as significant and necessary. Indeed the Naga Ho has actively wooed their representation as part of broad-based democratic support to sustain a just and transparent peace process.

If Naga society constructs women's activism in informal politics as non-challenging within the traditionally acceptable scope of action, the same cannot be said for NMA women activists attempting to enter formal politics. The NMA nominated a senior member, Ms Abeiu, for the town committee of Kohima, the Nagaland state capital. When the chairperson's post fell vacant, she contested and won, to the chagrin of many men. She explained her interventions as an administrator as an extension of women's work, for example in public hygiene. Only later did she take up legal literacy and human rights awareness (Banerjee 2001). Traditional notions of public and private space reassert themselves as post-conflict politics becomes more structured and hierarchical, and they block the space for women in institutionalised or formal politics. Increasingly though, there is a consciousness about the need to extend the struggle for rights to women's rights. Women like Dr Gina Shangkham, president of the Naga Women's Union, Manipur, are demanding space in the traditional decision-making structures of the Naga tribes. But others, like Ms Chanmaya Jajo of the Naga People's Movement for Human Rights, argue, 'Our people's history has taught us we can ill afford to pursue gender justice at the expense of justice for our communities' (Jajo 1999).

At issue is not only the postponement of the women's question till after the struggle. As Partha Chatterjee insightfully analyses, the closure of the discourse is inherent in the very nature of nationalist struggles that configure women as embodiments of tradition and the separateness of tribal/national identity (Chatterjee 1987). To challenge the tradition is to betray the struggle. Yet women of some Naga tribes have begun to raise the issue of property rights for women, particularly crucial given the structural implications of the growth of families headed by women. Paula Banerjee, in a study of women in the Naga struggle, shows that women are trying to appropriate traditional myths about Naga women as guardians of family land in order to legitimise culturally women's right to inherit property.

The societal upheaval caused by protracted conflict and the experience of loss has projected women into nontraditional roles in public space, but society needs to recognise and value women's activism; otherwise, after the conflict, marginalisation will follow mobilisation. Women need to make the transition into formal politics. If the unintended 'gains' from structural changes attendant on conflict are not to be lost, women must recover culturally enabling frameworks and build solidarity networks.

Civil War in Sri Lanka: Ambivalent Empowerment

Sri Lanka's civil war, now in its seventeenth year, has transformed the north and east of the island into war-ravaged zones under the shifting control of the Sri Lankan government and the militant Liberation Tigers of Tamil Eelam (LTTE). The Tamil minority's postcolonial political struggle for cultural and political rights against the unitarian, state-building policies of the Sinhala majority has become a full-blown, militarised, ethnic conflict revolving around demands for a separate Tamil state. The war has widowed 55,000 women and internally displaced more than 760,000 people, mostly women. Women now head a quarter of all households.

The Sri Lankan conflict offers an opportunity to analyse critically how the difficulty of assuming the burdens of nurturer, primary decision maker and income earner in women-headed households has set off unintended processes of desirable structural transformation (Kanapathipillai 1986). This process is particularly notable in the experience of displaced women. Despite the psychosocial traumas entailed, long-term displacement has provided windows of opportunity for experiments with identity and greater personal and group autonomy. Circumstances are certainly worse for displaced women, who are forced to live in refugee camps where privacy is nonexistent and levels of generalised violence, alcoholism and domestic violence are high; but displacement has also meant a liberating dislocation of caste and gender hierarchies. Traditionally, caste ideology frames the gender status quo in Tamil society.

Darini Rajasingham-Senanayke (2001), in a study of the Siddambarapuram refugee camp outside Vavuniya, demonstrated how displacement and the spatial exigencies of camp life eroded caste hierarchies and pollution practices, which had so limited Tamil women's mobility. Moreover, the need to assume the responsibilities of heading the household and generating income following the death or disappearance of their menfolk has obliged many women to challenge the traditional seclusion of unmarried Tamil women and the construct of the Tamil widow as inauspicious and polluting. Many young widows who have to go out to work are redefining the ideal of the auspicious, married, Tamil woman by refusing to be socially ostracised. To symbolise their determination, several young camp widows, or 'grass' widows of the disappeared in the town of Vavuniya and the eastern province of Batticaloa, defied tradition and wore the red *pottu* (vermilion forehead mark), an auspicious mark reserved for married Hindu women.

It is an ambivalent empowerment, for the women carry a burden of guilt about the empowering spaces opened up by their loss. They lack the cultural frameworks to legitimise these new, empowering structural transformations, prompting questions about the sustainability of these changes in the aftermath. The conflict has produced circumstances that tacitly sanction young, unmarried, Tamil girls going overseas with an 'agent' – someone who does not necessarily belong to their extended family network – who will connect them via a circuitous route to prospective husbands in the Tamil diaspora in North America or Europe. Once abroad, wearing the *thali* (golden neck chain) that is the symbol of marriage, the woman assumes the caste and ritual constraints of seclusion, which were typical of pre-conflict Tamil Hindu society. In the case of Muslim women from the war zone, the conflict has led to their veiling. Muslims interpreted the LTTE's order for their expulsion from Jaffna as the wrath of God for the un-Islamic ways of the women. (However, society sanctions the thousands of women working as domestic labourers in the Gulf.)

The conflict has significantly changed gender roles inside the family, but Shanti Sachidanand, a peace activist working with women in the affected areas, believes that these changes do not translate into legitimacy for women to use public space. For women to cross the line beyond the extended family network in search of economic and material benefits for their families, especially in the absence of male members, is socially sanctioned, but this permission does not extend to women entering public space (Sachidanand 2001).

The conspicuous lack of women engaged in political activity in the north and east is evidence of the absence of social sanctioning for this. In the early 1980s, Jaffna women organised the Mothers' Front, a largely middle-class movement of democratic protest against human rights violations. But militant groups stifled the Mothers' Front within two years, and its president was assassinated. Because the field of struggle is extremely militarised, women are reluctant to engage in political activity. Women cadres of the LTTE are the only politically active women in the north and east. LTTE propaganda calls them 'Birds of Freedom', but do they represent empowerment? More crucially, what impact has the assumption of nontraditional roles by the LTTE women had on the social construct of the Tamil woman?

Interrogating Agency: Militant Women Bearing Arms

The woman militant is a black hole in feminist discourse on the possibility of empowerment in conflict because she adopts the role of perpetrator of violence. The existence of women militants in the armed ranks of the Liberation Tigers, the Nationalist Socialist Council of Nagalim, and the People's War in Nepal compels us to come to terms with feminist assumptions about women and peace and gender dynamics in conflict. Writing about the women of the LTTE, Radhika Coomaraswamy (1997), the UN Special Rapporteur on Violence against Women, is categorical: 'I do not believe that inducting women into a fighting force is a step towards empowerment and equality; [it] signals the militarisation of civil society – a militarisation which in itself is inimical to anyone who believes in human rights.'

In the case of the LTTE, in contrast to the People's War in Nepal, the material conditions of declining manpower resources rather than the ideology of the movement created the space for women's induction. Nevertheless, LTTE discourse resorts to ideology to mobilise women recruits: it makes appeals to women's empowerment, as evident in slogans such as 'Women! Break barriers, expedite liberation', which they displayed during the annual celebrations for Malathi, the first martyr for women's mobilisation. Despite this celebration of armed women, there is no evidence that these women have autonomy in decision making. Inside LTTE ranks, there is no discrimination against women cadres in combat roles and they form the suicide commando units. But isn't that an extension of the self-sacrifice to which women are acculturated from birth? Should we see the valorisation of death over life as agency?

Arguably, ultranationalist movements like the LTTE, structured around anti-democratic models of decision making, are unlikely to empower women. Coomaraswamy (1997) claims that women in such movements are pawns, their liberation accepted only in so far as it fits the contours of the nationalist project, and thus after the conflict men can push them back into the kitchen. Rajasingham-Senanayke questions this denial of agency to LTTE women, arguing that over the past seventeen years there has been an evolutionary process of change; women have acquired positions of power in the areas under LTTE control, for instance in courts run by the LTTE. But we should be wary, for it is not empowering to run torture cells, dispense summary justice and mete out execution sentences. Recently, the patriarchal LTTE leadership encouraged its women cadres to form a separate political wing, but it is not clear that we can speak of the wing being open to gender-strategy politics as Sachitanandam (2001:65–7) suggests. The LTTE lists women as speakers at all its political meetings, but the question remains: can a fascist, ultranationalist force whose culture is one of intolerance and exclusion foster the democratisation of gender relations within its power structures? None the less, it seems likely that LTTE women may not return to the gender status quo in the aftermath without a contest.

The induction of thousands of young Tamil women into the LTTE's militant ranks and the privileging of the 'armed virgin' of the LTTE have radically transformed the Tamil woman's self-image. Traditionally, the iconic Tamil woman is auspicious, married, fecund. LTTE women's freedom of movement and equality of social and political commitment have challenged the stifling rituals and practices that oppressed the Tamil woman in a social system marked by caste, dowry, seclusion of the unmarried woman and sequestration of menstruating women. At first, only LTTE women rode bicycles and wore jeans while all other Tamil women had to sport long skirts, saris or half-saris. But history has a way of overtaking efforts to maintain the status quo – the restrictive dress code has not held.

The ability of the women's wing of the LTTE to shape new, empowering agendas for women is likely to be more ephemeral than its impact on more subtle transformations at the societal level. Indeed, Rajasingham-Senanayke (2001) argues that 'the greater challenge to the status quo comes less from women in fatigues who might be asked to do desk jobs after the conflict, and more from the women who refuse to erase the red *pottu* (symbol of marriage), the unsung civilian women'.

Women in Nepal's People's War: From Invisibility to Visible Protagonist?

A Maoist-inspired, peasant-based armed struggle has spread across more than half the landlocked Himalayan kingdom of Nepal. Several factors have predisposed the people to armed struggle: the acute, horizontal inequalities of caste, the regional deprivation and discrimination against indigenous communities and oppressed nationalities, and the continuing domination of the Nepali polity after the advent of democracy by a narrow upper-caste elite. Since the launch of the People's War in February 1996, the Maoists have set up what amount to base camps in their strongholds in the remote mid-western hills. However, with the government proposing emergency laws and raising armed paramilitary forces to combat the spreading Maoist revolution, we can expect much greater violence. Noncombatants, caught in the middle between the People's War and state repression, have become victims of abductions, arbitrary arrests, killings, rape and torture. Development, health and education activities have come to a standstill in the shrinking space available for humanitarian work between the Maoists and state repression. The People's War is strongest in the most backward and underdeveloped areas that are peopled by indigenous and minority communities. Two thirds of the revolutionaries come from Tibeto-Burman groups, especially the Magar community.

The ongoing People's War has transformed the lives of poor, illiterate, peasant women in the affected areas; from lives of invisibility the women have become visible protagonists. Drawn by the liberating, gendered ideology of the Maoists, women are flooding into their ranks as propagandists, combatants and area commanders. But the revolution in family and social relations is not confined to the revolutionary women. The women who remain to negotiate survival for their families are also creating new roles and new meanings with far-reaching implications for the traditional hierarchical structures of exclusion and sequestration that bind Nepali women. Women in Nepal rank at the bottom of the South Asia gender index, itself at the bottom of the world scale. Women from the Tibeto-Burman groups are culturally less restricted than upper-caste Hindus; as in any oppressed community, however, they suffer gender discrimination in addition to class, caste, community and regional oppression.

Women without Men Take on New Roles

In remote backward villages in the mid-western hills of Nepal, the epicentre of the conflict, the men are missing. The Maoist insurgency has denuded whole villages of men, and schools are without boys. The men have become *farari* (absconders), fleeing to the surrounding jungles or the cities of Nepal and across the open border into India to escape being picked up by the police or targeted by the Maoists. They leave the women behind. Women traditionally form the backbone of the semi-feudal subsistence agrarian economy. Men migrate seasonally in search of jobs: this time, the men have not come back.

The men have left Nepali women to negotiate the survival and security of their families with the police and the Maoists. Women have had to break tradition and take on the 'male' job of ploughing the land. Traditional society does not allow women to plough the land, on pain of social ostracism and punitive action. Women who now plough the land do not rationalise their action as necessitated by the absence of men. They explain it as a practical demonstration of 'there's nothing women can't do, if we have to do it'. It is an assertion of capability (Gautam *et al.* 2001). The absence of men has also opened up new opportunities for women to step into public life. When elections took place for the wards of the Mirule Village District Council, there were no men to contest positions. Illiterate peasant women came forward. All six members elected are women, including the chair.

These quiet, unintended structural changes could have a critical impact in the aftermath. In Gorkha, another district affected by the Maoist insurgency, the number of girls studying in village schools has increased dramatically. Where earlier few girls were seen, Sancharika, a Nepali women's organisation, claims that girls now make up 50 per cent of all students in Gorkha district village schools. One reason cited is that parents are sending sons outside Gorkha district to study in Kathmandu. They fear that Maoists will politicise their sons in schools and campuses under their sway. Also, boys are obvious suspects and targets of the police. The girls left behind come under the influence of the Maoists at school.

Women Combatants Engendering the People's War

One third of combatants in the Maoist strongholds in the People's War in Nepal are women. Both the ideology and the programmatic thrust of the movement appears to be pro-women. The Maoist party organ, *The Worker*, titled an issue on women, 'Fury of Women Unleashed'; it celebrates the participation of women at all levels, ranging from party committee secretaries and guerrilla squad commanders to local volunteers and propagandists (Reports from the Battlefield 1998). Women are involved in the People's War directly and indirectly, as cultural activists, members of village defender groups, couriers, guides and nurses, as well as visitors to jail and to the families of the martyred. Women are also combatants and spies. Some of the most violent actions against local 'tyrants' are associated with all-women guerrilla squads armed with *khukris* (traditional knives) and sawed-off muskets.

Leftist armed resistance movements tend to argue that the special conditions of revolutionary struggle make gender differences unimportant, that the process of liberating peasants and the proletariat will emancipate women from gender oppression. Is the Maoist movement in Nepal the exception? Analysis of the role of women in the Shining Path (Peru), the acknowledged model for Nepal's People's War, suggests that, despite the important presence of women at all levels inside the movement, the Shining Path was not capable of programmatically incorporating their gender interests; consequently, the relationship remained an instrumental one (Cordero 1998). Is Nepal's ultraleft movement an armed class struggle in which the women's question is not being postponed until after the revolution?

Just before the launch of the People's War, its political front, the United People's Front (UPF), released a memorandum of forty demands. Number 19 demanded that, 'Patriarchal exploitation and discrimination against women should be stopped. The daughter should be allowed access to property.' In an agrarian revolution, women's 'access to property' means women's right to land. Poor peasant women, the majority from the Tibeto-Burman ethnic minority groups, and some upper-caste Hindu and Buddhist women are flooding into the movement, drawn by the promise of its rights ideology and their desire to shake off the oppressive shackles of a religiously sanctified culture of oppressive rituals that exclude and degrade women. Hsila Yami, the former head of the women's front and the wife of Baburam Bhattarai, the political leader of the movement, claims, 'Women have more to gain from the movement than men.' She maintains that there is no discrimination against women at the political or military level.

Prachanda, the general secretary of the Communist Party of Nepal (Maoist), admits that before the launch of the People's War, they had not taken the women's question ' seriously', but he says that subsequently, with the dramatic importance of women's activism in the People's War, the party has incorporated the women's question ideologically and programmatically. Prachanda, in a wide-ranging interview with the *Revolutionary Worker*, mentions the laborious efforts made to bring illiterate, peasant women into the district leadership (Interview 2000). However, he admits that there are no women at the regional or central committee level. Indeed, the party has marginalised Pampa Bushal, who was once co-chairperson of the UPF. Presumably she is one of the 'bourgeois intellectual women' denounced by Prachanda.

There are forty to fifty women in the politico-military leadership of the district committees. Does this imply that women are gaining policy responsibility? The experience of women in high party posts in Peru's Shining Path counsels a cautious assessment of the degree of empowerment represented by women's access to the positions of area commander or party committee secretary in Nepal's Maoist movement.

In programmatic content at ground level, the Maoist struggle has given space for an anti-alcohol campaign, as well as for issues of sexual violence and women's exploitation. Prachanda steers clear of questions on abortion, which is illegal in Nepal, but engages the issue at the practical level of gender relations, for example in the context of Maoist women cadres who become pregnant and may be obliged to quit the movement. There is no inflection of a gendered discourse of women's rights. Yet, as women provide one third of the guerrillas in the areas where the Maoists are most active, issues of sexuality and maternity are critical. Prachanda mentions the practical difficulties of women guerrillas becoming pregnant and the provision of foster-care structures for children (Interview 2000). Gender-neutral discourses of revolutionary struggles often founder on issues of sexual morality and when women guerrillas become pregnant. It is noticeable that in socio-political revolutions, mothers are expected to leave their children behind, not fathers. In Nepal's People's War there is no questioning of the feminisation of parenting or, for that matter, of cooking.

Although the ideology of the movement has created space for women to take on new roles, women have also reshaped the movement by redefining the structure of women's roles. Most of the mass actions taken in the Maoist strongholds relate to justice for women: wresting back the land usurped from single women, mass action against liquor dealers, punishing rapists, and punishing men for polygamy. But this is essentially grassroots action. It is doubtful whether women have been able to redefine the programmatic agenda strategically at the ideological level or at the level at which policy is determined. The experience of women in the Telegana peasant movement in India, where women formed the backbone of the struggle but were pushed back into the kitchen afterwards, is a grim reminder of how fragile the social transformation during conflict can turn out to be in the aftermath.

Conclusion

Arguably, conflict is a terrain for renegotiating oppressive caste and gender hierarchies. In protracted conflicts, disadvantaged South Asian women's negotiations with those in power have, through historical shifts in the conflict, manifested variously as 'domestic activism' in the management of survival, as the political extension of 'stretched roles', as political mobilisation, and as induction into the ranks of militants. Despite their overwhelming presence at every level in the region's radical, nationalist or community identity struggles, however, women seem unable to sustain protagonism in conflict. The instrumental relationship of the leadership with women activists is starkly evident in the pattern of mobilisation during conflict and marginalisation in the aftermath. Part of the difficulty is that women themselves see their activity as nonpolitical, an extension of their domestic concerns, in other words as stretched roles. Women's language of support and resistance, which flows from their cultural experience (especially of being disempowered), further obscures their activism. Women's strategy of protest often uses the symbols of mourning and mother-hood for moral authority and political mobilisation. Moreover, South Asian movements, with the exception of the Maoist People's War in Nepal, have not attempted to or have been unable to integrate an autonomous struggle for women's rights. This contrasts with South Africa where a woman's charter was evolved in the process of struggle and where women were able to use the authority acquired in the process of struggle to enter formal political structures in the aftermath.

In South Asia, society invariably devalues, ignores and actively suppresses women's activism in public spaces outside their family networks; the same is true of women's agency in managing survival in households without men and women's experience in challenging and redefining an acceptable role for a good woman. Thus, in relation to ongoing conflicts in the region, it is critical to recognise, conceptualise and shore up the processes of transformation at national and international levels in humanitarian and development agencies. Agencies should assist in valuing politically women's activism in the informal spaces of power and in translating that activism into the authority that enables women to enter formal structures of power after the conflict. This transformation will assure a democratic and just peace process.

A more lasting transformative impact in gendered family and societal relations may come from the unintended structural social changes wrought by protracted conflict as a consequence of loss, of women having to cope without men. However, gains generated from the trauma of loss are particularly ambivalent, and enabling cultural frameworks and solidarity networks are needed to legitimise them. We need to validate ethically the gains-in-conflict discourse, without compromising the fundamental premise: peace is valuable.

CHAPTER 8

Liberated, But Not Free
Women in Post-War Eritrea

SONDRA HALE

A 'Postscript' is a fitting introduction to a discussion of the aftermath of war for Eritrean women. For them, the most immediate aftermath was another war against Ethiopia that continued until a peace agreement came into effect in December 2000. During that second war, which began in 1998 with skirmishes and developed into a full-fledged conflict by 1999, some 20 per cent of the Eritrean military combat force was comprised of women (in contrast to 30 per cent estimated in the first war).[1] However, a troubling event occurred on 11 March 2000 when the government announced that Eritrean women soldiers would leave the front lines, ostensibly for training programmes. This happened despite growing needs for military personnel resulting from the larger size of the Ethiopian army, heavy casualties, and draft dodging. Furthermore, the National Union of Eritrean Women (NUEW), also known by its Tigrinya acronym HAMADE (Hagerawi Maheber Dekenstio Ertrawian – National Union of Women Eritreans), supported the government act. Its president, Luul Ghebreab, argued that the wide-ranging skills development programmes should benefit women fighters.[2] Later reports from the field seemed to contradict the news reports. Clearly women remained in combat. Perhaps enforcement of the decision to remove them weakened because the fighting grew so fierce and the country was nearly overrun by Ethiopian troops. However, even the threat of removing women from the combat and other military roles that had enhanced their status in newly independent Eritrea does not bode well for women's future. At least one journalist asserted, 'the latest border skirmishes with Ethiopia threaten to undo many of the gains the women of Eritrea have made in a patriarchal society' (Hatch 2000).

Despite this possible negative turn for Eritrean women, there is some reason for optimism. On 27–29 November 1999, in Asmara, the NUEW convened a large international conference to commemorate its twentieth anniversary. Opening its doors to internal and external criticism was a forward-looking strategy, the impetus for which came from the new leadership of the organisation.[3] None the less, the NUEW refers to itself as 'the only women's organisation in Eritrea', a statement that needs to be explored for its veracity and, if true, for the wisdom of that situation (NUEW 1999).[4]

The Context

It does not bode well for any group of liberated women in a post-revolutionary situation that, to date, no liberation or revolutionary war, no matter how progressive its ideology regarding the emancipation of women – from Russia and China to Algeria, Vietnam, Cuba, Nicaragua, El Salvador, Guinea-Bissau, Angola, Mozambique, South Africa, and the Palestinian *intifada* – has empowered women and men to maintain an emancipating atmosphere for women after the military struggle and brief honeymoon are over. Despite this history, I am still interested in the emancipatory possibilities both for socialism and feminism, their combinations, and the contradictions that inhere.

In this chapter I focus only briefly on Eritrean women's actual participation in the liberation struggle of 1961–91 in order to emphasise some of the obstacles they face in civilian life (see Hale 2000 for more discussion). The period since the first war ended has been a time of state building and constitution creating, accompanied by the government's simultaneous attempts to maintain control and build democracy. The government is a one-party state, the Eritrean People's Liberation Front (EPLF) having assumed a new identity as the People's Front for Democracy and Justice (PFDJ).

I assume that the reader has some general knowledge of the situation for women in Eritrea and Ethiopia, and of the former's participation in the war of liberation. Eritrean and Ethiopian society – half Orthodox Christian, half Muslim – was very conservative with regard to the cultural positioning of women. In contrast, during the thirty-year liberation war for independence from Ethiopia, the EPLF developed one of the most enlightened views of women that we have seen. The EPLF was a syncretistic, independent, Marxist-inspired guerrilla movement and a secular, multi-ethnic, vanguard party. Women participated fully, not as substitutes, but as full-fledged citizens of revolutionary Eritrea. For example, close to the end of the war, women comprised more than 30 per cent of the fighting force and had served in all capacities.[5] This is not the usual history of military struggle, in which armies have used women selectively and mostly in jobs seen as extensions of their domestic labour. By most accounts, women experienced a high degree of emancipation while in the field, both in contested areas and in liberated zones, getting an education, including political education, learning new skills, and coming into a new identity. Women fighters were indeed icons of liberated women.[6]

Many factors went into making this a positive struggle for women, not the least of which was the active political education that took place at all levels, inside and outside the country, and in the liberated areas. However, after giving credit to the EPLF for a progressive gender ideology and a positive nod to their praxis, I now turn to a more detailed examination of the problems for women in Eritrea's attempt to build democracy in peacetime. We should bear in mind that it is easier to build the kind of camaraderie that might look like egalitarianism in the bunkers. Life in bunkers often looks like democracy, but life in a 'democracy' may seem like something else for women.

Thus I ask several questions in this chapter about democracy building and gender in newly independent Eritrea, in order to clarify what it might mean, in terms of theory, activism and policy, for a political organisation like the EPLF and its civilian counterpart to travel the route from liberation front – an organisation devoted to empowering the disenfranchised groups (women, peasants, youths, Muslims, workers) – to government assigned to control, monitor or contain these very groups. What is the impact on women when the government sometimes seems to assign itself the role of central policy-maker and activist on behalf of women and at other times relinquishes that role by handing everything over to the independent NUEW? The EPLF, the revolutionary organisation that led Eritreans to victory over the *dergue* (the Soviet-supported regime that overthrew the emperor, Haile Selassie) is in an unenviable position, as is its women's wing, the NUEW. Six years after liberation, the hard work had barely begun when the second war started. In this situation of the EPLF-as-government, many of the upper-class and middle-class women fighters, whether officially demobilised or not, now have government jobs, and less privileged women sometimes view them as bureaucrats. Another concern is that the NUEW is overburdened. Even though the organisation has sparse resources, responsibility for everything pertaining to women is being handed to it. Very little that is related to family life, children's health, divorce, violence against women, or the rigid gender division of labour is defined as part of the national agenda. Clearly we need to expand the definitions of common good, of national interests and of gender interests.

Other women's organisations have emerged, but these are not often coordinated in any national effort, and the NUEW often undermines them.

Theoretical Framework and the Policy and Activist Implications

In my work on Sudan,[7] one of my main analytical arguments has often been that men in most liberation movements, in the last half of the twentieth century, positioned women within the culture to serve the movement. Men expect women to maintain the culture or maintain the family, often as symbols of resistance or, just as often, because of fear of losing the 'original' or 'authentic' in the face of unusual situations such as war. One effect can be to freeze the culture, imped-ing the natural change process. A second effect is to romanticise the role of women: as mothers, as mothers of liberation fighters, and as the 'keepers of the hearth'. Another related process of liberation fronts has been to expect women to represent the 'morality' or central ethic of the movement (Hale 1996).

This set of propositions does not seem to hold in the same way for Eritreans. Rather, women fighters are being abandoned to cope with civilian life in a highly traditional culture and are, practically by default, being expected to maintain a high level of social morality and traditional values. In a way, we could say that civilian Eritrean society was frozen during the war. That is, while the combatants and other fighters in the liberated zones envisioned and carried out transformations in economic, political, class, ethnic and gender relations, the rest of society held on to an unchanged concept of being Eritrean, preserving extant cultural practices and behaviour. Therefore, although there was no clear demarcation between the liberated zone and the rest of society (as there was constant flux across the borders and regular interaction), very different sets of behaviour prevailed. Although civilian society was mobilised to a considerable extent for clandestine and underground war activities, private life and family life were exalted, even romanticised.

Furthermore, because EPLF fighters had sacrificed 'normal' family life for a life in the bunkers, the 'old ways' held a certain appeal for both genders when they returned to civilian society. Romanticising and exalting private life encourages people to overlook the harsh reality that private life is frequently the site of the greatest oppression of women.

In the Eritrean case, although ideological rhetoric said otherwise, the EPLF's lack of attention to the constraining processes that Eritrean women were encountering in post-liberation family life amounted to the abandonment of certain social gains that EPLF women had experienced in the field. Among these gains were free social relations with men, relaxed social customs and habits, including of dress and hairstyles, the lack of social pressure toward marriage and childbearing, and the collapse of the conventional gender division of labour.

As a left feminist activist I have been concerned with some of the negative processes occurring with regard to feminist agendas in many movements for fundamental transformation. How can we analyse why and how things fall apart for women? Bearing in mind that when the struggles end, politics and political parties may be in place, but not policies and policy mechanisms, one task might be to explore the internal dynamics of these movements and the contradictions within the structures of the revolutionary organisations themselves. This would include examining the nature of the military struggle, the role of women in that sphere (both as regards long- and short-term revolutionary strategies), the relationship of the movement to 'traditions', and the manner in which the symbolism and metaphors of the revolution served women's agendas.

Like many feminists who work within a Marxist framework, I have not given up on the 'promissory note', the implicit contract between women and socialist movements that conceived of women's liberation as an integral part of the revolution (Kruks *et al.* 1989). But I am highly critical of the hegemonic Marxist approach to most revolutionary situations and of the nearly facile solutions prescribed for women. I argue that the post-war situation for the EPLF and PFDJ is a supreme test to see if one of our brightest case studies of gender egalitarianism in wartime can be converted to civilian life. Can the EPLF succeed in applying the same gender, race and class ideology that it developed in the bunkers? What kind of activism would make that happen? Can civil society develop out of this situation?

In 1994 and 1996, to answer some of these questions from the point of view of Eritrean women, I collected the oral histories of women fighters. I interviewed some three dozen women, including both famous and less famous women fighters. I talked with the pioneer warrior Worku Zerai, Judge Letebrahan Kasai, and 'Gwande' (Asmarat Abraha), another famed warrior. I asked these women of the EPLF who had served at the front to narrate their experiences in the field and, more important, to reveal their stories about returning to civilian life.[8]

What Do Women Fighters Say about Being Civilians?

I asked the women fighters about their problems as civilians in a society that had not yet built a civil society and about the organising strategies they are now using. One fighter complained thus:

> [Our families] were happy at first that we came back alive. But after a year it changed. We have very different ideas from the rest of society. Women must stay at home and take care of their children, not go out and talk with men. We do not accept these traditional ideas of our parents, but it is difficult to change them. It is very hard for us because we were used to equality in the field.

I wondered at the time what strategies the NUEW has for enabling these fighters to transfer consciousness-raising skills to older-generation Eritreans, to women who had not gone into the field or to traditionalists. When the war ended, did consciousness-raising as a political strategy end, too? Perhaps it is time, I argued at the NUEW conference in 1999, to revive some of the pedagogical skills used in the military struggle: in the consciousness-raising groups, during military training, at special seminars on gender, class, ethnicity and religion, at cultural shows, and in the Zero Schools. I knew that every platoon had had a military leader and a political leader. The latter had the task of facilitating political education. He or she would bring political and theoretical questions to the frequent group meetings. Fighters discussed racism, sexism and other forms of inequality. These were multi-class, interethnic, multi-religious and gender-diversified groups. They used some of the pedagogical strategies of Paulo Freire (1979) and the criticism/self-criticism processes of Mao Tse-tung and early Euro-American feminists. A great deal of consciousness-raising, self-education and mutual group edification resulted.

Another fighter, who had spoken eloquently about how effective they had been in the field as organisers and teachers, seemed discouraged:

> On the surface they [civil society] accept the [progressive] ideas, but underneath they do not accept equality for women. To change our parents, our society, we have to change their ideas. There is a struggle over the major differences between us. When we try to explain, they do not accept easily. When they saw that in practice we fought against the enemy, they could accept that. But they insist that we must [also] be married and bear children – and stay home and take care of our children.

Then, like most of the women fighters, she ended her statement hopefully: '... if we struggle more, we will succeed.... Women need to be educated more to become like us.' I asked other fighters and officials about the role of education. We had discussions about educational policy and about the idea that education is not a panacea; it is not going to solve as much as most people think it will. Other fighters also argued against the idea that those who had not been fighters needed to be more like the fighters. Some agreed that the diverse paths to empowerment and emancipation might be stressed in the NUEW training of organisers.

I had assumed that women fighters who came from families where a number of relatives had gone into the field would more easily be incorporated into civilian life. But a few of my interviews contradicted this. For example, one woman fighter commented:

> My mother is not a fighter; all [the other members of] my family are
> fighters, so my mother lets us do as we want. But when my brother got
> married, she restricted his wife [for example, from going out to the city
> with her]. She said, 'Now she is my daughter and your brother also said
> she should not go out, so I won't let her go out now that she is married.'
> We argued, but she did not agree. She knows that we are outside her
> authority and says we can do as we want, but not our brother's wife.

I reflected with other fighters on the absence of NUEW work with
the men, who seemed to be backsliding into traditional roles. It
seemed, in the example above, that it was the brother's responsibility
to help liberate his spouse. What had happened to his EPLF fighter
consciousness? There is no adult education on these matters for men
in civilian life.

Women fighters raised many concerns that underscored their view
that traditional marriage laws and customs are oppressive whereas the
EPLF marriage code is liberating.[9] Many whom I interviewed described
campaigning while in the field against the marriage of very young
adolescents and children, and now in civil society. One told me about
women's activism during the war and after:

> We have started to work against too-young marriage, for example. We
> carried out research and began to use the media [she used the word
> advertised], newspapers, radio/TV, etcetera to give evidence against
> young marriage. We have worked through the Department of Social
> Affairs. We tried this organising in the rural areas first, but no one
> accepted our ideas.... But then they began to see all the problems young
> girls were facing; they could not survive that way. They became infected
> easily with different diseases and were exposed to dangers ... we have to
> change these customs.

Yet, when I asked during a group interview with ex-fighter students
at the Teacher Training Institute what organising strategies they were
using, they expressed only two ideas: educating women and using the
media. Unable to use the same tactics that they used in the field where
their authority was much greater *vis-à-vis* the countryside, they
seemed puzzled. I wondered, what does it mean to use the media?
What are the messages that should be carried? By whom, and how
should they be disseminated?

Despite valiant organising efforts, many ex-fighters also feel spent and overwhelmed, even as they carry on. They feel overwhelmed by the relatively larger civilian population; many have to deal with extreme poverty, not to mention the consequences of the new war, which curtailed badly needed social programmes.[10] The government demobilised women veterans of the first war before the men because women were often the last fighters to enter the war. By 1997 they had demobilised some 12,000 of the 51,000 women soldiers. They gave each fighter 10,000 birr (about $2000, or 10 months' salary) on demobilisation.[11] Yet unemployment was very high. With no jobs, it was hard to see how reintegration of veterans into civilian society would take place.[12] A high percentage of the women fighters were from the rural areas; they had changed so much that it was impossible for many of them to return to their villages. Of these 12,000 demobilised fighters, half are reported to have divorced. The situation of divorced women fighters can be grave: they may be left alone with children, very little money, no job, and little or no education in the case of village women; they may be unable to return to their villages, and are quite probably unmarriageable.[13]

Even women who are married complain that their partners have become traditional.[14] If the women have jobs, they are overburdened with domestic labour, as men who, in the field, had cooperated in subverting the gender division of labour are now balking at performing 'women's' tasks. Child care is a major concern.

The contemporary situation of the women and children demobilised after the war is bleak and calls out for strenuous policy formation and activism. At the 1999 NUEW conference we discussed unions or associations of divorced women. Why not provide child care by using the displaced elderly and disabled fighters as care providers? This way no one is a charity or welfare group.

A number of participants at the 1999 NUEW conference stressed the need to build a new generation of organisers, younger women who are fresh and willing to take on the odds. Older fighters could be consciousness-raisers, entrusted with training new cadres, while recognising the younger generation's need to do things differently. Now there is too much emphasis on the women fighters holding on to the limited power that they have in the society and trying to replicate themselves. This is typified by the old, not the new leadership of the NUEW.

During my interviews I wondered why no one talked about labour unions, not even teachers' unions. I asked people about the formation of syndicates and work cooperatives. Forming all-women's unions or getting women into positions of power within unions might be useful strategies at this point. A state or state agencies can never take the place of unions. It may be the case, however, that Eritrean women will have to form their own unions, some of which might resemble the Self-Employed Women's Association (SEWA) in India.

The National Union of Eritrean Women after the War

Like a great many of the progressive movements of the twentieth century, Eritreans, early in the struggle and under the wing of the EPLF, developed a strong women's organization, the NUEW (or HAMADE). However, in 1993, just after independence, there was a crucial shift when the NUEW, which claims between 100,000 and 200,000 members, declared itself independent from the EPLF, making it officially a nongovernmental organisation (NGO). During the national struggle, NUEW members had worked on recruitment for the movement, on consciousness-raising in the villages of the liberated areas, and on international and national propaganda (NUEW 1994a, 1994b; Wilson 1991). In the years from independence to the election of the new leadership in 1999, the programme of the NUEW empha-sised representing women in the development of a new constitution and actively developing new marriage, family and labour laws. At the same time, NUEW activities involved literacy campaigns, health issues, working to eradicate female circumcision, polygamy and prostitution, as well as seeking to secure women's land rights and parental leave, developing cooperatives, training women for leader-ship roles, offering vocational training, lobbying for child care, and developing rural credit programmes (NUEW 1999).

The current programme, under Luul Ghebreab's leadership, is slightly different in its approach. There is more emphasis on women in power and decision-making, and a more international outlook with regard to international conventions such as CEDAW (the Convention on the Elimination of all Forms of Discrimination Against Women) and women's rights as human rights (NUEW 1999:3–4). In line with international mandates, there is a call for attention to the girl child, attention to the environment, an insistence on the salience of women's health issues and a campaign against violence against women. Also, for the first time, NUEW is paying attention to women in situations of armed conflict, recognising that women and children suffer the most from such crises as war (NUEW 1999:8–9). This is a clear change from the war and immediate post-war periods when even the NUEW participated in romanticising the roles of women in the war. By the time the second war started in 1999, however, it was nearly impossible to carry out a reassessment of women's role in the war. Criticisms of the first war effort would have been too politically sensitive.

The NUEW is beset internally and externally with questions about its independence from the EPLF/PFDJ and its legitimate status as an NGO. I discovered some disparity of opinion on the degree of affiliation that now exists between NUEW and the EPLF/PFDJ. An issue only discussed in private circles, which did not emerge openly in the 1999 conference, was the question of how much autonomy is needed and how tightly the EPLF/PFDJ will continue to control the NUEW.

The Organisation and Its Discontents

It has been clear to me that the EPLF and NUEW have revolutionary potential beyond the military struggle. Yet I have some reservations. I will discuss only a few of them here.

To begin with, many observers and participants in the debates, myself included, are concerned about the NUEW's relationship to other women's groups. How many women's organisations would be optimal in any one country? In the Eritrean context, other women's organisations have emerged, but these are often not coordinated in any national effort, and can easily end up in an adversarial position *vis-à-vis* NUEW. Is it more effective for women to have many organisations, perhaps functioning under one umbrella group? This issue did emerge at the 1999 anniversary conference. Not raised was whether this is a time for a 'women's movement' that is more self-interested, mainly invested in improving the lives of women and not so focused on national concerns. Or, to turn that question on its head, is it time to define all women's issues as 'national issues' or interests for the common good?

Considering the beleaguered, overstretched condition of the NUEW, there may be a need for other women's organisations and agencies, for a division of labour. Yet the NUEW monopolises women's issues, defining them in particular ways, and possibly sabotages other organisations engaged in gender work. One such organisation, Bana (meaning 'dawn' or 'brightness'), the Eritrean Women's War Veterans Association, is designed to form cooperatives among demobilised women fighters, but it was undermined by the NUEW and seemed, at one point in the mid-1990s, to be on the verge of collapse. The relationship between the Gender Unit of the Department of Reintegration for Demobilised Fighters, popularly referred to as Mitias, and the NUEW does not seem to be one of cooperation. There is little or no coordination among these various gender or women's units connected with government departments, causing suspicion and competition for government resources.

The girls' and women's section of the National Union of Eritrean Youth and Students (NUEYS) was also undermined by the NUEW and finally collapsed. A person I interviewed, who was for a brief time a staff member in that section, gave me a paper that the organisation had published on women in Eritrea and asked that I not show it to anyone in the NUEW. These are not positive signs and follow from the bureaucratisation of the NUEW and other governmental and quasi-nongovernmental organisations.

Class and Ethnic Hierarchies

Women fighters revealed in interviews some attitudes that suggested the distance they had travelled, but also suggested that new hierarchies had been created among women. For example, there was a tendency to consider all traditional culture to be 'backward' (a frequently used term), to attribute these 'undesirable' customs to the rural areas, to the lowlands, and to Muslims, and to assure me that education is the panacea and that educated people are mostly progressive. What emerged was a stereotypical, value-laden bifurcation of the society into highland Christian and lowland Muslim, with education designated as the key to making the Muslims more like the Christians. But if education is the answer, the problem may be exacerbated because many of those I interviewed complained of the recent neglect of social issues, including education.

Related to these elitist social attitudes, women EPLF fighters have a deportment and a behaviour that tell us they are, somehow, outside the culture. This attitude developed over thirty years of living in bunkers and in isolated, sealed-off liberated areas. The EPLF succeeded in developing a remarkable degree of political and cultural hegemony that resulted in an 'us' and 'them' mentality. Women fighters repeatedly used expressions such as 'We have to educate them.' For all the attempts to break down class, race, ethnic and religious distinctions, the dichotomy between the 'enlightened vanguard' and the unenlightened was distinct. Although the new leadership of the NUEW seems committed to dealing with these attitudes, they remain embedded in the majority of the membership. Perhaps the peacetime establishment of mandatory national service, which will require urban youth to work in rural areas, will be effective in breaking down rural/urban and mental/manual labour dichotomies.

Education

As I have indicated, education was viewed as a panacea for a gender egalitarian society. That would point to the importance of the national curriculum, which is still in the development stage. Although it will be based on the Marxist-inspired curriculum of the Revolutionary Schools, or Zero Schools, established in the field, much has been scrapped on the grounds that it is too difficult and not palatable for some social and religious groups. The problem with this accommodation is that it dilutes the old Revolutionary School readers and syllabuses, which were more direct in their discussions of the oppression of women. In the new readers, women are not singled out for special consideration or affirmative action in reversing old stereotypes. Educational policy that is explicitly aimed at re-education, as the Zero Schools were, with curriculum geared toward eradication of class, race, ethnic, gender and religious difference, does not have the luxury of kowtowing to conservative social and political interests.

Having said that, my perusal of the new school readers revealed that they are comparatively enlightened in terms of the various roles people are portrayed as playing in society; for example, women and men are depicted as occupying any job, and boys and girls both do housework. What is not said in the readers is portrayed in drawings.

As for adult education, for which the EPLF and NUEW were famous during the first war, the literacy training that the NUEW is designing for small groups throughout the country presents an opportunity for a pedagogy of the oppressed, which will provide a liberatory education. However, there is no indication that theory has become praxis. Currently, literacy training incorporates very little political education, perhaps a reflection of demands for political moderation being made by the local NGOs with which the NUEW is working.

One of the problems in developing a national curriculum is its centralised nature. A decentralised, localised curriculum would open up opportunities for schools, once again, to develop a curriculum that emanates from small-group structures, consciousness-raising and liberatory pedagogy.

Politics, Equal Representation and the Constitution

Despite the egalitarianism of the field situation during the war, there was inequity in the numbers of women in high-ranking, decision-making positions, and this continues in the post-liberation period. Thus, notwithstanding the lip service paid to political equity at high levels, quotas in various areas of politics and twenty years of NUEW existence, equity has not been achieved.

The NUEW National Report, in a revealing table, underscores the lack of women in various government posts: women make up 22 per cent of the national parliament, 11.8 per cent of serving ministers, including the Minister of Labour and the Minister of Justice, 85 per cent of deputy district administrators, and 16 per cent of judges; but there are no women provincial governors or first secretaries in international embassies (NUEW 1999, table 1:4). Women's representation at the regional level (the Zoba Assembly), however, exceeds the quota set aside for women (NUEW 1999: table 2:4).

The EPLF's contention that politics should be 'gender-blind' led to the exclusion of any specific, affirmative action clause in the new constitution, ratified in 1997. It remains to be seen if the constitution is constructed in such a way that gender equity can be pursued in the courts.[15]

Coexisting with the 'Traditional Order'

One contradiction within the structures of revolutionary organisations and their various wings is in the strategy for dealing with the traditional religio-kinship structures. Few liberation organisations are so secularised as to aim at obliterating, through administrative assault or revolutionary legalism, the very social fabric on which the society was built. It will be instructive to observe how the Eritrean government, in a society nearly half Christian, half Muslim, will deal with aspects of *sharia* law and such Islamic practices as polygamy, or with Christian customs that run counter to EPLF ideology.

Generally, most Third World liberation movements strive to coexist with the traditional order, rationalising that the revolution will be based on the concrete conditions of the society. In general this means that, at a fundamental level, there is not a great deal of difference in the gender ideologies of the state, which is seldom secular, and various parties, when these 'concrete conditions' relate to Christianity, Islam, traditional culture, the gender division of labour, and issues of sexuality.

What Kind of Organisation is the NUEW?

I have some questions about the NUEW's stress on literacy campaigns, the formation of cooperatives, and a 'development mentality' that partially relies on NGOs. This amounts to a fairly conventional and moderate approach to women's emancipation. Have these approaches worked? The professionalising of the NUEW (a necessary corollary of participation in the international feminist agenda) may have its positive side, but although staffed almost entirely by fighters, it has become the establishment, removed from the people and viewed by some as just another bureaucracy. It is a bureaucracy overburdened with work and yet, perhaps necessarily, selfish about sharing responsibilities with other agencies. The NUEW has engaged in a journey that has taken the organisation from dependence on the decidedly Eritrean agenda of the central movement to an international women's agenda that brings also a new reliance on international money. How does this fit into the context of a movement and country renowned for self-sufficiency?

It is still too soon to tell how independent the NUEW will be. Many questions arise. Can women and feminists be more effective infiltrating mass organisations and undermining their sexism, or is independence a necessity? Is there a need to develop a women's movement that emanates from, but radically transforms, indigenous structures such as women's popular culture and networks and their struggles as workers in the home and neighbourhood, a movement that emanates from both strategic and practical gender interests? And how is that done? The EPLF/PFDJ's current stress on the economic over the social raises further questions. With international organisations imposing policies such as structural adjustment on fledgling governments like Eritrea's, there is little hope that social and economic concerns will be appropriately conflated. And now there is the second war. Where does that leave a national women's organisation?

Some Policy Implications

Decisions by the NUEW and the state to deal with the difficulties women are having in the public domain are problematic. Although the new Eritrean constitution and the national school curriculum reveal some erosion of the affirmative and proactive gender egalitarianism for which the EPLF had been known, my interviews with women fighters revealed more severe problems in their private lives. Civilian women ex-fighters now have to deal with the persistence of some oppressive personal status laws, the erosion of the egalitarian gender division of labour that had been developed during the military struggle, a breakdown in the socialisation of children as 'free-spirited', and a return to stricter adherence to religio-kin dictates.

In their public lives, women are relying too much on the NUEW and the government to teach them, offer them skills, give them credit, help them relearn a family economics all but lost in the war years, train them for leadership positions, and find them jobs. Groups of women may fare better by being independent from both the NUEW and the government. Bana, the cooperative of demobilised fighters mentioned earlier, provides a good example of what can be done.

Using their 10,000 birr demobilisation compensation bonus as a kind of investment, Bana members can buy shares in various projects. Bana stresses individual self-sufficiency rather than the communal interdependence that was stressed in the field. The cooperative began with a fish market, then a bakery, and will try to expand into a garment factory.

Fighters had no money in the field: the government took care of all their material needs. The consequence is that families are not managing their resources well. As one might expect, the money and material problems that families are having now account for a number of divorces. Government and NUEW policy-makers might address these household economic problems by offering workshops in household economy.

Conclusion

Summarising the situation for women in Eritrea, an EPLF woman fighter delivered one of the most powerful statements I heard in my interviews: 'As for us, upon re-entering [civil] society, we find that we are liberated but not free. In the field we were not liberated, but [we were] free.'

We can see the contradictions and dilemmas of a state ideologically committed to constructing an egalitarian society, free of class, gender, ethnic or religious distinctions, but facing immediate economic problems and multiethnic tensions. Is success possible? Will women always suffer with the existence of a vanguard party or the development of the state and state apparatuses? Can policy and activist strategies offset these processes without undermining them?

Key questions, outlined earlier, remain as yet unanswered. What might it mean for a political organisation and its civilian counterpart to travel the route from liberation front – an organisation devoted to empowering disenfranchised groups like women, peasants, youth, minorities and workers – to a government assigned to control, monitor or contain these very groups? In terms of feminist theory building, what does it mean for women who have shared in a liberatory military struggle when the state variously assigns itself the role of central policy-maker and activist on behalf of women or entirely relinquishes that role, handing everything over to the national women's organisation? Can women achieve the goal of consolidating their wartime gains most effectively by depending on the state or by depending on their own women's organisations?

In most societies, men position women within the culture to serve male-dominated institutions. Likewise, in political movements men position women to serve the movement. Men expect women to preserve the culture or the family, often as symbols of resistance, or to maintain 'authentic' culture in the face of chaos and violence. Older women often become the enforcers. Eritrean women who actively participated in the war escaped this pattern, but it affected women who did not serve in the field. These civilian women, the 'keepers of the hearth', participated in freezing the culture. Women returning from military service found themselves facing similar expectations. The roles they had played in combat were romanticised along with their roles as mothers, as mothers of liberation fighters, and as the 'keepers of the hearth'.

The pressure on former fighters to revert to traditional norms is a familiar pattern in liberation struggles. In post-war situations the men need the labour of women, but they need to channel it into 'appropriate' tasks for the common good, such as reconstruction, economic recovery and replenishing the population lost in the war. The devastation imposed on Eritrea by the outbreak of a second war swiftly expanded the demand for such service in the common good. The country requires a great deal from all citizens, state control over public utilities and various institutions, and sacrifices from women and men. For women this takes the form of upholding the fabric of Eritrean society, no matter how traditional that may be.

Acknowledgements

This chapter is based on research conducted in 1994 and 1996 and a return trip to Asmara in November 1999 for the conference celebrating the twentieth anniversary of the National Union of Eritrean Women (NUEW). I would like to thank the NUEW, which gave me an affiliation, my two research assistants, Edna Yohannes Hadera and Selam Araya, my daughter, Alexa Almaz Hale, for setting up appointments with women fighters and acting as my consultant in 1994, and my other daughter, Adrienne Hale, for assisting me in Asmara in 1996. Thanks also to Abrehet Goytom, Aster Solomon, Kifloum Kidane, Dr Bereket Habteselassie, Worku Zerai, Aynalem Morcos, Tigisti Mehreteab, Elsa Yacob and many other Eritreans. Various units at the University of

California, Los Angeles, provided research funds: the Center for the Study of Women, the African Studies Center and the International Studies and Overseas Programs.

Notes

1. The estimates for the first war have remained constant in government, NGO and journalistic accounts at 30 per cent (See 'No Easy Walk to Freedom' 1998). Estimates of women combatants in the second war range from 15 per cent (Gilmore 1999a, 1999b), to 20 per cent (Smith 1999), to 25 per cent (Jenkins 1999).

2. See, for example, 'Eritrean Government Takes Women Soldiers from Frontlines' (2000), and 'Eritrean Women Soldiers Leave Frontline' (2000). Both of these were posted the same day on Dehai-News, an Eritrean internet listserv. The withdrawal of women combatants from the front lines is a mystery, but theories and political gossip suggest that too many women had been captured or killed, although figures are not available (Gilmore 1999a, Smith 1999). The casualty figures are very high, so one can imagine that a large number of women have been killed. It may well be, however, that it is the fear of their capture that propelled the decision. See a report from Mekele, Ethiopia, 'Eritrean POWs, including Women, Wait For War's End', dehai-news@primenet.com (1999).

   The term 'fighter' was used in the 30-year war to refer to anyone who was struggling in any form as part of the EPLF; the phrase 'in the field' referred both to areas already liberated and to those being contested during the struggle.

3. The 'doors' were not completely open. Attendance was by invitation only; each ministry was invited to send two representatives. The format was mainly formal, with order strictly observed. Small breakout groups were occasions that invited critical thinking about the organisation. However, the presence of government officials and the old regime of the NUEW sprinkled throughout the conference hampered some of the discussions. The conference themes were conventional and chronological: The Status of Women in Traditional Eritrea; The Role of Eritrean Women in the Liberation Movement; The Status of Women in the Post-Independence Period; and Future Strategies for the Advancement of Eritrean Women. I was amazed, however, at being invited to present a paper, as it was known that I had published some critical pieces on the NUEW (e.g., Hale 2000).

4. The NUEW is the only national women's organisation, but there are other gender units in the government and a few other struggling women's groups, such as Bana.

5. Furthermore, it is estimated that one third of the 65,000 Eritreans who died in the first war were women (Fisher 1999).

6. Most of the sources on the role of Eritrean women in the war are scattered journalistic writings (e.g. Grinker 1992). The only full study of women warriors to emerge during the war is Wilson (1991).

7. My work in Sudan, extending over decades, has been both academic (teaching and research) and activist (as a human rights advocate). Currently, for example, I am a founding member of the International Women's Committee in Support of Nuba Women and Children and a member of Darb Alintifada, a left activist forum. See Hale (1996).

8. The interviews began at the Asmara Teacher Training Institute from 12 to 15 July 1994. The interview with Worku Zerai took place on 25 August 1996, with Asmarat Abraha on 22 July 1996 and with Letebrahan Kasai on 13 August 1996. Interviews were conducted in English and Tigrinya.

9. An English translation of the EPLF programmes, the marriage code, statements on women and a seminar on romantic love can all be found in the appendices of Wilson (1991).

10. The EPLF combatants, men and women combined, were only some 3 per cent of the total population (information obtained in 1994 from the Research and Information Section, Embassy of Eritrea c.1994).

11. Fighters received varying amounts, depending on how long they had served (Embassy of Eritrea c.1994).

12. In 1995 it was estimated that some 41,000 men and women were unemployed (Klingebiel et al. 1995).

13. A number of sources have mentioned the high divorce rate (e.g., 'No Easy Walk to Freedom' 1998). Nearly all of my interviewees in 1994, and especially by 1996, commented that nearly half of the demobilised fighters who married in the field were divorced.

14. This is a quote from the journalist Ruth Simon in a documentary film on Eritrean women fighters by Eva Egensteiner, 'When the Dream Becomes a Reality? Nation Building and the Continued Struggle of the Women of the Eritrean People's Liberation Front', University of Southern California (1995).

15. The 'gender-blind' statement was made in an interview I conducted in July 1996, in Asmara, with three members of the Constitution Commission. At the time a final draft was about to be presented to the public for discussion and public education. The interview was with Zahra Jabir Omer, Tsega Gaim and Mehret Iyob. Most of the statements were from Mehret Iyob.

CHAPTER 9

Rape in War and Peace

Social Context, Gender, Power and Identity

TINA SIDERIS

How can women use a post-conflict transition to democracy to move beyond reconstruction of pre-war gender relations to real social transformation? We confront this basic question because the promise of democratic change holds hope of social relations free of discrimination and violent control and opens the space for women to agitate for equal access to social, political and economic power. But the enormity of the task that the question implies overwhelms us. It is especially overwhelming when one considers that, in spite of the growing strength of women's voices and the achievements of their struggle for equality everywhere in the world, violence continues to be a feature of relations between men and women and constitutes one of the primary risks to women's lives and their physical and mental health.

It is generally accepted that in any particular instance the causes of violence against women are complex and multiple. The causes include general levels of social violence, themselves multidimensional. Nevertheless, acts of violence perpetrated by one individual against another occur in a context specified by inequality in power. The structural inequality of power that exists between men and women across societies creates the conditions for the social control of women. Thus, while general societal violence, that is, the levels of violence prevalent in a specific social situation, may limit the degree of violence used to control women, violence against women reflects relations of domination and subordination.

By relations of domination and subordination between men and women, we mean more than antagonism between individual men and women, or particular groups of men and women. Unequal relations of power between men and women suggest a set of social practices, beliefs, ideas, values and speech that promote male domination and superiority and female subordination and 'secondariness' (Rowbotham 1983:27). This discourse intersects in complex ways with discourses of class, race and ethnicity, becoming manifest in specific forms of social control and discrimination across societies and within cultures at particular historical moments.

We can begin to understand women's internalised sense of submission or secondariness if we accept that society constructs the sense of oneself as a man or woman – that not only internal representations of primary relationships produce the self but also the social world and culture, which is internal and external to the individual. Equally, dominant discourses of gender fail to provide men with alternatives to superiority and the necessity of control. This becomes most clear when particular circumstances pose threats to masculinity. The reassertion of manhood appeals to predominant values and ideas, which reaffirm superiority. In the process of reasserting domination, extremely violent forms of sexual control are enacted.

If the social is 'inscribed' on human subjects, then it is fair to argue that there are not only *inter*cultural but also *intra*cultural variations in subjective experiences of masculinity and femininity (Young 1996:43). Within the dominant discourses of male domination and feminine subordination, particular social forces – material, ideological and institutional – frame divergent experiences of what it is to be man and woman and elaborate the violent features of gender relations. This suggests that attempts to combat sexual violence require an understanding of gender roles, the relative power of men and women, material conditions and socio-cultural practices in specific situations and localities.

This chapter examines the experience of sexual violence in particular contexts, war and peace, amongst a distinct sector of women, Mozambican women refugees.[1] It draws on work with marginalised groups of rural women who survived rape in war and peace. By examining the social context in which women are violated, the chapter attempts to promote an understanding of how specific conditions impact on women's interpretations of their violation, create the limits and possibilities to challenge the inequalities they experience, and promote the necessity of superiority and control in men.

In situations of peace, rape tends to be privatised. In the context of war, the socio-political content of rape is more obvious. When women recognise rape as a weapon of social control and cultural destruction, they are able to avoid the negative effects of 'privatisation of the damage' (Becker *et al.* 1989:81). However, recognition of the socio-political content of rape does not necessarily translate into action to challenge the balance of power in women's social relations. The social conditions in which women live provide both constraints and opportunities for resisting the inequality in power that exposes them to gender-specific violence.

The Struggle to Combat Gender-based Violence

Countries emerging from organised conflict and effecting a transition to democracy have a tendency to adopt a rights-based approach to sexual violence. South Africa provides a good example. The constitution protects the rights of women, and a relatively high number of women hold government posts. Yet statistics on violence against women reveal alarmingly high rates. In 1998, the official statistics indicated 99.7 reported rapes per 100,000 people (Vincent 2000). Dominant explanations attribute the extremely high rate of sexual violence in South Africa to societal violence. The predominant approach to combating violence against women emphasises the implementation of progressive legislation and the protection of individual rights. Democratic transition has heralded changes in legislation that provide survivors of sexual violence with increased possibilities of protection and justice. The state has conceived victim empowerment programmes that prioritise rape, sexual abuse and family violence. These programmes aim to improve implementation of the law and to provide individual survivors with counselling and support.

In a country emerging from repressive governance, such constitutional and legal protection of individual rights is a significant achievement. It is important that the government acknowledges sexual violence as a problem requiring intervention. There is no doubt that the legacy of state repressive violence, the social insecurities created by transition, and the structural violence embedded in poverty all contribute to generally high levels of social violence. Research shows that it is the poorer sections of the population that face the most interpersonal violence (Vincent 2000). At the same time, there is ample evidence that attitudes promoting male control and subordination of women in sexual and gender relations are directly related to sexual violence against women.

For example, a recent study of violence in sexual relationships amongst youth in the town of Umtata in the eastern Cape concluded that 'men perceived that girls should be sexually available for them and that sex was their "right" in a relationship; thus [the] "taking" of sex which was not freely offered, by force if necessary, was legitimised'. Further: 'Violence against women *per se* was not perceived by men as an essential aspect of masculinity ... however the leverage it gave men in controlling women was' (Wood and Jewkes 1998:38).

Critics of the rights-based struggle to combat violence against women concede that legal reforms have resulted in greater protection for survivors of rape and battery, more fairness in their treatment, and some changes in attitudes. Nevertheless, they argue, these changes have not addressed the social conditions that give rise to rape and battery, namely sexual inequality and the oppression of women as a group (Caringella-MacDonald 1988; Romero 1985; Collins and Whalen 1989). Thus, they argue, the legal reformist approach to sexual violence adopts a discourse that assumes a consensus of interest and ignores the socio-political conflict that relations of power produce.

Returning to the South African example, is it accurate to say that unequal relations of power between men and women have not been contested? There is evidence to suggest otherwise. For example, in the 1990s women came together to lobby for representation in the structures that were negotiating a political settlement and transition, and thus challenged male-dominated discourse on women's place and role in shaping national political issues. In the transition phase, women have successfully taken up positions – political, economic and professional – previously reserved for males. Marginalised rural women are coming forward to report experiences of rape and battery, suggesting subtle shifts in consciousness about the legitimacy of sexual violence perpetrated against them (Masisukumeni Women's Crisis Centre Annual Report 1998–99).

In this sense, domination and subordination are not static. Power is a contested terrain and is contextually based. Thus women may experience domination in the home but greater equality in extra-domestic spheres of work. Further, women are not passive victims of their circumstances. They resist and reflect on their experiences of oppression and violence. Consciousness shifts but not in a progressive linear direction. Resistance, reflection and shifts in consciousness are multidimensional and contradictory, framed by the particular conditions and circumstances in which women live (Rowbotham 1983).

In order to understand the choices women make we need to understand their specific experiences of oppression and the possibilities open to them. For example, changes in impoverished rural women's perceptions of the legitimacy of intimate partner violence may not translate into challenging male domination in the household. Nor can it be said that a collective political consciousness has developed amongst these women. Yet individual women are contesting unbridled control and exploring options to limit the violence, by reporting experiences of violence. The endurance of battery displayed by many of these women is a product of the material and socio-cultural constraints of their life conditions rather than some kind of false consciousness.

If women reflect on their experiences, then it is reasonable to argue that specific forms and conditions of sexual violence may open up possibilities for shifts in consciousness. Can we categorise experiences of rape or battery? For example, is the experience of rape for victims the same in war and outside it (Nordstrom 1991)? Differentiating between rape in war and peace carries the danger of prioritising sexual assaults so that rape that is used as a tactic of ethnic cleansing evokes moral outrage, yet forced sex in the privacy of family life is accepted (Nordstrom 1991). I argue, based on my research with women war refugees who were raped, that the context of war specifies the forms that sexual violence takes and frames the way it is experienced and understood. This does not imply that I am suggesting a 'hierarchy' of rapes.

Rape in War and Peace: Same Category, Different Experiences?

The paradox about rape is that it is a political act, which has far-reaching social ramifications and violates one of the most basic and intimate experiences individuals have of themselves. Thus individual victims experience a political phenomenon in a deeply subjective way. Burt and Katz (1987:58) explain this very clearly when they say, 'Rape may be a social/political phenomenon, but its reality is acted out in an intensely personal and personalised way.' In the context of war, rape, both in its aims and its effects, perhaps more than any other act of violence perpetrated by one individual against another, highlights the political intention of interpersonal violence.

Nordstrom (1991) uses the term 'dirty war' to describe warfare in which civilian populations and their social and cultural foundations are strategic targets. She argues that in the context of the dirty war, sexual attacks are tactics of intimidation and instruments of social destruction.

> Rape, as with all terror-warfare, is not exclusively an attack on the body – it is an attack on the 'body-politic'. Its goal is not to maim or kill one person but to control an entire socio-political process by crippling it. It is an attack directed equally against personal identity and cultural integrity. (Nordstrom 1991:8)

Rape, when used as a tactic of social destruction in war, takes specific forms. It is perpetrated on a mass scale. Women are abducted and used as sex slaves. Rape is often perpetrated in public, in the presence of family and compatriots. Other forms of torture usually accompany it. In its most perverse form, rape involves the relatives of the victim in the assault (Nordstrom 1991; Akina Mama wa Afrika 1995; Sideris 1999). For example, during the war of destabilisation in Mozambique, widespread reports from men and women explained how rebel soldiers used the husbands of rape victims as *mattresses* upon whom the perpetrator took his victims (Sideris 1999).

In the context of war, the facts that large numbers of women are violated, and in public and perverse ways, combine to undermine social stability. Sexual violence perpetrated on a mass scale threatens the continuity of family and community (Magaia 1988; Nordstrom 1991).

In-depth interviews with Mozambican women refugees who were raped during the war in their country reveal that they made a strong link between rape and social fragmentation. They argued that when one woman was raped, the whole community felt the rape. They pointed out that those present were also dehumanised. Relatives and compatriots, who were drawn into the public degradation of the rape victim by their witness to the attack and their participation in the assault, were shamed and humiliated. Illustrating the ways in which rape resulted in the breakdown of family and community functioning, these women described with deep concern cases of men who rejected women who bore the children of RENAMO rapists.

The attacks on individuals and the breakdown of families and communities constitute only part of the threat to social stability. The ways in which women are raped pervert social norms and in this way threaten social and cultural integrity. Women are raped by children of their communities. Men are forced to participate in raping their wives. Women who watch their husbands being murdered are taken by force to be the concubines of the murderers.

These kinds of terror tactic constitute an attack not only on individual women, their families and communities, but also on the overall social system. Thus, the discrete event of rape is fundamentally linked to the process of social and cultural destruction. When rape is one of the weapons used to destroy society, acts of sexual violence take on a special significance. The individual act of sexual violence is related to the destruction of social order for victims and nonvictims alike.

The intimate nature of the assault involves rape victims, albeit forcibly, in their own violation. Rape engages the victims in human sexual interaction. Thus the sexual content, which implies familiarity and communion, leaves the victim feeling like a participant in a repulsive sexual interaction (Metzger 1976; Agger 1989; Dahl 1993). In war, when rape takes place on a mass scale and rapists so evidently use it as a weapon to attack the social system, victims are left feeling that they are 'active agents' in the corruption of social norms (Scarry 1987:47).

Rebel soldiers abducted the Mozambican women referred to above; many were held in captivity for long periods lasting up to six years. The women spoke of being made the 'wives' of the rebels for whom they had to provide sex and perform domestic tasks. Performing these activities made the women feel like active participants in their own ill-treatment and in the perversion of social norms (Scarry 1987; Agger 1989; Dahl 1993). In the words of one of the women:

> They [RENAMO] were killing our people – we were seeing them. Then they were coming to us as husbands. Can you afford to face such a thing?

At the camp I was chosen to be the wife of the commander. And others together with my children were given as wives to other soldiers. We feel it because the RENAMO were showing us guns that if we don't do these things – sleep with them and cook for them – they will kill us. We did these things. So that was a terrible thing to happen to us. What has happened to us – our properties have been damaged, our bodies have been damaged. Everything – our life has absolutely changed because of RENAMO. The spirit has been damaged. (Sideris 1999)

Thus in the context of massive social conflict, the trauma of rape for individuals is made up of the violation both of the body-self and of the social body. This is not to suggest that victims of rape in the context of war do not experience extreme personal anguish and emotional suffering. Post-traumatic stress disorder symptoms, existential injuries, spiritual damage, depression, anxiety, somatic problems, fear, shame and humiliation are well-documented outcomes of rape in war (Agger 1989; Groenenberg 1993; Lunde and Ortman 1992; Sveaass and Axelsen 1994; Sideris 1999; Van Willigen 1984).

There is an added dimension to the suffering in the context of war. The trauma of rape is multidimensional. Victims respond to the lived experience of a discrete incident of violence, and to the social destruction of which it is an integral part. This interdependence of the individual and social dimensions of the trauma of rape in war provides victims with an opportunity to avoid privatisation of the damage and to recognise the socio-political intent of the attacks.

The point can be more clearly illustrated by a brief examination of the well-known tendency amongst survivors of rape towards self-blame. With few exceptions (Frazier 1990), studies investigating attributions of responsibility report that self-blame is common amongst survivors of rape. One explanation put forward for the tendency among rape victims to blame themselves is that women are socialised into the victim role and therefore accept responsibility for negative life events (Meyer and Taylor 1986). Self-blame and societal blaming of rape victims are closely linked by feminist explanations to social myths about male and female sexuality that cast women as seductress and men as victim of their uncontrollable sexual instincts (Herman 1993; Koss and Burkhart 1989; Lebowitz and Roth 1994).

In contrast, research with Mozambican women war refugees showed that they attributed causal responsibility for the sexual violence they suffered to external factors (Sideris 1999). The following comment is typical: 'I blame the war. I don't blame myself because this thing didn't happen to me only. We were so many who were raped. I should question myself if this happened to me only.'

The large majority of the Mozambican women interviewed accepted neither characterological nor behavioural self-blame for the rape that was perpetrated during the war. They demonstrated a realistic understanding of the fact that, where the whole social environment is under attack and social institutions disintegrate, personal and behavioural changes provide scant protection against external threats.

These women did, however, express a deep sense of shame rooted in those socio-cultural constructions of sexuality that assign value to the sexual purity of females. It is clear that feeling ashamed is not necessarily accompanied by accepting causal responsibility. Both shame and self-blame may be rooted in social constructions of women and their sexuality. It seems that the context in which rape occurs and the forms it takes can override socially held beliefs. The sense of being intimately known and exposed, which plays an important role in producing shame, is part of the lived experience of rape. Yet despite feeling spoiled, worthless and devalued by rape, the Mozambican women were quite capable of assigning responsibility to the source of the violence and were thus able to avoid privatisation of the violation.

Hence research with one group of women survivors of sexual violence in war reveals that they experienced and understood the social content of rape. The context in which the rape was perpetrated allowed these women to reject responsibility for the rape – a considerable achievement given the strength, in their societies, of social beliefs that tend to blame women possessed by another for failing their husbands and fathers (Brownmiller 1975; Meijer 1985). Of course, this rejection of responsibility does not necessarily translate into collective or organised political resistance.

War: Gender Roles and Gender Identity

The conditions of war make the political intent of sexual violence evident for men and women. For example, reports on political conflict in KwaZulu Natal, South Africa, during the late 1980s and early 1990s show that sexual violation and humiliation were common forms of punishment meted out to women who allegedly consorted with the enemy, punishment meted out by both ANC comrades and Inkatha warriors (Hassim and Stiebel 1993).

Feminist scholarship has been in the forefront of theorising the links between dominant notions of masculinity, war and militarisation. Conventional wisdom defines war as a male affair that excludes women. In practice, although they are direct targets of war, the power structures that decide the terms of battle and settle its spoils exclude women. Thus, the institutions of war constitute exclusive male clubs, which are defined by hierarchy, authoritarian control, aggression and violence.

Membership in the military club also confers the identity of hero: men who give up their lives for ideals, soldiers who protect property and the vulnerable, braves who take up arms to liberate their people from oppression. Brownmiller points out that 'ordinary men are made un-ordinary by entry into the most exclusive male-only club in the world' (1975:31). Thus militarisation, which draws on the most aggressive and violent features of notions of masculinity, provides men with a heroic identity. This combines with real experiences of courage and conviction to give many soldiers, guerrillas, comrades and warriors a sense of meaning and direction, of playing a special role in society.

Women may also draw on traditional gender roles and identities to survive both during war and in the aftermath, even though the domestic sphere is a principal site of battle. For example, the Mozambican women referred to above argued that they derived a source of strength from their mothering roles. They distinguished two ways in which their roles as caretakers, nurturers and homemakers made them feel strong. First, they attributed the actions they took to save and protect others to the fact that they are women. They argued that they acted with humanity, maintaining a morality that honoured life, despite a context in which people were being killed and degraded. The following statement by one of the survivors illustrates the point.

A woman, even if it's bad, she cannot run and leave her children. She prepares to die with her children. Being a mother makes a woman strong because you must look after other people. As a woman I managed to get some money and to go and fetch my mother to bring her here safely. (Sideris 1999)

Second, these women suggested that being mothers allowed them to re-create homes and families, that is, to re-establish some normal functioning in the aftermath. They argued that men do not have the skills and endurance to sustain a home in the face of difficulty.

Women survivors of the conflict in Lebanon have described similar experiences. '[I]n some ways war is easier for women. Whatever the situation, even in shelters, they are busy, looking after the children, managing the house. Men, meanwhile, have lost their role, if they cannot go out to work' (Bennet et al, 1995). Women from Somaliland make similar observations when discussing the effects of war on gender roles: '[N]owadays, women seem to be better at work than men. They are all on the move, bustling about to make ends meet. Men seem to have lost their bearings about their family concerns, lost confidence in their abilities to maintain their families' (Bennet et al. 1995).

Paradoxically, these examples suggest that the male-dominated arena of war can present serious threats to masculinity. Acts of sexual violence strike at traditional notions of men's protection of their wives, daughters and mothers. The overall social destruction inherent in dirty wars leaves men with few opportunities to implement traditional roles as providers. Thus war leaves men with either an eroded sense of manhood or the option of a militarised masculine identity with the attendant legitimisation of violence and killing as a way of maintaining power and control.

It is reasonable to argue, on the basis of the evidence above, that situations of war can result in a shift in gender roles while at the same time provoking a retreat to conservative notions of masculinity and femininity. To survive, women take on roles previously reserved for men without always challenging social relations in the domestic sphere. Men whose masculinity is threatened are forced to find ways of reasserting their manhood.

These twists and turns in gender roles and identities are elaborated in different ways by the nature of the conflict or repressive situation and by the relationship of groups of men and women to the conflict, which is itself determined by social background. Under apartheid rule in South Africa, for example, gender intersected with race so that white femininity played a fundamental role in sustaining the militarised identity of white males.

Sexual Violence in the Aftermath

Similarly, the nature of the conflict and the history of repression specify the demands and priorities of reconstruction in the aftermath. Projections of the future include varying degrees of emphasis on the participation of women in public life. We observe variations in emphasis on economic reconstruction, reconciliation, development of democratic political structures and processes, and legislative reforms. Across societies, women play a pivotal role in social reconstruction by virtue of their unique relationship to the domestic sphere, whatever the policies on women's participation in political institutions.

Yet although women play a crucial role in reconstructing society, and transition may effect greater participation of women in decision-making structures, available evidence shows that sexual violence continues in the aftermath. But the conditions of transition specify the particular domain of sexual violence, the forms it takes, and the way it is experienced and understood. For example, although statistics, particularly in South Africa, show that rape takes place on a mass scale, rape is not perpetrated in public. Evidence reveals that the greatest number of rapes takes place in the private realm of the family and intimate relationships.

The private nature of sexual violence, the fact that it takes place in the context of intimate relationships, which imply love and reciprocity, and the emphasis placed on containing general levels of social violence, tend to obfuscate the socio-political content of sexual violence. Interventions are aimed at protecting individual rights, addressing the privatised damage of individual survivors, and changing the behaviour and relationships between individual men and women in particular families. Sexual violence is located in antagonisms between men and women, in the inner world of domestic life rather than in the discourse that legitimates male domination and female subordination.

The privatisation of sexual violence, reinforced in the context of peace, makes it more complicated to address. Society defines the domestic context as personal and treats it as peripheral to broader political processes, even though it is essential to social reproduction (Dubish 1986). This ideology makes it difficult to penetrate the inner workings of domestic life and results in a tendency to avoid intrusions, which may shift the balance of power in the family. The reluctance of police officials to intervene in cases of domestic violence, even where laws are in place to protect the victims of abuse, is telling. Thus although changes in laws may provide women with increased protection against abuse and greater access to justice, they are not sufficient to change the attitudes and beliefs that affect the implementation of legal justice for survivors of sexual violence.

The necessary and important focus on legal reforms in post-war reconstruction also tends to diffuse attention from other fundamental social issues. Women survivors of war and repression who lose access to housing, land and the traditional methods of subsistence and who have unequal access to employment opportunities are left without the relative autonomy to resist violence in intimate relationships and have limited options for using legal protection. Poverty increases vulnerability to gender-specific violence. Evidence in South Africa demonstrates that poor and marginalised women are at greater risk of sexual violence.

A woman living on the margins of rural South African society explains the problem in this way:

> We are suffering as women. A man can go and sleep out and come back in the morning. When he comes he'll expect you to say, 'Oh! are you back baby.' You make tea for him. You don't say anything. Even if you quarrel – you can't say to him, 'You were out with your girlfriend!' You can't say that because you will be beaten like hell. It is his home. Where can I go? (Sideris 1999)

As indicated above, women are not simply passive victims of their circumstances. Countless individual women have resisted the complex web of power relations that confronts them to remake their lives with some dignity. Lacking access to formal employment, women have created the informal sector to support themselves and their dependants. In South Africa, some rural women seized opportunities offered by government policy to supply low-cost housing by accessing government subsidies collectively to construct homes for themselves. Mozambican women with access to land on the outskirts of Maputo developed successful vegetable-growing cooperatives that were the principal suppliers to the capital city's markets during the late 1980s and the early 1990s.

Even in the overall social context of male domination, there are particular circumstances in which such women represent a threat to men. Economic underdevelopment, with high levels of poverty and unemployment, is one such environment. The traditional sense of manhood derived from being a provider is thwarted without the dignity of work. In situations of post-war reconstruction, this frustration can merge with the eroded sense of manhood produced by subjection to violence in war. Any resistance or challenge to power in the one area where men can assert their manhood, that is, in intimate relationships, further threatens masculinity and can lead to ever more violent and perverse attempts to maintain control.

Workers at a rural rape crisis centre, for example, report growing support from men in denouncing rape, in particular stranger rape. The same men express concern when women contest men's power in the home. Men whose partners are employed demand full control of their wives' salaries. Some of these men have complained to the centre that they are being abused because their working wives no longer perform their domestic tasks with the same efficiency. Women who do not meet these demands are at high risk of violent abuse (Masisukumeni Women's Crisis Centre, personal interviews, 1999).

It is too simplistic to argue that economic empowerment is sufficient to combat effectively violence against women. History is filled with evidence to the contrary. Even in societies in which women exercise some control over economic resources, ideologies can exist that devalue women and promote female subordination. In other words, material conditions and ideology do not always correspond. Many women collude with practices and promote ideas that favour male superiority particularly in the household because of the belief in upholding culture and tradition.

It is equally true that even though overall men may have greater access to public power, this does not necessarily give all men the same access to material and productive resources. The socio-economic vulnerability of both men and women can intersect with cultural and socio-political practices to exacerbate violence against women and limit the possibilities for resistance and change.

Framing the questions within a South African context highlights some key issues. Immediate questions include: what is the everyday life experience, in underdeveloped rural areas, or former comrades, or freedom fighters, and their sons and brothers, who today are still immersed in poverty, have very limited employment opportunities and thus no real role in reconstructing the nation? How do these men construct a masculine identity? Do intimate sexual relationships provide them with one sphere where they can sustain an identity defined by control, where they can have a sense of group belonging by engaging in competition and camaraderie with other men? Is the domestic arena the one remaining area where they can still have a sense of power and superiority?

In general, neither the language nor the process of post-war reconstruction sufficiently acknowledges the changes and crises in gender roles and identities that situations of war can effect. Soldiers, activists and freedom fighters are demobilised rather than demilitarised, for example. These men are generally left with few alternatives to militarised masculinity, and in real terms they very often have neither the skills nor the opportunity to play a positive role in the reconstruction of their communities. Determining ways in which these ordinary men can be involved in the construction of alternative notions of masculinity and play a part in reconstruction is crucial in transition periods if we are effectively to address discourses that legitimate violence against women.

The question arises of why most men in South Africa have been reluctant to fully adopt gender discourses that promote equal rights for women. Is it because investment in the new order, in alternative identities, is nonreciprocal and threatens their last remaining power base, offering them nothing in return? Answering these questions requires an understanding of micro-dynamics that goes beyond sexual attitudes and the dynamics of sexual relations, extending to the broader range of life experiences of ordinary men who are dealing with the legacy of repressive violence and the insecurities of transition. Of course, gender-based violence implies a relationship, and clarification of these questions requires an understanding of the micro-dynamics of gender relations. Perhaps, as Hale (1999) has argued, workshops on the household economy would be fruitful.

At a more general level there is not much substantial evidence to show that post-war governments have taken an opportunity to use the obvious socio-political content of sexual violence in war to challenge in public forums the socio-cultural values and political practices that legitimate violence against women. The South African Truth and Reconciliation Commission (TRC) is a case in point. Before pressure from outside groups, the TRC did not include a gendered perspective in its reconstruction of human rights violations. Even after it instituted women's hearings, there is evidence to suggest that many women did not see the TRC as an appropriate space in which to describe personal violations, especially the sexual assaults and torture they experienced under apartheid repression.

Research conducted with female political activists suggests that socially constructed conceptions of women and their sexuality contributed to the reluctance of women to make submissions. Several women who were interviewed expressed the fear that publicly revealing experiences of sexual assault could result in their being stigmatised and devalued in their own communities (Goldblatt and Meintjes 1996). Thus the TRC, a body and process that in part symbolised the ushering in of a culture of human rights, did not effectively challenge those attitudes and beliefs that discriminate against women and control their sexuality.

Conclusion

The forms that sexual assaults take make it easier to mobilise moral outrage at rape in war than to challenge the privatisation of sexual violence in the aftermath, when society defines violence against women in terms of antagonisms between men and women in personal, dysfunctional relationships. To develop strategies to combat violence against women in both of these circumstances it is necessary to locate gender-specific violence in context – the context of subordination (Romero 1985). Subordination creates the conditions for the perpetration of sexual violence. Yet subordination is neither static nor uncontested. It is elaborated in different ways by class, race, ethnicity and culture within and across space and time. In this sense, then, context shapes gender-specific violence, the forms it takes, the way women and men experience and understand it, and the possibilities for resisting it.

The important role that context plays in specifying sexual violence calls for integrated approaches to combating violence against women. Such approaches need to address the overall social context by tackling issues such as legal reforms, equality and citizenship as well as the specific manifestations of power and oppression in different social contexts. The latter require locally specific interventions that take into account how particular material conditions and ideas, beliefs and values intersect to determine exposure to violence.

Note

1. I conducted interviews with Mozambican women refugees between 1995 and 1998 in Block A, Mangweni, and Schoemansdal villages in Mpumalanga province, South Africa, as part of my doctoral research.

CHAPTER 10

Between Love, Anger and Madness
Building Peace in Haiti

MYRIAM MERLET

The title I have chosen for this chapter about the problems my country, Haiti, has with violence against women, contains words that appear on a poster that my organisation, ENFOFANM (Organisation for the Defence of the Rights of Women), published on the occasion of the Beijing Conference in 1995. We borrowed the expression 'love, anger and madness' from Marie Vieux-Chauvet (1968), the Haitian feminist novelist, to express the range of feelings women have when confronting the difficult task of building peace.

Women have learned, through their biological functions, which are reinforced by their socialisation, to be the bearers of love – love of life, love of what is human. Women are taught to love others, but not themselves. Yet this love has enabled women to see the world differently. It has allowed them to transform their anger – an anger stemming from their painful experiences as women – into what may seem in many respects like madness: faith in the possibility and the necessity of establishing a new order, and investing in the building of that new order.

My aim here is to show how Haitian women's organisations, 'between love, anger and madness', are attempting to make the best they can out of the difficult situation that Haiti has endured for more than a decade, in order to build something else. Though full-scale armed conflict does not exist in Haiti – that is, conflict between different political factions or between Haiti and another state – one can nevertheless argue that for several years the conditions under which Haitians have been living can qualify as a war situation. And, as in every warlike situation, women are the first to be targeted.

Historical and Economic Background

Because location and context are important to an understanding of the geopolitical stakes and the terms of the problem of violence, let me begin by situating Haiti. Located halfway between Cuba and Puerto Rico, one hour's flight from the Florida coast, the Republic of Haiti shares the island of Hispaniola with the Dominican Republic. Haiti, a small, densely populated country of 8 million people, is a former French colony that attained independence in 1804 after a long slave revolt and a bloody war of independence. Some people believe that this warlike past still determines current violent practices that taint social relations both between individuals and between individuals and the state. I doubt this. Apart from the fact that similar situations do not necessarily produce this effect, I think that violence is a cultural phenomenon resulting from certain conditions prevalent in a society and that it tends to become dominant. In the case of Haiti, violence is noticeable in interpersonal relations and in the relations between power structures and citizens, male and female alike.

Haiti has a very stormy political history. Since independence, the Haitian nation has been building governing institutions with considerable difficulty. For thirty years, from 1957 to 1986, the country lived in the grip of the Duvalier dictatorship. This dictatorship, of the bloodiest kind, provoked the mass exodus of thousands of Haitian men and women to Africa and to the great metropoles of North America and Europe.

Since the fall of the Duvalier dictatorship, Haiti has been going through what is commonly referred to as a transitional period, meaning a transition to democracy. To clarify the foundations of present-day Haiti's political situation, it seems appropriate to list a few historical milestones in the period since 1986.

Populist struggles, which were supported by the intervention of foreign powers, particularly the United States, resulted in the fall of the Duvalier regime in 1986. In these struggles against state authoritarianism, women were fierce resistors as well as victims. The following year, Haiti adopted a new constitution which (*inter alia*) establishes legal equality between men and women and pays special attention to women's status. The constitution held leaders of dictatorships in the background for ten years.

A multitude of interim governments succeeded the Duvalier regime. The presence of high-ranking army officials, presaging the supreme control the army would continue to have in political affairs, characterised the governments of the years 1986–90. During this period, the government of Leslie Manigat (1988), which emerged after a massacre perpetrated during elections, created a Secretariat for the Status of Women.

In 1990 the interim president, Ertha Pascal-Trouillot, the first woman president, organised the first free and democratic elections. Those elections, carried out with the assistance and under the supervision of international monitors, resulted in the election of Jean-Bertrand Aristide. The population in both the countryside and the cities gave Aristide, a parish priest, a landslide victory. Women's participation in the elections was especially notable, although the state authority responsible for organising them included only one woman. Of the 2,032 candidates, only 164 were women, mainly at the local government level. Only three women ran for the senate, and none won a seat; three of the thirteen women who stood as deputies were elected and thirty-four were elected as mayors. This was only the second time that Haitian women had been able to exercise their citizenship since they won the right to vote in 1957. Women were appointed to high office in the new government, assuming posts as ministers, members of the presidential and ministerial cabinets, and directors of public services. During the seven months of its life, this constitutional regime made overtures to other Caribbean countries, including Cuba (with which diplomatic relations had been broken off at the instigation of the United States). The Haitian government took steps to become a member of Caricom, the Caribbean common market, and to join the Lomé Convention, which links the European Community with developing countries.

In 1991, marking the army's refusal to accept the pursuit of democracy, a military *coup d'état* overturned the democratically elected government. This very violent *coup d'état* for the most part targeted the working classes. It also revealed the army's refusal to allow the poor majority to consolidate a permanent presence on the national political stage. Violence against women, particularly gang rape and forced rape by a close relative, were among the weapons used systematically by the putschists. Popular resistance, by women in particular, matched in intensity the atrocities committed. Examples of this resistance included the publication of the newspaper *Ayiti Fanm* (Women of Haiti) by the feminist organisation ENFOFANM in August 1991; the first national meeting opposing violence against women; women's organisations documenting cases of human rights violations, particularly violations of women's rights; the organisation of resistance; and different forms of protest on both the national and international levels.

In 1996, under the banner of a multinational armed force (which in reality consisted mainly of American GIs), the constitutional government returned to power. The new government disbanded the Haitian army. This era, called a 'return to constitutional order', saw the establishment of the Truth and Justice Commission, but did not bring people the reparations they expected. In particular, no compensation was paid for specific violations of which women had been the victims, although women's organisations had done their utmost to document cases and to submit them to the authorities. Moreover, women disappeared from the centres of power. The only ministerial post occupied by a woman was that of the new Minister for the Status of Women and Women's Rights. During this period of military occupation, women's organisations condemned the military's sexual abuses of women, and in particular of little girls. The government made no attempt to follow up the complaints filed. This government did, however, support the Beijing Platform for Action (UN 1996).

Despite new presidential elections in 1996, women continued to be excluded from the centres of power. However, the women's movement did push the parliament to vote and ratify the Inter-American Convention on the Prevention, Punishment and Eradication of Violence Against Women (Convention of Belém do Pará) and to declare 3 April the national day of the Haitian Women's Movement.

Following a series of crises, the government resigned. More than a year later, without establishing mechanisms for reconstituting the legislature, the president dissolved parliament and appointed a prime minister by fiat. The nation continued to wait for a return to constitutional order, and the president announced new elections.

Four factors strongly influence the situation in July 1999, which can be summed up as a general structural crisis affecting every area of national life. The first is the new mode of international military occupation, consisting of a rotation of different occupation forces. The second is the imposition of certain socio-economic policies by the World Bank and the International Monetary Fund (IMF). These economic 'reforms' rest on the easing of restrictions on markets and the privatisation of public companies. International cooperation proves to be the main conduit for implementing these IMF reforms. This control of the Haitian economy has all the more impact because the weakness of national production makes Haiti totally dependent on foreign countries. The third influential factor is the institutional crisis at the state level: seven months without a parliament, and the legislative body has failed to ratify a government as stipulated in the constitution. The fourth is the fragmented, unstructured nature of Haitian society.

This situation has had serious consequences for people's living conditions. In the grip of runaway inflation and a drastic devaluation of the local currency, people see their living conditions deteriorate every day. The majority of the population is impoverished. These phenomena are the direct results of the implementation of structural adjustment policies. Civil society, which has taken an activist stance in the past, has experienced difficulty in developing appropriate responses and organising as a real force for change.

Violence against Women's Bodies

It is on the basis of the above history that I affirm that Haiti is a country at war, and has been for quite a long time. This is a war against the people, a war against modernity, against the establishment of the new order that the whole of Haiti's population so clearly wants, a war against the establishment of a state of law and justice. We are certainly not in a formal war nor in a situation like that of the *coup d'état* of September 1991, but our predicament is comparable to that of a country at war. A report by the World Bank (1998), analysing the country's economy over the last forty years, describes the Haitian socio-economic situation in those terms.

Looking more closely at the period of the *coup d'état* (1991–94), I want to emphasise certain acts of violence that victimised women. The army used the systematic rape of women as a regular political weapon.

It is important to examine here the phenomenon of 'forced rapes'. Men, under threat, were induced to rape their sisters, their daughters, their mothers. Subsequently, women denounced the military and their henchmen and implicated them as rapists, but the acts of those men who were 'forced' to rape went unchallenged. Although society has condemned the phenomenon of 'forced rape' as such, it has not made these rapes the subject of analysis, reflection or detailed study. Yet the very horror of such a situation raises questions that, although painful and disturbing, cannot be ignored. By not properly addressing this question, the Truth and Justice Commission has heightened the shame that attaches to the memory of these acts.

In a situation of widespread repression such as the Haitian *coup d'état*, which created circumstances akin to war, the military use sexual violence against women as a punitive and intimidating weapon. This weapon targets women of course, but also affects men who are implicated in the situation with regard to the women they generally consider their 'possession'. We have observed a distinct correlation between the use of violence as a political weapon and the phenomenon of domestic violence, with domestic violence increasing in line with the numbers of acts, the forms of violence and the degree of cruelty reported.

Violence against women is a daily phenomenon. The women of Haiti, like those of all patriarchal societies, must face violent situations every day, both in the isolation of their home and in public places. Let us look more closely at this phenomenon and at the responses of women and women's organisations.

The lack of reliable official national statistics on violence against women limits any attempt to evaluate the situation in Haiti. The situation is exacerbated by the isolation and silence imposed upon women, few of whom dare to expose the violence of which they are victims. Haitian society remains complicit with those who consider violence against women a normal, everyday fact to which one reacts according to an accepted threshold of tolerance. Society does not regard violence as a shattering occurrence but as a phenomenon that it would like to pass off as a characteristic expression of Haitian culture.

Nevertheless, women's groups have conducted consciousness-raising activities, contributing to a very widespread dissemination of information. As a result, more and more women are daring to report

TABLE 10.1 CASES OF VIOLENCE REPORTED BY KAY FANM[a]

Type		Numbers		Percentage
Physical Violence				
Beating			31	
	by spouse	28		
	by others	3		
Knife wounds			1	
Other physical cruelty			26	
	by spouse	26		
Sub-total			58	60%
Rape				
Young girls and adolescents			29	
	by individuals	28		
	gang rape	1		
Adult women			3	
	gang rape	3		
Sub-total			32	33%
Murder and attempted murder				
Attempted murder	by spouse	3		
Murder	by spouse	2		
Sub-total			5	5%
Sexual harassment			2	2%
TOTAL			97	100%

a. The data was gathered in the period September 1997 to May 1999.

the extreme demands to which they have been subjected. Encouraged by these women's efforts, women's organisations are systematising the recording and processing of the data.

The Belém do Pará Convention defines violence against women as 'any act or conduct, based on gender, which causes death or physical, sexual or psychological harm or suffering to women, whether in the public or the private sphere'. With this definition as a guide, Haitian women's organisations are recording and cataloguing data related to four broad categories of violation: physical violence (beating, injury and other physical cruelty), rape, murder and attempted murder, and sexual harassment (see Table 10.1).

Kay Fanm (the House of Women), a Haitian feminist organisation based in the capital, Port-au-Prince, is mainly involved in the struggle to end violence against women. Kay Fanm offers women victims of violence and cruelty such services as temporary shelter, escort to court, and physical and psychological health care. A review of the data Kay Fanm gathered in the period from September 1997 to May 1999 is helpful in building a picture of the region close to the capital. As 85 per cent of their figures are relevant to that area, most of the cases concern women who used the organisation's services. The data represent only a tiny portion of a far larger phenomenon, but I reproduce these partial statistics because they make it possible to outline the profile of violence against women in Haiti and to measure the results of the work of women's organisations against violence.

According to these figures, violence against women in Haiti consists above all of such physical acts as beating and other acts of cruelty – 60 per cent. In most of those cases, the violence is the act of the spouse; we are therefore dealing with conjugal, domestic violence. Rape, primarily the rape of little girls and of adolescents from seven to sixteen years old, stands second on the list – 33 per cent. Let me stress that these figures represent only a tentative picture of the phenomenon, for they represent only reported cases. In the period reviewed, there were no reports of the rape of an adult woman by an individual; nor was a single case of conjugal rape reported. Despite the enormous efforts of women's organisations to encourage women to break the silence, it is easier to expose sexual violence perpetrated against little girls and adolescents than violence of which adult women are victims. There were only two reported cases of sexual harassment.

Violent Systems – Economic and Political

In addition to interpersonal violence, the economic and political systems have a violent impact on women. Like women in many market economies that have not yet reached a certain level of development, Haitian women find themselves working in the most sensitive areas, those that exist precisely to absorb the shocks of the market. The types of violence that result from the economic structures to which Haitian women are subject are to be found above all in the relation of needs to goods and to production. Women have needs and are simultaneously producers and consumers of goods. But the relation of production to satisfaction of needs is far from equitable.

At the production level, there is a general tendency to consider women as the producers of market goods. Haitian women like to say that they are the *poto mitan*, the central pillar holding up the economy. So we emphasise the courage of women agricultural producers, who represented 50 per cent of all agricultural producers in 1991, performing the least valued jobs because of the sexual allocation of work in the rural milieu. Women's daily wages are half those of men in this sector. We praise the courage of women traders who move merchandise throughout the country, especially in the least profitable rural areas. Although 77 per cent of traders in 1991 were women, men hold the monopoly on the profitable trade of export goods. Women traders are exposed to physical and psychological violence in the form of both gang violence and violence from the authorities in marketplaces where merchandise is distributed. We deplore the execrable working conditions of women workers on factory assembly lines; in 1991 women represented 70 to 75 per cent of workers in manufacturing, a sector that seems to be moribund in today's context of Haiti's integration into the global economy. But we do not breathe a word about the women who work as domestics. Let me note again that the figures at our disposal are outdated.[1]

Haitian women are very involved in the workforce, but like all women in the world, Haitians are first and foremost producers of nonmarketed goods.[2] It is their domestic labour and production that enables all citizens, men and women alike, to survive. This production is all the more important in that it offsets the lack of market production in both the formal and informal sectors. But it is accorded no formal value, goes unrecognised and is hidden. No one even mentions it.

Haiti is a poor country, subject to a poverty that even outdated statistics cannot hide. Women are the most affected by this poverty. They are the poorest of the poor and, following a current worldwide trend, every day more and more women become yet poorer. This feminisation of poverty is a phenomenon so important that it worries the big multinational organisations, generally insensitive to the lot of populations. They worry because this feminisation of poverty threatens, in a disturbing way, the well-being of families (in the narrowest sense of the term) and hampers a certain model of development based on globalisation and structural adjustment policies. Haitian women are most often the sole providers for their families. Recorded female single parenthood runs at over 50 per cent. Practically all Haitian women run the risk of finding themselves single parents because serial monogamy of women and polygamy of men characterise the structure of marital unions. So the women are solely responsible for fulfilling the family's needs. Perhaps Haitian women are called pillars of the family because their own needs are one and the same as those of their family, which on average comprises five to eight people and often even more. Yet women face an overwhelming need for the most basic goods affecting their survival and that of their entire family.

Thus economic violence against women shows up in terms of their unfulfilled basic needs; it can also be seen in the very bad conditions under which they produce market and non-marketed goods and in the system under which production by women is valued only barely or not at all; overall it is clearly displayed in the feminisation of poverty.

Women Fighting Back

Gender stereotypes, which have striking psychological and cultural connotations, are at the base of violence against women. Power relationships become entrenched in a definite hierarchical order. On the basis of social differences between men and women in roles, behaviour, and mental and emotional structures, women find themselves at the bottom of the hierarchy. These differences are socially produced; they are the cultural models on which violence against women is based. Violence passes through all acts and activities that embody these models. Space prevents me from dwelling upon the expressions of violence in Haiti that stem from these models. I will simply say that this form of violence reaches its peak during the three days of carnival each year when women bear the brunt of the 'merrymaking'.

Women and women's organisations have not sat by passively when it comes to countering this violence. Since the fall of the Duvalier dictatorship, women, like many other groups of social activists, understood that they had to come forward so that changes did not take place at their expense. We commemorate the renaissance of the women's movement on 3 April 1986. On that date, women showed their potential for protest in support of their demands: 300,000 women demonstrated in the streets of Port-au-Prince and some provincial towns. Their demand was clear and simple: 'We want to be present in all areas of decision making – policy will no longer be made without us'. Their highly political demand was accompanied by others of a more socio-economic nature relating to women's poverty and to sexual violence.

The protest against sexual violence was the one that most stirred women into action, then and now. Women's organisations are conscious that every analysis must recognise the unequal power relations between men and women if they are to propose workable solutions. The specific issue of the violence done to women by the forces of repression was thus one of the main spearheads in condemning the military dictatorship that began with the *coup d'état* of September 1991. At that time, women's organisations were able to expose and highlight the specific character of violence against women, and a coalition of more than one hundred women's organisations convened the First National Meeting Opposing Violence against Women. At this meeting more than three hundred women analysed and condemned the violence of which they were victims and sought to organise networks to struggle against the phenomenon.

With this action and those that followed, women's organisations put the struggle against violence affecting women on the nation's political agenda. Witness, for example, the interest that was stimulated by the sessions of the International Tribunal on Violence against Haitian Women in November 1998. The principal media of the capital and provincial towns covered events widely, carrying excerpts from the three-day meeting and continuing to discuss the issues raised for more than two months.

Despite some difficulties, and going beyond even the diversity of the women's organisations involved, Haitian women conceive their fight as political action on a global scale. They are committed to taking on the very foundations of women's oppression, foundations that are also the basis of the social structure. Women's organisations have understood that they must be present in all arenas, particularly in order that development policies, as they are being formulated, explicitly take into account issues relating to the equality and equity of the sexes. The basic aim of the women's fight is to build democratic institutions, democratic structures that must be realised through plans of action clearly reflecting the problems of equality and equity, whether this takes place through interventions on the national scene or in the arena of international forums.

Women's collectives are consolidating and moving toward more systematic organising in such diverse forms as initiative committees, ad hoc committees, reflection groups and action groups. The most recent experiment to date is that of the Committee of Women's Organisations to Negotiate with Members of Parliament. This committee, which brings together more than twenty organisations including the three principal feminist organisations (ENFOFANM, Kay Fanm and SOFA – Haitian Women's Solidarity), has started a process of negotiation with members of parliament in order to introduce changes in the texts of certain laws that are particularly unfavourable to women; it also aims to make adjustments in national budgets with the idea of effectively dealing with the socio-economic needs of women.

This kind of action is the fruit of a long process of maturation in the course of which women's organisations have learned to base their action on strategy. The process itself has demystified certain areas of struggle. Thus, in contrast to the period 1986–1990, when women's organisations, did not invest effort in political arenas, now they no longer reject such direct involvement. We have built a strategy of struggle extending to all arenas, which is based on concerns of a legal nature. The status of women returns to the centre of discussion and action in women's organisations, as it was in the era of the Feminine League of Social Action (the first Haitian feminist organisation) in the 1950s.

Despite the difficulties inherent in the struggle and in seizing opportunities that are presented in a difficult context, women's organisations are finding many ways to make women's voices heard. In so doing, they are showing new ways to construct a new society that rejects the idea that differences are unavoidable sources of inequality, and that recognises respect for life and what it costs to produce a human being. Giving birth and maintaining life are responsibilities incumbent upon women. In developing awareness that taking on such responsibilities is a matter of choice, and a basic choice for life, women prove to be in the best position to lead the entire society to mobilise for the struggle to respect life in dignity, equity and justice. It is precisely because they are aware of being bearers of life, because they are in the position of giving love, that women – out of their madness of believing in life – can transform their anger into love.

Acknowledgements

I salute the initiative of the African Women's Anti-War Coalition in my own name and in the name of the activists of the women's movement in Haiti. My sisterly greetings go to all women who are committed to the difficult task of looking at war in another way precisely in order to construct peace in a new way.

I thank Danièle Magloire of ENFOFANM for her help in producing this chapter. Without her, the text would have remained a series of disparate ideas.

Notes

1. In 1994 a projected 54 per cent of Haitian women were economically active, a relatively high figure for Latin America and the Caribbean. Women work overwhelmingly in the sales sector (846 women per 100 men, according to the 1990 census) and are underrepresented in professional, technical and related fields (65 women per 100 men), a fact probably related to women's very low literacy rates (51 per cent) (UN 1995:143, editors' note).
2. According to the 1990 census, 38 per cent of women are employers or own-account workers, 37 per cent are unpaid family workers, and 44 per cent are employees (UN 1995:148, editors' note).

CHAPTER 11

Caring at the Same Time

On Feminist Politics during the NATO Bombing of the Federal Republic of Yugoslavia and the Ethnic Cleansing of Albanians in Kosovo, 1999

LEPA MLADJENOVIC

This chapter is an attempt by a feminist activist working in Belgrade to understand the responses possible for feminist counsellors and peace activists in the situation created by two simultaneous aggressions in the spring of 1999: seventy-seven days of North Atlantic Treaty Organisation (NATO) bombing of the Federal Republic of Yugo-slavia, and the ethnic cleansing of Kosova[1] Albanian citizens by the Serbian military, police and paramilitary forces. As a feminist coun-sellor working with women survivors of male violence, my observa-tions are based on personal experience – my own experiences and those of the women I work with. I am interested in emotions, how they develop and how they lead to the shaping of women's everyday politics. As an anti-war activist I am interested in how the dominant political discourse intervenes in our emotions and our politics. The dilemmas, questions and actions I write about here are the outcome of my own politics and emotional place. The question I asked myself throughout this period – as I walked home from work in a city in complete darkness that was waiting for bombs to fall, a city in which some people were standing in front of the gates of their houses waiting and others were descending into shelters – the question I asked is how, while living in Belgrade in the midst of the NATO bombing, one continues to care about other citizens who, at the same time, and because it was the same time, are being victimised and ethnically cleansed. (It was the same time because Milosevic could carry out ethnic cleansing only at the time NATO was bombing the country. I explain this below.)

Background: The Region

The Socialist Federal Republic of Yugoslavia, known now as former Yugoslavia, consisted of 22 million inhabitants and six republics in which there were twenty different ethnic groups; three groups (Serbo-Croatian, Slovenian and Macedonian) had the status of constitutive nations, and the others had the status of ethnic minorities. During the rule of President Tito (1945–80) and until 1990, Yugoslavia was a nonaligned socialist state. After the fall of the Berlin Wall in 1989, parties with a nationalist programme won the first free elections in six regions. This opened up the possibility for the division of the Republic into independent states. The second element in the break-up of Yugoslavia is connected to the fact that Slobodan Milosevic, who was then the new president of Serbia, did not agree with the idea of independent states. He used military force to oppose the separation of Slovenia, Croatia, Bosnia and Herzegovina, launching attacks by the Federal Army from Belgrade. The war started in the summer of 1991 with ten days of aggression in Slovenia. Serbian-led Federal Army soldiers opened fire on Slovenian soldiers protecting the Slovenian flag – the symbol of the newly independent state of Slovenia.

After the unsuccessful attempt to stop Slovenia from becoming independent, Milosevic led the Federal Army into Croatia on the pretext of protecting ethnic Serbs, who made up about 30 per cent of the population of Croatia in 1991. In 1992, Serbian soldiers moved into Bosnia and Herzegovina against the Muslim ethnic population and against the Croat ethnic population, again using the pretext of the need to protect Serbs. Simultaneously the Croatian Army moved into Bosnia and Herzegovina to fight against Muslims and Serbs in order to cleanse the territory for its own occupation.

In 1995 the Dayton Peace Agreement ended the war in Bosnia, Herzegovina and Croatia. Milosevic then moved his soldiers to fight the Albanian ethnic group in Kosovo, which was at that time officially part of Serbia. The deliberate construction of hatred against Albanians mounted with daily killings of ethnic Albanians in Kosovo in 1998. In 1999 Milosevic did not want to stop military and police violence in Kosovo and did not want to sign the so-called Rambouillet Agreement that provided for UN/NATO protection of Kosovo. Milosevic's refusal to sign this agreement meant NATO air strikes on the entire

Federal Republic of Yugoslavia, which at that time included Kosovo, Montenegro and Serbia. Immediately the NATO bombing started, the Serbian Army and police began their cleansing operation against ethnic Albanians in Kosovo. Through the course of the seventy-seven-day NATO air raids on the Federal Republic of Yugoslavia, Serbian soldiers and policemen used force to expel 848,000 of the 1.9 million citizens of Albanian nationality in Kosovo from their homes. Serb soldiers and policemen forced 90 per cent of the population that remained in Kosovo to move out of their homes and hide. Serb soldiers and policemen burned some four hundred Albanian villages in Kosovo, completely destroying 67,000 houses and ruining another 50,000. Ethnic cleansing by Serbian soldiers and policemen created 529 mass graves and caused 2,108 deaths; only 19 per cent of the dead have been identified. Data have revealed records of around 11,000 names of dead or missing persons of Albanian nationality. In comparison, 6,200 people of all nationalities are known to have died during the Second World War in Kosovo. The NATO bombing killed around 1,000 people in Serbia and Montenegro. The number of Serbian dead or missing in Kosovo is about 1,200; most were probably killed by the Albanian Liberation Army.[2] The NATO bombing stopped after seventy-seven days when Milosevic agreed to let UN/NATO forces protect Kosovo. The expelled Kosovo citizens of Albanian nationality returned and citizens of Serbian nationality were forced to leave; about 200,000 fled to Serbia and are still there.

Background: The Author

Since the 1991 outbreak of war in the former Yugoslavia, it has been my custom to introduce myself with a statement about where I come from. I have a Serbian name and I live in Serbia. That implies a privileged position in the context of the pro-fascist Serbian regime that has systematically ostracised non-Serbs in the past nine years. It means that I live in a state the government of which has started four wars in the region – with Slovenia, Croatia, Bosnia and Herzegovina, and then Kosovo.

In the past nine years I have, directly and indirectly, witnessed different levels of exclusion of the 'Other' manufactured by the Serbian regime. Examples extend from ethnic cleansing in Bosnia in

1992, through concentration camps, rape brothels, mass killings, looting, and the seizing of cities to the fact that 4 million of the 22 million inhabitants of Yugoslavia have been forced to leave their homes. In the spring and summer of 2000, the Milosevic regime embarked on campaigns to hunt down opposition parties, NGO human rights networks and the OTPOR (Resistance) student movement, declaring them 'state enemies' and 'traitors'. This harassment came to an end only when Milosevic 'died' politically in October 2000. As Zarana Papic (1999:187), a feminist anthropologist from Belgrade, says:

> The series of wars in former Yugoslavia is a series of culturally, politically and militarily produced hatreds. Milosevic's power system is based on producing, transforming and handling hatreds to its own ends. Social hatreds demand a defined list of emotions that should be followed by how we deal with the Other: 'do not trust them', 'do not talk to them', 'do not touch them', 'be suspicious of them', 'despise them', 'spit on them'.... This is an example of politically and culturally constructed racist antagonism. Yes, racist first, because race/ethnicity/nationality today is, in fact, a political category – an instrument of the 'definitive Other' with whom life together is no longer possible.

Insisting on Constructionism

When I and my fellow feminists use the term 'Other', as in the above quote from Papic, we usually follow the thinking of Simone de Beauvoir, the First Lady of Constructionism, and we insist in our work that nationalism does not come from soil and blood but from state power, that hatred against women is not embedded in women's bodies but in the patriarchal order, and that racism does not spring from someone's skin colour.

Using this thesis when thinking about the world during the bombing in Belgrade raises many questions. How does the political attitude of a woman shape her own emotions, especially fear? How does the emotion of fear influence our political thoughts? If the aim of the Serbian regime was, among other aims, to create a social consensus of fear during the NATO bombing, how did knowledge of this policy influence the feeling of fear itself? If Milosevic tacitly accepted the NATO bombing in order to create the conditions for carrying out his military plan of cleansing Kosovo of Albanians, who is the original generator of the fear of NATO bombing? Is it the man who provoked the NATO bombing, or NATO's bombs themselves, or both, and if both, in which ways?

Rules for Dealing with Trauma

Feminist counsellors start their work with a few ethical principles. One of them is that women's experience is a law for the counsellor. This means that counsellors take women's experience as it is presented. Our search for the truth implies creating conditions in the counselling session that encourage a woman to tell her story with her own interpretation and values. Conditions that enable women to feel trusted and heard allow them to say as much as they can, at that moment, about how they felt and what they experienced in critical situations. A woman must be able to express herself, let go, identify and tell the emotions she feels. This phenomenological approach implies that the counsellor does not judge or interpret the emotions, but begins her work with getting to know them in order to work through them. 'Remembering and telling the truth about terrible events are prerequisites both for restoration of the social order and for the healing of individual victims' (Herman 1992:2).

This therapeutic principle implies that every experience and emotion has its unique value and that one does not compare experiences. Non-comparability of experience also means that feminist counselling does not believe in a hierarchy of pain. Each pain is *the* pain for the woman concerned, whatever its cause. In wartime it is extremely important to distinguish the hierarchy of crimes from the hierarchy of pain. This phenomenon of hierarchy is a basic principle of the functioning of the patriarchal system; it is pervasive and well internalised by women. Patriarchy persists, in the social space of wartime, through the hierarchy of pain. As a result, many a woman slips into the so-called circuit of guilt, into the cycle of accusing other women, of making other women feel guilty for being lesser victims than she. Thus patriarchy works to divide women. 'You have two men killed in your family, I have four.' The opposite patriarchal mechanism prescribes the inferiority of pain, which means that some women, internalising the hierarchies, feel their pain is not worth talking about or listening to, and they never ask for help. For this reason the therapist uses validation as a technique for supporting women, making it possible for them to accept and make space for their emotions, whatever they are.

On the other hand, in order to restore the social history that is necessary for the healing of women survivors of war, it is important to identify the hierarchy of war crimes, to recognise, for example, that the Albanian population in Kosovo was exposed to numerous war crimes by the Serbian regime during the seventy-seven days of ethnic cleansing and NATO bombing. It is common for at least one side in a war not to issue any data on war crimes committed against the Other, whilst exaggerating data on war crimes committed against its own population. The Serbian regime followed this pattern so that, from the point of view of the 'case of Serbia', it cannot be said that the Serbian population knows about the war crimes committed by the Serbian military. To this day, probably more than 80 per cent of Serbs do not know the facts about the ethnic cleansing of Albanians in Kosova described here.

Third, from our own experience and from theoretical work on trauma, it is clear that, until the truth is recognised, the process of healing does not start and the individual has great difficulty in hearing the experience of the Other side. What is the truth at this moment? For political therapists the truth is a story told by the victims – to truth commissions and to human rights organisations that collect stories from the victims in order to build up a full picture of the facts of crimes in one region. Truth and pain are therefore connected, which also means that my pain is my truth, but your pain is not my truth. If we have a situation in which there are two aggressions, and if my pain and my truth do not give me space for your pain and your truth, can we still create the emotional and cognitive space to hear and care about the Other during two traumatic events that take place at the same time? For example, while I was bombed by NATO, my country-men killed other countrymen and -women of mine in Kosovo.

We know that there have always been women in wars who invented the impossible, who cared about 'enemy' women who were also in the war. Following this women's tradition, the feminists and anti-fascist activists turned conventional 'motherly caring' into the political act of caring for the Other, even during the self-made, self-organised raptures of Serbian, pro-fascist nationalism during the seventy-seven days of its double war. These women organised care for

Serbian women and at the same time they did everything possible to care for the Other – for Albanian women.

Resisting the Role of Victim

During these seventy-seven days I grappled with how to resist the role of the victim, when every day the acts that produce fear pressed in upon me – the fears of other women, the fearful sounds of bombing, the state news, the darkness in the streets. If I think only of myself, isn't the Serbian regime using the NATO bombing to cast me precisely in the role of the victim, more victimised than any other victim? Every hour Serbian TV told us, 'Never in the world before has there been a longer period of bombing by a more powerful enemy.' If one decided to adopt the victim position then the pain of the Other was erased from memory, and the Serbian regime could carry on with its killing–cleansing plans without anyone even asking, 'How come?' Am I then a victim or an accomplice? If someone decides to take on the position of victim, how far is she/he from being the executioner?[3]

Work

The Autonomous Women's Centre Against Sexual Violence (AWCASV) where I work undertook phone counselling of fearful women from 24 March to 13 June 1999. Immediately after the first day of bombing, the distinction between public and private disappeared. The fear of bombing became a public emotion. Therefore the centre decided to change the ethics of its work in this particular situation and to call women in their homes and ask them how they felt, specifically about fear. There were 713 phone counselling sessions in those seventy-seven days. The counselling was done with women from forty-three towns in Serbia, Montenegro and Kosovo.

Fear in Serbia and Montenegro

We observed, from the data collected in our phone counselling, that in the first month about 87 per cent of women from the Serbian and Montenegran regions we talked to were in some state of fear, ranging from very little to extreme forms of fear. About 30 per cent experienced severe fear; they lived in cellar refuges, did not go out on the streets, feared every sound or open space, and felt helpless. 'I fear terribly,' 'I can't concentrate,' 'I sleep at my friend's place,' 'With the sound of sirens I feel nausea,' 'I have lost weight and my psyche has broken in pieces,' 'My emotional state varies from one moment to another,' 'I am nervous, I go from the cellar refuge to my flat three times a night,' 'My menstruation has been with so much blood, more than ever'...

> Tonight the bombs fell somewhere close to us. I woke up suddenly and I panicked, I did not know what to do, I had to take sleeping pills. They hit some antennas. During the day I function, sometimes I have stomach aches and go often to the loo, and when the night falls I am afraid, you don't know where they will hit. (Belgrade, 1 April 1999, M.)

By the second period, the months of May and June, about 67 per cent of the women had already adapted to the sounds of bombing and had created ways to deal with the situation.

> I am better now; I left for a village near Kragujevac with my children because one hears the detonations less. In the beginning I thought that each bomb will fall on my head and I was very afraid, but after some time we all got used to it. Children in the neighbourhood organised them-selves; when there were sirens they stopped playing for a while and later they went out again. (Kragujevac, 3 May 1999, N.)

Fear in Kosova

NATO also bombed Kosova, but Albanian women said that they were not as afraid of the bombs as they were of the Serbian police and military ('blue', 'green', and 'masked'). 'We do not go out during the day, the fear is inside the bones,' 'I don't know what to tell you, I am still alive,' 'I fear being raped twenty-four hours a day,' 'I fear they will come in at every moment and take us all,' 'We sit together in darkness every night, I cannot sleep or eat, but I still have cigarettes and coffee.' We made the telephone calls to Kosova in the first two weeks. Afterwards, most of the women we knew had been deported or did not have working telephones. We remained in contact throughout the seventy-seven days with two families. We heard the stories of the forced deportations to Macedonia and Albania afterwards. The Serbian government had deported more than 700,000 Albanian citizens, and in a matter of a couple of days they became refugees.

> Every day the fear grew. All the Albanian people waited. I can't explain how we felt nights while we waited for them. I have not slept more than two hours a day, every time I thought they were coming I was restless, I did not want them to come while I was asleep. The tenth day it happened. Through a hole in the curtains we saw three Serbian policemen who said to our neighbours, 'Tell the rest of the neighbours we are coming in thirty minutes.' All of my family, all thirty of us, children and our old mother, we walked down the street, it was an image I will never forget. It reminded me of images from the Second World War of the deportation of Jews. First, there were hundreds and then thousands of us down the main street in a queue that stretched to the train station. All this time the police shouted and cursed at us not to run away.[4]

In a few cases we dialled telephone numbers at random and talked to people of Serbian nationality living in Pristina. Their statements revealed that they were afraid of the bombing, but still not overly afraid. They told us they were expecting something positive for themselves when it was all over. In one case a Serbian man on the phone from Pristina said, 'Why are you asking us how are we, we are alright, we are celebrating my brother's birthday, and when this thing stops we'll be allright' (Pristina, 8 April 1999, N.N.).

What We Learned

The emotions of the Serbian population in Kosova toward the NATO bombing were different from those of the Albanian population, because the Serbian police told the Serbs that they would be 'finally liberated'. In talks with Serbs they revealed their state of waiting for something, which possibly influenced their feelings of fear. (The Milosevic regime completely deceived the Serbian population in Kosova. At the end of the NATO operations, when UNMIK, the UN international force, arrived, 200,000 people of Serbian, Roma and Bosnian ethnic identities had to leave Kosova. The Serbian regime forced them first to hate Others and then to run away from the hatred the Others returned. Their testimonies reveal how the Albanian army threatened them in order to force them to leave their homes. This situation followed the NATO bombing campaign and thus is outside the scope of this chapter.)

The Albanian population, on the other hand, was in a completely different position at the same time and in the same towns in Kosova. The forced deportations, mass killings and mass lootings, the burning of villages and news about rapes created terrible fear among them. They stated that fear of the Serbian police was their dominant fear.

Without Fear in Belgrade

I was interested in the 12 per cent of women who said during our phone counselling that they felt little or no fear. If we look closely at their answers we can see who they were: some were older women who had lived through the bombing of Belgrade in the Second World War, which according to their statements was much more destructive and dangerous; some were women refugees from the wars in Bosnia and Herzegovina and Croatia who had arrived in Serbia as part of a group of 400,000 between 1991 and 1995. Some stated that they had already experienced the fear of war, so this bombing campaign was of no interest to them; others said they were reliving the trauma of war and felt very intense fear. Some were activists in the peace movement who, instead of fear, felt rage towards the Serbian regime, which they felt was responsible for the fear and which demanded fear at every moment of daily life. They refused to feel fear as a way of protesting at the regime's intentions and deeds. These women were feminists, anti-war activists or active anti-fascists and most of them were informed about war crimes in Kosova. One of them said, 'I hold Milosevic responsible for each and every bomb that NATO drops on this territory. Every time I hear the sirens I curse him. I am very angry.'

The Regime's Construction of Fear

Although the bombing process itself creates fear, the Serbian regime used every possible mechanism to increase that fear.

Blackouts

The officials ordered complete blackouts, banning the turning on of city lights in any place in the Federal Republic of Yugoslavia. They told people that the blackout would make their houses invisible to the 'enemy who wants to target them'. The average citizen had no way of knowing that this information was incorrect, that the targets were calculated on computers in NATO bases far away. This type of reasoning was successful because it rested on people's memory of the bombing technology of the Second World War. Dark streets created more fear among people everywhere in the region. This method of constructing fear was very successful.

Propaganda about targets
The Serbian regime constantly produced propaganda saying that the real NATO target was the Serbian population, not only the military facilities, factories, bridges and other sites. Milosevic's aim was to deepen fear by convincing the population that each 'Serb is under threat by NATO'; the population had no access to NATO's public statements, which stressed that the targets were not people but Milosevic's military strategic points.

Social pressure
Given the social consensus of fear, the local community exerted great pressure on people committing acts that revealed their lack of fear. Thus if curtains did not cover lighted windows, if music was played too loud, if individuals walked at night with no urgent need to be on the streets, the local community interpreted these and other acts as 'traitors' deeds'. In other words, every Serbian citizen was expected to be in a state of fear, and anyone deviating from this consensus was subjected to social pressure.

Banning independent media
The Milosevic regime banned independent media, which meant that every article had to go to the Ministry of Information for approval. One month after the beginning of this double war, the regime killed independent journalist Slavko Curuvia, which created more fear.

Declaration of Martial Law
Along with other acts, the declaration of martial law made illegal all gatherings of people, private and public, as well as any activity that

opposed the Milosevic regime. This added to the mounting sense of fear, since nongovernmental meetings and other types of gathering became 'dangerous'.

These examples show the complexity of constructing fear. On the one hand, bombs falling on towns can themselves create fear; on the other hand, much of the fear felt in Serbia was very much a consequence of the regime's construction of fear. This fear campaign was designed to fill the citizens with emotions that paralysed them and kept them from thinking about the Other. Our work shows that there were women in a very serious state of fear living in towns on which (by chance) not one bomb was dropped in the entire period.

Caring at the Same Time

At the Autonomous Women's Centre Against Sexual Violence we started from the fact that during the seventy-seven days of bombing and ethnic cleansing almost everyone was living in a state of fear – the counsellors, our women clients and the activists in Serbia and Kosova – and that it was our duty as feminists and counsellors to try to take care of the different groups of women living in fear. One can approach the politics of 'caring at the same time' in different ways: from the principles of strictly professional therapeutic ethics, from the principles of feminist ethics, or from anti-war principles. I will begin discussing the logic of caring for them and us at the same time by describing the activities of the centre during the bombing campaign.

Phone counselling of women living in fear

Five counsellors and six volunteers made a total of 713 phone calls to women in 43 towns. The women we counselled had different ethnic names: they were Albanians, Bosnians, Croats, Jews, Roma and Serbs. We documented all of the work and will publish it in a book on women's experience of war.

Transistor radios

For women in Serbia who wanted access to news other than the regime's news, the centre provided transistor radios run on batteries. Our aim was to support women who wanted to be informed other than by the Serbian regime's hate–fear propaganda. (The transistors had medium-wave bands for news in the Serbian language transmitted from other countries.) Many women and international organisations were involved in this project.

Workshops

The women's centre organised weekly workshops on fear for the women who did the phone counselling – ourselves, activists, friends, volunteers and all the drop-ins.

E-mail communication

The women's centre was in constant e-mail communication with women from around the world who sent us messages. We estimated that we received more than 2,500 messages of all kinds, and about 200 support messages from all the continents, for women in Serbia as well as for women in Kosova who could not be reached at that moment. International women's solidarity was very moving and important.

News from the internet

Activists at the women's centre kept us informed by constantly reading news on the internet. This meant that we were able to inform women who called us and asked for the latest news on the bombing and on ethnic cleansing (always on both wars). It was our rule to give out only facts because the war propaganda produced huge numbers of fear myths. ('Belgrade will look like a carpet, it will be destroyed by bombs,' etc.)

Reports on women's lives

The women's centre e-mailed reports to women from around the world with whom they had corresponded on the situation in Belgrade as well as the scenes related to us by witnesses on the phone in Serbia and Kosova.

Twelve-hour hotline

The women's centre operated a hotline for activists of any woman's network in the region who called us for any reason whatsoever. On the first day of the bombing campaign, we sent information about our work by e-mail and fax to women's groups in Serbia and Montenegro; we included information on 'How to talk with a woman who feels fear.' In the first three weeks the hotline was open practically fourteen hours a day and on weekends as well; afterwards it operated twelve hours a day on working days.

Bicycle support
The women's centre also supported women who were afraid to go out to buy cigarettes, bread or medicine. A group of activists on bicycles were on duty for this work.

Feminist reading support
The women's centre mailed feminist reading materials to women in other towns in Serbia, because some women said they were bored not being able to go to work. (Usually we sent the latest issue of the *Feminist Notebooks* published by the centre.)

Packages to Pristina
The women's centre sent a few packages to friends in Pristina, Kosova, via a human rights activist who was brave enough to go there during the ethnic cleansing.[5]

Visits
Activists of the women's centre paid a few visits during the bombing, first to women activists in Novi Sad, near Belgrade, where there was heavy bombing, and next to Budapest, Hungary, to visit women from Serbia who had left their homes in fear and created a small group there. A third visit was to Kosovar Albanian women activists who, after being deported from their homes and exiled to Macedonia, started to work in the refugee camps there. This encounter strength-ened our sisterhood with feminists of different women's groups from Kosova with whom we had been collaborating for years; it also showed that Milosevic's war was not our war and that there are activists in Serbia who care about 'Albanian sisters'.[6]

These examples demonstrate that as women's centre activists and counsellors, we worked on different levels to support ourselves, to support women in the region, to support women in the so-called Other, 'enemy' region, and to communicate with the international women's community.

I believe that one way to overcome the role of victim as it was constructed by the Serbian regime for the Serbian population in the spring of 1999 was to carry out the feminist politics of caring for oneself and the Others at the same time. Some of us resisted the social consensus of fear and hatred by breaking the Milosevic-made isolation at every instant: in our thoughts, which were open to the voices of all women, of each ethnic name and each war situation; in our emotions, which were open to fear and anger and pain and laughter and music; in our behaviour, which was to walk the streets night and day and to travel outside the city and even the country; and in our politics, by asking each other, How are our friends from Kosova, naming each one. Not to isolate oneself from anyone was a deliberate decision – not from our Albanian sisters, not from our Serbian sisters or our international sisters, not from our own sisters, and even not from oneself as a sister.[7]

If we accept the ideology of nationalist isolation and stop searching for facts – facts of Serbian crimes as well as facts about the love that exists on the other side – then we can trap ourselves in Milosevic's patterns of Serbian self-glory and of Serbs being surrounded by 'enemies'. That locks us into an arena with lions. If we slip into a discourse of 'ours' being more important and better than 'theirs' (child, woman or man, black or white, mad or sane, lesbian or heterosexual), that is the end of the idea of civil society, that is the end of the idea of beauty in diversity, of the politics of different and equal. It erases the possible beauty in ourselves, because suspicion and mistrust of Others has taken its place.

A year after the war, a Serbian woman asked an Albanian woman, looking her directly in the face, 'How can I trust you?' The Albanian woman told her, 'I will tell you my story and you decide.' If a woman describes her dilemmas out loud maybe she can start changing. The possibility of civil society is present even during wartime, when it is least possible. I believe that solidarity in wartime is one of the maps of hope and acts of reality that announce the future of democracy. And in every war we have examples of those who support each other, Other as 'other than me' whoever she or he may be, or Other as the 'enemy Other', the 'Other gender', the 'Other nationality', the 'Other race'. Taking care of oneself and the Other equally opens the issue of the children we take care of, the students, and the neighbours with whom we deal. Is our child automatically better than the Other child, because he or she is 'ours' (whatever that means)? Taking care of ourselves and Others at the same time also breaks down the classic women's role, which ordains that a woman should take care of others first and only if there is time left over take care of herself. 'Women eat last.'

The logic of taking equal care overcomes nationalism and breaks fascism in its logical core of hatred of the Other. Taking equal care can also be a step in transforming into a passionate choice of justice for women the hierarchies of patriarchy and hatred of women, which are too often internalised to self and externalised to Others. Caring equally means I value equally myself as a woman and the Other as a woman, in the way that I value all women and men. I believe that taking care equally of ourselves and Others when it is possible, even if barely possible, is an act of feminist political life; it is working toward the end of all discrimination. I believe that we can create the end of discrimination, the end of patriarchy, in the small choices we make now, in wartime and peacetime. Every step we choose can be a political step towards this end.

Acknowledgements

I thank my three friends who helped me to write this chapter and gave me political and sisterly support as well as help in the English language: Slavica Stojanovic, Madeleine Rees and Yulia Krieger. I also wish to name all the anti-fascist feminists who were active in the Autonomous Women's Centre during the seventy-seven days. Some worked on the computer, some rode bikes, some worked the phones, and some cooked for us. We shared a political understanding of caring for each other and the Others: biplane male tin, bobbin macaroni, boas janjucevic, brankica grupkovic, cica simic, desa drobac, diana miladinovic, divna matijacevic, mila popovic, milica gudovic, olga marinkovic, stanislava otacevic, tanja kuprecanin, teodora tabanki, tviti ljubinkovic, zorica gudovic, zoka rajic.

Notes

1. The name Kosovo comes from the Serbian language, the name Kosova comes from the Albanian language. Serbs and Albanians have lived in Kosovo/a for centuries and I have chosen to use both of these names randomly in my text.

2. The Albanian Liberation Army was a rebel group fighting for the independence of Kosovo (editors' note).
3. The political dramaturge, Borka Pavicevic, director of the Centre for Cultural Decontamination in Belgrade, said in a lecture at the Centre for Women's Studies during the course on 'Political and Cultural Responsibility', on 11 February 2000, 'The one who chooses to be a victim will become the executioner.'
4. Igballe Rogova, feminist activist from the women's group Motrat Qiriazi from Pristina, Kosova. This is part of her testimony of deportation from Pristina, published by the women's centre in a book of women's experiences of war in 1999.
5. Natasa Kandic, director of the Humanitarian Law Fund in Belgrade, a nongovernmental organisation, was the only human rights activist who worked in Kosovo during the bombing. The women's centre collaborated with her and she carried packages from us to friends who remained in Pristina, Kosova, and from friends in Pristina to us.
6. In my short report I describe my visit to Albanian friends expelled from Kosova to Macedonia (Mladjenovic 1999:238–41).
7. The black feminist lesbian poet, Audre Lorde, is cited on the T-shirt of the Boston Area Rape Crisis Center (617-492-RAPE): 'I am not my sister's keeper, I am my sister'.

CHAPTER 12

Healing and Changing

The Changing Identity of Women
in the Aftermath
of the Ogoni Crisis in Nigeria

OKECHUKWU IBEANU

1994 was just another year for many people, but not for the Ogoni of Nigeria. It was the year that their thirty-seven year struggle for survival and resistance against exploitation came to a head. In that year the popular Movement for the Survival of Ogoni People (MOSOP) imploded by turning against itself, marking the beginning of half a decade of systematic state repression in which large numbers of Ogoni people either died or became displaced.

Recently we have seen many accounts of the Ogoni conflict, rendered by academics, activists, advocates and apologists for military rule. Activists and advocates place human rights and environmental issues on the front burner (Human Rights Watch 1995; Earthaction 1994), while apologists emphasise law, order and state security dimensions of the crisis. Several academics, mostly social scientists, have offered explanations for the crisis and its implications for state and society in Nigeria. They have in particular explored issues such as the roles of oil companies and state officials, the minority and federal questions, and the military–authoritarian character of the Nigerian state (Ibeanu 1997; Osaghae 1995). In the din of these accounts, the voices of women have been mute. More important, few serious intellectual accounts of the post-conflict situation of women are available. This chapter seeks to provide a starting point for filling these two lacunae. It explores violence against Ogoni women and how this is shaping or reshaping identities in the post-crisis period.

Identities and Social Action

'Identity' is a concept that social anthropologists, psychologists and

189

political scientists have used in analysing socio-political behaviour and action. It has gained particular currency in the Third World following both the end of the Cold War and the subsequent rash of communal conflicts and contestations of state legitimacy. Analysts say that identity defines a person's sense of belonging to a group, which in turn determines political behaviour. It serves as 'rallying and organising principles of social action within the civil society, and in state–civil society relations' (Jega 2000:14). Another common notion among analysts of identity is that of 'multiple identities'. Reminiscent of the role theorists of the 1960s, this idea suggests an individual's concurrent and equal adherence to many identities, which structure social roles and social action. The critical issue, and the subject of theoretical speculation, is 'which sort of identity has the most significant impact or bearing on a person's behaviour' (Jega 2000:15). A common suggestion is that identity is situationally determined depending on what issues are at stake.

A number of issues remain unresolved in the current interpretations of the interface of identities and social action. First, it is not clear whether identities are natural or only socially constructed. Thus Jega (2000:14) argues that both 'physiological givens', like gender and age, and sociological characteristics, like ethnicity, nationality and religion, create the basis for identity. However, one has to problematise the role of biological categories in defining identities. Even a seemingly obvious physiological given like race is socially constructed. Gender is by no means a physiological category, as Amadiume (1986) has shown.

Second, it is not clear whether group identity is self-defined or other-defined. Social exclusion by others could be as strong a basis for identity formation as self-consciousness on the part of a group of its difference from others. For instance, the growing dichotomy in many African societies between natives and settlers, which has been the basis of numerous conflicts, results from both the awareness of natives and settlers that they are different, and the ascription of settler status to 'settlers' by 'natives'. In addition, a third party can catalyse an identity. Huntington (1968) reports that as late as the 1950s, Igbo politicians in Nigeria were touring parts of Igbo country trying to convince people to accept a pan-Igbo identity because the British colonialists categorised them as such, and because parallel identities had emerged in other areas of the colony. Above all, external forces could shape the particular meaning(s) that an identity has for its members. In Burundi, the competitive ring that the colonialists gave to their division of the people into Tutsi and Hutu became the basis of relations between the two groups (Gahama *et al.* 1999:83).

Debate continues in the research literature on whether identity is structural or only instrumentalist. That is to say, we do not know if identity is an end in itself, for instance a feeling of pride in belonging to an identity, or a means to an end. The prevalent tendency is to instrumentalise identity, linking it to competitive behaviour in situations of scarcity (Nnoli 1978). Consequently, Jega (2000:15) limits identity politics to the pursuit of material benefits in the context of competitive politics. Although this may be a strong inclination, we know that in Africa many groups, especially ethnic minorities, are staking a claim just to be recognised as different from others. The struggle for self-determination is not necessarily targeted at material benefits. In many cases, people are asking for things that others take for granted, such as the right to speak a traditional language or bury their dead in the customary way.

Fourth, related to the instrumentalisation of identities, some analysts make the Hegelian distinction between identity-in-itself and identity-for-itself. They portray identity as something formed first; subsequently its bearer develops a consciousness that then leads to social action. This goes to the heart of philosophical distinctions between consciousness and being, idealism and materialism. Identities are not first formed and thereafter projected into social action. Rather, they are formed and transformed in social action. As Jega (2000:15) rightly argues, identity transformation is a continuous process framed in praxis.

Other questions that prevalent analyses of identity have not answered satisfactorily include the following: Are there collective interests uniting people who share an identity, or is identity just a subjective, emotive feeling that an individual has towards his/her group? Is identity necessarily behavioural, that is, externalised action, or only attitudinal, that is, an internal feeling that may or may not translate into a behavioural pattern? Is identity only relevant in other-directed behaviour, or does it structure behaviour towards group members, for instance by defining rules of reciprocity and a stable system of mutual expectations?

There are also questions about multiple identities. Although it is true that people have concurrent identities, one should not reduce their importance to situational dynamics in a voluntaristic manner: that is, people willingly choose what issues are crucial and therefore what identities they should defend. Such a voluntaristic interpretation cannot be fundamental. There are always principal and subsidiary contradictions in any social context, which are defined not subjectively by individuals but objectively by social ensembles in struggle. This is not to suggest, as do the dominant instrumentalist notions, that identities are necessarily competitive. Identity action could also be cooperative and 'win–win' depending on the interests and actions of social forces. An extension of the instrumentalist-pluralist interpretation of identities is to privilege cultural identities over economic ensembles, especially classes, since classes become one of many possible identities. In the process, multiple identities become a veritable instrument for avoiding questions of class domination, and class struggles are conveniently banished from analysis.

In addition, the interface of multiple identities and instrumentalism contains a fundamental contradiction of logic. Apart from the unresolved issue of explaining what identity is central in social action, given multiple and equally weighted identities, it is problematic to argue that in a given situation one identity rises and subsumes all others. How do we explain individuals who do not toe the line of the presumed dominant identity? For instance, how do we explain the so-called vultures who 'acted against' Ogoni interests in the struggle with Shell and the Nigerian state?

Healing and Changing

That women are targets of violence during conflicts is widely accepted. However, the frequent portrayal of violence against women during conflicts as episodic or epiphenomenal, the inevitable by-product of conflict, is inadequate. Instead, violence against women during conflicts should be seen as a phase of a continuum. In most societies, whether in conflict or not, women are continuously subjected to aggression, both direct and indirect. Indeed, in many cases violence escalates in post-conflict situations (Turshen 1998:1). To appreciate this fact, we should not see violence exclusively as a direct or objective act. Instead, in many cases it is also structural. Structural violence is an indirect form of violence exerted through channels that are not immediately visible as violent. It involves such social conditions as exploitation, domination, repression and discrimination (Kassim 1991; Nnoli 1978). Viewed structurally, we also see that not only the enemy inflicts violence on women in conflict situations. Community leaders, husbands, women's organisations and family members can be involved. Further, looking at violence structurally we avoid the instrumentalist treatment of identity that addresses gender and sexuality separately from questions of economic exploitation and class domination. As Gilliam (1991:218) has strongly argued, this separation is elitist and a reproduction of bourgeois ideology.

An epiphenomenal portrayal of violence against women during conflicts tends to lead to a static conception of healing in the post-conflict situation. Seeing violence as exclusively objective leads to thinking that healing occurs when objective violence is eliminated and victims are recompensed materially. In contrast, a structural approach to violence yields a holistic understanding of healing that addresses not only the immediate physical and psychological impacts of violence but also more structural issues like access to resources, reconciliation, reintegration and long-term peace building. Such an approach to healing is not static but dynamic. It recognises that victims of violence may have changed because of their experiences during the conflict. Consequently, the demands of healing should go further than mere restoration of pre-conflict conditions. This point is particularly relevant in addressing gender issues in the aftermath of conflicts. We know that women's wartime experiences sometimes serve as the forerunner to challenges delivered to structural gender inequalities in post-conflict situations. This occurred in both the Biafra–Nigeria war and the liberation war in Zimbabwe. Thus, there is a dialectical relationship between healing and changing: healing must address change, and change must be a basis for healing.

Preliminary data from ongoing research on the Ogoni crisis form the basis of this chapter. The research covers issues of security, livelihood, displacement and social movements. Much of the data comes from the responses of 100 women to a questionnaire; the sample was drawn from the Ogoni communities of B-Dere, K-Dere, Bera, Biara, Bua, Deeyor, Lewe, Luawii and Okwale. In addition, we conducted oral interviews for the larger research project upon which we have also drawn. Our data collection strategy aimed at giving emphasis to the voices of women themselves, ensuring that they expressed their particular perceptions. Supplementary data come from secondary sources such as private and public documents.

We adopted the categories of violence that appear in the final report of the West African Workshop on Women in the Aftermath of Civil War (Turshen 1999). Field experience then led us to modify the categories. Experience also suggested to us six categories of perpetrators of violence against Ogoni women, namely security agents, community leaders, husbands/relations, women's organisations, government officials, and other communities. Security agents include military and paramilitary forces, intelligence agents and the police, all of which Nigeria's military governments used to repress the Ogoni. The category 'community leaders' comprises notable members of Ogoni communities, including chiefs, professionals, leaders of organisations and youth leaders. The category 'government officials' includes political appointees and public servants at the local, state and federal levels of government; it also includes officials of oil companies, since oil-producing communities do not make a distinction between government and oil companies, for good reasons. Finally, 'other communities' refers to neighbouring communities with which the Ogoni had conflictive relations during the period, including the Okrika, Andoni and Ndoki. As we shall see, some observers suggest that government often incited these communities to create conflict with the Ogoni as part of a policy of aggression and repression against the Ogoni.

The Ogoni Crisis

The Ogoni are one of more than 247 ethnic minorities in Nigeria. They are one of several ethnic groups occupying the oil-rich Niger Delta in the States of Delta, Bayelsa and Rivers. Other ethnic minorities in the area include the Ijaw, Itsekiri, Andoni, Ikwerre, Kalabari and Egbema. Ogoniland is in Rivers State, located southwest of Port Harcourt, the capital city of the state. With an estimated population of 500,000 and a land area of about 700 square kilometres, Ogoniland is one of the most densely populated rural areas of

Nigeria (approximately 715 persons per square kilometre).

Traditionally, the Ogoni are organised into six kingdoms, namely Tai, Eleme, Gokana, Babbe, Ken-Khana and Nyo-Khana. Each kingdom had a traditional head called the Gbenemene. Principally, the Ogoni speak two closely related but distinct languages, namely Gokana and Khana. Farming and fishing are the dominant economic activities in the area. However, several years of crude oil exploitation, leading to environmental degradation, have contracted these two activities tremendously. Consequently, white and blue-collar engagement of Ogoni in the petroleum industry has grown rapidly.

It is important to appreciate recent patterns of Ogoni encounters with the Nigerian state as a background to understanding the Ogoni crisis. These encounters, though dual in expression (the Ogoni against the state), are triangular in content, involving the Ogoni, state officials and petrobusiness. The conflicting conditions of security posited by state officials and petrobusiness on the one hand and by the Ogonis on the other set the limits of Ogoni encounters with the Nigerian state in the 1990s (Ibeanu 1997). The Ogoni do not make a distinction between petrobusiness and state officials. In fact, the interests of petrobusiness and state officials interlock so much that separating them may be only conjectural. Security for state officials and petrobusiness means an uninterrupted production of crude oil at 'competitive' (read: low) prices. Informed by a pro-growth ideology, the concern of state officials and petrobusiness is the production of petroleum to satisfy the demands of accumulation. This is paramount irrespective of the negative impact crude oil production has on the local environment and populace. This principal condition for security posited by state officials and petrobusiness had two corollaries. The first of these was the maintenance of Nigeria's military regime, for petrobusiness relied on the authoritarian regime to ensure an uninterrupted supply of oil in the face of restiveness in oil-producing communities like Ogoni. The second was the need to ensure that a coalition of oil-producing communities did not emerge. In other words, because there was always the possibility that grievances would spread from one community to another, aggrieved communities had to be isolated from one another and encouraged to pursue their claims separately. Therefore, state officials and petrobusiness sought to prevent a link-up and escalation of the struggles of oil-producing communities. They executed this divide-and-rule strategy in two ways: by repressing single communities and by setting the oil-producing communities against one another.

The Ogoni condition for group security is the maintenance of the carrying capacity of the environment, that is, the ability of the land to support the population. Unsustainable exploitation of crude oil, with its devastation of farmland and fishing waters, threatens resource flows and livelihoods. The Ogoni therefore link the protection of the environment with survival.

When livelihoods are threatened, a feeling of deprivation ensues. A people who feel deprived also feel anxious about their livelihoods. Such people are insecure. Therefore, a condition of security for the Ogoni is the elimination of deprivation, especially because they are keenly aware of the great wealth accruing to Nigeria from crude oil. The issue is justice in the distribution of resources which, for the Ogoni, means that a good part of the wealth generated from their land should return to them. The Ogoni in the 1990s became a target of state violence as a result of the conflict between their conditions of security and those of the state and petrobusiness. In turn, the Ogoni mobilised to resist state violence, rather than capitulate to it. The consequence was the spiral of violence in Ogoniland between 1990 and 1998.

During the period, state violence against the Ogoni took four major forms. First, it took the form of harassment of Ogoni leaders through surveillance, arrests and detention. From 1991, when the Ogoni struggle began in earnest, their leaders became regular victims of the state's security and intelligence agencies. On many occasions, the agencies detained and questioned the then leaders of the popular Ogoni rights movement MOSOP, such as G. B. Leton, Chief Kobani and Ken Saro-Wiwa. In January 1993 they arrested the men in Lagos. In April 1993 they arrested Saro-Wiwa twice. On 21 June 1993, they arrested him again with two other MOSOP activists, N. Dube and K. Nwile. On 13 July, they brought criminal charges against them (Human Rights Watch 1995; Ibeanu 1997). In December, they arrested Ledum Mitee, another MOSOP leader, and detained him without charge. Between May and June 1994, following the murders of four Ogoni leaders, they arrested several hundred people in Ogoniland (Human Rights Watch 1995).

Second, the state used violence against the Ogoni by encouraging violent conflicts between the Ogoni and their neighbours and then using the conflicts as a pretext to repress the Ogoni. The government readily proclaimed such clashes to be ethnic clashes. But the frequency of the clashes (among erstwhile peaceful neighbours), the extent of devastation, and the sophistication of the weapons employed, convinced many independent observers that 'broader forces might have been interested in perhaps putting the Ogonis under pressure, probably to derail their agenda' (Claude Ake, quoted in Human Rights Watch 1995:12). Between July 1993 and April 1994, there were at least three such conflicts between the Ogoni and their neighbours – the Andoni in July 1993, the Okrika in December 1993, and the Ndoki in April 1994. In each case, the security forces blamed the Ogoni. These conflicts resulted in the destruction of many villages, loss of life, and the creation of refugees.

Third, state violence against the Ogoni involved setting the Ogoni against themselves. From early 1993, it had become clear that the military government sought to divide the Ogoni and set them against one another. The obvious target was MOSOP. The people themselves knew this. Following the Wilbros affair in April 1993, some Ogoni accused some of the leaders of MOSOP of selling out to the government in the negotiations taking place at the time. The rancour this generated had hardly died down when MOSOP decided to boycott the presidential election scheduled for 12 June. By then it was obvious that the leadership of the movement had split in two, apparently under pressure from the military regime. One group, led by Dr Leton, Albert Badey, Dr Birabi, Chief Kobani and chiefs Samuel and Theophilus Orage, argued that the boycott decision negated an undertaking MOSOP had given the Babangida government during negotiations going on at the time. Subsequently, both Leton and Kobani resigned their positions as, respectively, president and vice-president of the movement. They accused Saro-Wiwa of being brash, confrontational and authoritarian, claiming that he had created the National Youth Council of Ogoni People (NYCOP) as a private army to intimidate and eliminate his enemies. They also accused him of planning to kill thirteen Ogoni leaders, some of whom later died on 21 May 1994.

The deep divisions and tensions inside MOSOP, which the government clearly aided, came to a head on 21 May 1994 with the killing of

Chief Edward Kobani, a former commissioner in the Rivers State government, Chief Albert Badey, a former secretary to the state government, Chief Samuel Orage and Chief Theophilus Orage. One can see the beginnings of these divisions in the events following 21 June 1993 when security agents arrested Ken Saro-Wiwa in connection with the boycott of the presidential election. In reaction, Ogoni youths, probably members of NYCOP, went on the rampage. The Andoni, their neighbours, later used their demonstration to justify an attack on such Ogoni villages as Kaa in August 1993. Many MOSOP members loyal to Saro-Wiwa rejected a subsequent peace accord brokered by the Rivers State government. Exchanges of angry letters among leaders of the movement followed until some leaders of Gokana, one of the five kingdoms that make up the Ogoni ethnic group, repudiated MOSOP and Ken Saro-Wiwa in the so-called Giokoo Accord of March 1994. At that point, MOSOP's complex internal tensions exploded, producing a struggle of Ogoni against Ogoni.

Finally, state violence also took the form of direct repression using the armed forces and police. There were widespread reports of the security forces carrying out extrajudicial killings, flogging, torture, rapes, looting and extortion against the Ogoni. The Rivers State government established an Internal Security Task Force under Major (later Lt Col) Okuntimo. His job was the systematic use of violence against the Ogoni. Indeed, Okuntimo bragged on prime-time national television that the army taught him 204 ways of killing people, but he used only three against the Ogoni. Between May 1994, when the four prominent Ogoni personalities were killed in the town of Giokoo, and early 1995, the security forces summarily executed at least fifty Ogoni. Earlier, in April 1993, in what has become known as the Wilbros affair, a detachment of the 2nd Amphibious Brigade based in Bori shot at least eleven Ogoni, among them a woman, at Biara. The Ogoni were protesting at the laying of a pipeline from Rumuekpe to Bori. Major U. Braimah of the brigade claimed that his men were carrying out duties directed by the military government. The Ogoni conflicts subsided only with the overthrow of General Sani Abacha in June 1998. His successor, General Abubakar, made democratisation and reconciliation the bedrock of his regime, which terminated with the inauguration of a civilian democratic government on 29 May 1999.

The Ogoni Crisis and Violence against Women

As in most conflicts, Ogoni women were specifically targeted during the crisis. They were victims of sexual violence by security forces and invading fighters from neighbouring communities, but also victims of violence executed by their own people. Our respondents testified that during the crisis Ogoni women suffered all nineteen forms of violence that we indicated to them (Table 12.1).

Our evidence shows that violence against Ogoni women during the crisis was widespread. Ninety-nine per cent of respondents to our questionnaire were either victims of violence or knew victims. Among the 70 respondents who did not suffer violence personally but knew women who suffered, 44 women (63 per cent) said that the victims were their relatives. Thus, about 73 per cent of our respondents either were themselves victims of violence or had relations who were victims.

Table 12.1 also shows that security forces – army, police, intelligence agents, etcetera – were the worst culprits committing violence against Ogoni women. Our respondents recounted 2,356 'hits' or separate incidents involving violence, and identified the security forces as involved in 1,112 of the events (47 per cent). The second-worst culprits were government officials (27.7 per cent); the next worst were neighbouring communities (14.2 per cent). Clearly, security forces were the villains in the Ogoni crisis. Fifty per cent or more of our respondents identified them as having committed 16 of the 19 acts of violence that we categorised. Table 12.1 indicates the proportionally large number of security force members involved in the most violent assaults such as systematic rape (71 out of 98 cases), shootings and killings (92 out of 148 cases), sexual slavery (73 out of 99 cases), forced pregnancy (70 out of 91 cases).

These figures appear to support our position that the Ogoni conflicts had to do with state violence, sometimes executed by instigating conflicts between the Ogoni and their neighbours. The role of community leaders in violence against women needs serious analysis. Even though community leaders ranked fourth out of the six agents of violence, respondents identified them as being involved in seventeen out of the nineteen types of violence. A third of respondents associated them with verbal abuse, nearly a quarter linked them with imprisonment and detention, while a fifth said that they were involved

TABLE 12.1 VIOLENCE AGAINST OGONI WOMEN DURING THE CRISIS

Type of violence	Hits*	Main Perpetrators (ranked by number of hits)					
		Security agents	Community leaders	Husbands/ relations	Women's organisations	Government officials	Other communities
Verbal abuse	205	66	30	-	1	51	57
Harassment and intimidation	194	90	9	-	3	62	30
Imprisonment or detention	193	82	23	1	-	64	23
Destruction of property	178	89	16	-	-	41	32
Denial of access to resources	173	62	5	-	-	72	34
Shooting and killing	148	92	1	-	-	28	27
Dispossession of property	143	68	2	-	-	36	37
Discrimination by social institutions	140	43	19	-	3	55	20
Denial of education	135	35	6	1	1	75	17
Beating and flogging	124	91	-	3	-	24	6
Sexual slavery	99	73	1	-	-	7	18
Systematic rape	98	71	1	-	-	21	5
Abandonment**	91	27	6	20	1	35	2
Forced pregnancy**	91	70	-	-	-	13	8

Forced labour	89	64	1	-	1	19	4
Rejection of women victims of rape	86	17	18	36	1	11	3
Forced prostitution	75	49	1	-	-	22	3
Betrothal for economic reasons	51	17	4	7	-	16	7
Forced marriage of widows by husband's relations	43	6	8	26	-	-	3
Total hits	2356	1112	151	94	11	652	336
As % of total hits	100.0	47.2	6.4	4.0	0.5	27.7	14.2

* The number of respondents indicating that Ogoni women suffered each form of violence. The total possible 'hits' for each row (act of violence) is therefore 600 (100 respondents multiplied by 6 perpetrators). The difference represents respondents who did not think that Ogoni women suffered the form of violence.

** Both ranked thirteenth in terms of most frequently reported incidents of violence.

TABLE 12.2 VIOLENCE AGAINST OGONI WOMEN AFTER THE CRISIS

Type of violence	Hits*	Main Perpetrators (ranked by number of hits)					
		Security agents	Community leaders	Husbands/ relations	Women's organisations	Government officials	Other communities
Verbal abuse	180	63	27	6	1	36	47
Discrimination by social institutions	133	38	15	2	3	58	17
Denial of acccess to resources	125	38	2	-	1	61	23
Denial of education	114	26	1	2	1	68	16
Beating and flogging	97	75	-	-	1	17	4
Destruction of property	94	55	4	1	-	22	12
Dispossession of property	90	42	4	1	1	23	19
Rejection of women victims of rape	79	11	21	36	2	6	3
Sexual slavery	78	42	-	1	2	20	13
Forced prostitution	77	50	2	-	-	23	2
Forced pregnancy	67	47	7	5	-	3	5
Abandonment	57	12	1	16	1	23	4

							Total
Forced marriage of widows by husband's relations**	2	2	4	25	7	8	46
Systematic rape**	3	9	-	-	-	34	46
Betrothal for economic reasons	4	16	3	1		15	39
Total hits	172	387	20	96	91	556	1322
As % of total hits	13	29.3	1.5	7.3	6.9	42.0	100.0

* The number of respondents indicating that Ogoni women suffered each form of violence. The total possible 'hits' for each row (act of violence) is therefore 600 (100 respondents multiplied by 6 perpetrators). The difference represents respondents who did not think that Ogoni women suffered this form of violence.

** Both ranked thirteenth in terms of most frequently reported incidents of violence.

in discrimination against women. These figures suggest that violence against Ogoni women may not be a transient phenomenon associated with the conflict. If leaders and other members of the community are deeply involved, then gender-based violence is bound to be a more lasting problem.

Our respondents seemed to agree on the increasing role of community leaders and other community members in violence against Ogoni women. Table 12.2 indicates that as the conflict wound down, the role of security agents and other communities in violence against Ogoni women declined. Simultaneously, community leaders, husbands or relations and local women's organisations became increasingly involved in violence against women. They were particularly engaged in verbal abuse of women, discrimination in resource allocation, the ostracising of women who were victims of rape during the crisis, abandonment and forced marriage.

After the crisis, the role of security agents and other communities, measured as a percentage of total incidents, declined by 5.2 and 12.9 percentage points respectively. By comparison, the role of husbands and relations increased by 3 percentage points, the role of women's organisations by 1 percentage point, and the role of community leaders by half a percentage point.

Some of the respondents explained that these increases express reprisals against people thought to have cooperated with the 'enemies' during the conflict. These are the so-called 'dere', the Ogoni word for vulture, which is used in this context to express the belief that these people worked to sabotage the Ogoni cause. That may be so, because post-conflict policy in Ogoniland has scarcely emphasised the rebuilding of social capital. Yet rebuilding social capital is crucial to the task of post-conflict economic reconstruction. This is because the essential prerequisites of social organisation and collective action, such as a stable system of expectations, trust, norms of reciprocity, civic networks and good neighbourliness, are destroyed in conflict situations, especially in intra-community conflicts. Rebuilding social capital includes contending with the culture of impunity, which invariably accompanies conflicts. Among other things, this involves coming to terms with the atrocities of the conflict period, including restitution where necessary, and also limiting personalised reprisal in the aftermath.

TABLE 12.3 SUPPORT FOR WOMEN VICTIMS OF VIOLENCE

Support	Very effective (2)	Effective (1)	Not effective (0)	Score	Rank
Personal efforts and friends	64	23	5	151	1
Religious groups	43	49	0	135	2
Human rights organisations	31	43	10	105	3
Forming and joining women's organisations	38	20	8	96	4
Family/extended family	25	32	11	82	5
Community	7	33	21	47	6
Local government	5	5	45	15	7
State government	2	3	52	7	8
Oil companies	0	4	60	4	9
Federal government	0	1	54	1	10

TABLE 12.4 SUPPORT FOR WOMEN BEREAVED IN THE CRISIS

Support	Very effective (2)	Effective (1)	Not effective (0)	Score	Rank
Personal efforts and friends	51	27	7	129	1
Religious groups	44	22	19	110	2
Human rights organisations	29	37	16	95	3
Forming and joining women's organisations	32	19	14	83	4
Family/extended family	21	32	12	74	5
Community	9	25	24	43	6
Local government	4	5	41	13	7
Oil companies	2	3	57	7	8
State government*	0	3	50	3	9
Federal government*	0	3	52	3	9

* Both ranked ninth

However, other respondents argued that the *dere* theory is only part of the story. They think that with the violence over, the traditional/structural discrimination against Ogoni women is re-emerging. This seems to coincide with our earlier observation that violence against Ogoni women is not episodic or epiphenomenal arising only with the conflict, but a structural/endemic problem. This view led us to ask respondents if the vulnerability of women to violence has reduced 'a lot', 'a little' or 'very much' since the end of the crisis. Interestingly, more than two in every three respondents (68 per cent) said that women's vulnerability has declined only a little.

In fact, there are strong indications that the communities, as collectives, may not be giving support to the women who were the most victimised by the crisis. We asked respondents about support for women who either were victims of violence or bereaved in the crisis. We were seeking to assess the effectiveness of various support agencies such as women's organisations, religious groups, the family, human rights groups, community, government, oil companies and personal efforts. We asked whether these were 'very effective', 'effective' or 'not effective'. In analysing the responses, we scored each response (for example, 'very effective' 2, 'effective' 1, 'not effective' 0). We then totalled the scores for each response category and ranked them (Tables 12.3 and 12.4).

These tables show that the victims of the worst violence depend essentially on themselves rather than the community and family. Although it is understandable that government and oil companies scored low, the low rating of community and family is deeply suggestive. It seems to confirm that Ogoni women suffer traditional, community-based discrimination. This is also suggested by our findings on the taking of traditional titles. Such titles are recognition of the contributions that individuals make to the community, and as such, they serve to enhance the social standing of titled persons. We asked respondents if women hold traditional titles in their communities. Only 35 per cent said that they do. Worse still, only 14 per cent of respondents said that they held such titles themselves.

Crisis and the Changing Identity of Ogoni Women

In spite of these difficulties, it would be wrong to assume that Ogoni women were mere passive victims of the crisis. In the course of it, their identity changed in many positive ways, in terms both of how they perceived themselves and of how others defined them. This is to be expected because as social categories, identities are dynamic, and identity transformations usually accompany periods of upheaval and rapid social change. Prior to the Ogoni crisis, gender relations in Ogoniland were no different from those that obtained in most traditional Nigerian societies, which are predominantly patriarchal formations. Women did not enjoy the same social, economic and political rights and opportunities as men. This lopsidedness permeated both traditional and modern economic and political structures (Ibeanu and Nzei 1998). In the contemporary situation, Ogoni women found themselves in a male-dominated economy in the Niger Delta, centred around the petroleum industry, which further entrenched the exclusion of women by depressing the traditional areas of female economic activity such as farming and petty trading. This identity of powerlessness was often contested by women in intermittent revolts against petrobusiness, which has congealed the inequities of gender relations in the Delta (Turner and Oshare 1994). Often it is in the context of such struggles that women reclaim their dignity and transform their identity. The Ogoni crisis was no different.

There is, generally, a positive feeling about the future position of the Ogoni woman in her community. Many men and women feel that the crisis raised the profile of Ogoni women. Our respondents shared this attitude, as shown in the questions and responses analysed in Table 12.5. Over 60 per cent agree that the crisis enhanced respect for Ogoni women, who are widely praised for their positive contributions to the Ogoni struggle, which ranged from laying down their lives to mobilising and fundraising. Women were central in the mobilisation process. For instance, when MOSOP organised the 'One Naira per Ogoni' fund raising campaign in the early 1990s, from which millions of naira were realised, a majority of the contributors were in fact women. Apart from their role in mass mobilisation, many Ogoni women were in the front line with their menfolk. Many lost their lives, as in the shooting in Biara over the Wilbros affair.

As a result of this enhanced profile, a number of traditional stereotypes about women have been challenged. Women's active participation in the Ogoni struggles against the militarist Nigerian state and

TABLE 12.5 IMPACT OF THE CRISIS ON
THE SOCIAL POSITION OF OGONI WOMEN

	Yes %	No %	No response %
Generally, would you say that the crisis has enhanced respect for women in your community?	63	30	7
Do you think that the crisis increased women's confidence in dealing with issues confronting them in the community?	82	11	7
Has the crisis contributed to reducing traditional and cultural discrimination against women in your community?	61	30	9

multinational oil companies challenged the notion that women are weak and should be submissive to men. Some 61 per cent of our respondents believe that the crisis has contributed to reducing traditional and cultural discrimination against Ogoni women. However, the deepest change seems to have occurred among Ogoni women themselves, namely in how they see their identity in Ogoniland. More than 82 per cent of respondents to our questionnaire think that the crisis has increased the confidence of Ogoni women in dealing with problems confronting them in the community. This is reflected in the rise in numbers of women's organisations in Ogoniland during and since the crisis. Although women's organisations in Ogoniland are still in their nascent stages, in future they are likely to become the basis for reconstructing the identity of the Ogoni woman at the political, economic and cultural levels.

Conclusions

On 29 May 1999, the long phase of military dictatorship in Nigeria, which began in December 1993, ended. Clearly, the military did not leave of its own accord. A coalition of democratic forces in civil society brought about the end of military rule. The Ogoni and their mass organisations rank high among the democratic forces that sent the military packing. Unfortunately, the experiences of the heroines of the Ogoni struggles have not received the attention that they deserve. This chapter is a modest attempt to begin that process. Many Ogoni women suffered untold violence in the hands of security forces, government officials and neighbouring communities, including rape, imprisonment, forced pregnancy, denial of access to resources, and beating. Such violent acts are not mere episodes related to the crisis. Instead, violence against Ogoni women pre-dates and post-dates the crisis. The structural character of violence against women needs to be realised if proper healing and closure of the bitter experiences of Ogoni women during the crisis are to be achieved. An important step in achieving this is a realisation that Ogoni women have been changed by the experiences of the crisis. Healing must take cognisance of this change. In the final analysis, those concerned for the healing of the Ogoni woman in the aftermath of the crisis must face the inevitability of changing gender relations in the direction of equity.

Note

1. Ken Saro-Wiwa, a poet and political activist, was executed by the Abacha regime on 10 November 1995 (editors' note).

CHAPTER 13

Ambivalent Maternalisms
Cursing as Public Protest
in Sri Lanka

MALATHI DE ALWIS

> Today a hundred and fifty shot
> Yesterday seventy blasted
> Even the poet becomes numerate ...
> The map erupts with gigantic bubbles of blood
> Bursting and flooding the lacerated terrain
> Jean Arasanayagam

During the years 1987 to 1991, Sri Lanka witnessed an uprising by nationalist Sinhala youth (the Janatha Vimukthi Peramuna – JVP)[1] and reprisals by the state that gripped the country in a stranglehold of terror. Although the militants randomly terrorised or assassinated anyone who criticised them or allegedly collaborated with the state, the state similarly, but on a much larger scale, murdered or 'disappeared' anyone they suspected of being a 'subversive'. These included thousands of young men, some young women, and several left-wing activists, playwrights, lawyers and journalists who were either monitoring or protesting against the state's violation of human rights. Bodies, rotting on beaches, smouldering in grotesque heaps by the roadsides and floating down rivers, were a daily sight during the height of state repression from 1988 to 1990. It was in such a context that women formed the Mothers' Front, a grassroots Sinhala organisation with an estimated membership of over 25,000 women, in July 1990 to protest against the 'disappearance' of approximately 60,000 young and middle-aged men.[2] Their only demand was for 'a climate where we can raise our sons to manhood, have our husbands with us and lead normal women's lives' (*Island*, 9 February 1991). The seemingly unquestionable authenticity of their grief and espousal of 'traditional' family values provided the Mothers' Front with an important space for protest unavailable to other organisations critical of state practices.[3]

As Rita Manchanda notes in Chapter 7, the categories of 'gains' and 'losses' are particularly value-laden and complicated. In fact, they take on additional significance when used to evaluate a concept such as motherhood – which I define here as encompassing women's biological reproduction as well as their interpellation as moral guardians, care-givers and nurturers – and its corollary maternalism, which is the mobilisation of this concept. Since the potency of maternalism, like most hegemonic formations, lies in its resiliency and malleability, it has also engendered a certain predictability in feminist debates on motherist movements, both nationally and internationally. Over several decades, feminists have continued to frame their arguments about maternalised protests in terms of binaries that posit that the mobilisation of 'motherhood' either essentialises or empowers women, or that it produces either victims or agents. Maternalist feminists such as Jean Bethke Elshtain (1987), Ellen Key (1909), Catherine Reid (1982), Sara Ruddick (1980, [1989]1995) and Olive Schreiner ([1911] 1978) are among proponents of arguments that women's crucial contributions to the cause of peace is through their mobilisation of 'preservative love' (Ruddick 1984). These feminists have privileged the family as the core of moral humanity and called for women to remain at home and launch their battles against (masculinised) militarism and liberal individualism from within such a privatised and feminised space (Elshtain 1981, 1983a, 1983b, 1987). On the other hand, feminists critical of such arguments have suggested that such assumptions only reinforce the notion of biology as woman's destiny and legitimise a sex-role system that, in assigning responsibility for nurture and survival to women alone, encourages masculinised violence and destruction (see for example, di Leonardo 1985; Enloe 1989; Hartsock 1982; Houseman 1982; Lloyd 1986; Stacey 1983).

Although I myself have been implicated in such binary thinking in the past, my work with the Mothers' Front has made it increasingly clear to me that such dichotomous thinking has only debilitated political praxis rather than advanced it. We have become so caught up in the binary logics of our arguments that we have failed to see beyond them or out of them; such dichotomous thinking has not only obfuscated the differences that exist within the category of 'motherhood' but it has precluded our questioning why 'motherhood' is deployed in the first place.

In this chapter, I would like to focus on an especially spectacular public practice of the Mothers' Front that not only created a space within which women could articulate their criticisms about a repressive regime but also made fraught any quick and simple categorisation of these women either as victimised mothers or as idealised mothers.

Ritualised Cursing

The Kaliamman Kovil, a Hindu place of worship at Modera, a suburb of Colombo, sits atop a slight promontory overlooking the Indian Ocean, which crashes against the rocks below with a muffled roar. This *kovil*, part of a larger temple complex, with a main shrine for Lord Ganesa as well as other Hindu deities including Siva and Parvati, exemplifies two religious orientations – those of Buddhists and Hindus. As Gombrich and Obeyesekere have observed, the latter group, who are mainly Tamils, come primarily to worship Lord Ganesa and the other deities in the main temple (though they do propitiate Kali as well), while for 80 per cent of all Sinhala Buddhists who visit the temple complex, the Kaliamman shrine is the primary goal (Gombrich and Obeyesekere 1988:141).[4] On the afternoon of 23 June 1992, this shrine became the site of an extraordinary public spectacle – a *deva kannalawwa* (beseeching of the gods) by the Mothers' Front, who chose to hold their action on that day because it was President Premadasa's birthday.

After the second National Convention of the Mothers' Front, which was held in Colombo, the members of the Mothers' Front were bussed to the Kaliamman Kovil by the Sri Lanka Freedom Party (SLFP), organisers of the Convention.[5] On their arrival at the shrine, however, a padlocked gate and a battalion of policemen standing guard greeted the women. Not to be deterred, SLFP member of parliament Alavi Moulana instructed the first group of women to break their coconuts outside the *kovil* gates.[6] Almost simultaneous with this and the loud chanting of '*sadhu, sadhu*' that rent the air, the gates were hastily opened by a somewhat chagrined senior police officer, though access to the inner sanctum was still denied. The small *kovil* premises soon became packed with members of the Mothers' Front who, apparently oblivious to the presence of the police, the press, politicians and curious onlookers, dashed coconuts on the ground, lit lamps, tore their hair, struck their heads on the earth and wept and wailed and beseeched the goddess to locate their 'disappeared' and punish those who had brought such suffering upon them and their families. 'They didn't take just one of my sons, no, they didn't even stop at two, they had to take all three of my boys', intoned one woman, '[m]y own boys that I carried in my womb, fed with my bloodmilk (*le kiri kala*) and nurtured for the past 20 years.... Even if these beasts (*thirisan*) live freely now, may they suffer the consequences of their actions unto eternity, in all their future lives.' Another moaned and muttered: 'May they suffer lightning without rain (*vehi nethi hena*),[7] may their families be ground to dust.' Others called out the names of the perpetrators, including that of President Premadasa, and cursed them. Asilin, one of my neighbours whom I had accompanied to this protest, was chanting over and over again, 'Premadasa, see this coconut all smashed into bits, may your head too be splintered into a hundred bits, so heinous are the crimes you have perpetrated on my child.' Another woman wept, saying, 'Premadasa, I bore this child in my womb for ten months – may you and your family be cursed not for ten days or ten weeks or ten months or ten years or ten decades but for ten aeons.'

To ward off the women's curses President Premadasa sought refuge in an elaborate counter-ritual, the *kiriammawarungé dané* (feeding of milk mothers), an archaic ritual that is now connected with the goddess Pattini.[8] On 23 June, the day of his birthday and the commencement of one of his pet projects, the *gam udawa* (village reawakening) celebrations – and also the day that the Mothers' Front had chosen for their *deva kaññalawwa* – he offered alms to 68 (grand)mothers (*Silumina*, 28 June 1992). At the conclusion of *gam udawa* and another *deva kaññalawwa* organised on a much smaller scale at Kalutara (south of Colombo) by the Mothers' Front, on July 3rd 1992,[9] he offered alms to 10,000 (grand)mothers while the North Central Provincial Council Minister for Health and Women's Affairs, Rani Adikari, chanted the *pattini kaññalawwa* to bring blessings on the president, the armed forces and the country (*Daily News*, 6 July 1992).[10] Though the commonly held belief is that Pattini is predominantly a guardian against infectious diseases, she is also the 'good mother' and ideal wife whose chief aim is to maintain 'a just and rationally grounded society' and can thus be read as a counterpoint to the goddess to whom the Mothers' Front appealed – the 'bad mother' and evil demoness Kali who deals with sorcery and personal and familial conflicts (Gombrich and Obeyesekere 1988:158–60; see also Obeyesekere 1984).

Such rituals disturbed not only President Premadasa but even the urbane Minister of Industries, Science and Technology, Ranil Wickremasinghe, who warned, 'If your children have disappeared, it is all right to beseech the gods. After all, if there is no one else to give you succour, it is fitting to look to one's gods. But if one conducts such *deva kaññalawwas* with thoughts of hate and revenge, it could turn into a *huniyam* (black magic) and backfire on you' (*Divaina*, 28 July 1992). Wickremasinghe's junior minister, Paul Perera, thought it fit to direct the Mothers' Front to a Sinhala proverb: '*Wadinnata giya devalaya hise kada watena dinaya wadi aathaka nowanne*' – the day will soon dawn when the temple at which you worship will fall down on your head (*Lankadeepa*, 28 July 1992). Nevertheless, despite such dire warnings and counter-rituals by the government, President Premadasa was blown to smithereens by a suicide bomber before a year was out. A few days after his death, a beaming Asilin came to see me with a comb of plantains (considered to be an auspicious gift): 'He died just like the way I cursed him', she said triumphantly.

Situating Sorcery within Maternalist Politics

Cursing is usually assimilated within the broader category of sorcery in anthropological discourses on demonism in Sri Lanka, which also encompasses the more spectacular rituals associated with spirit possession.[11] Defined as a 'technique of killing or harming someone, deliberately and intentionally' (Obeyesekere 1975:1), sorcery is perceived to function as 'a regulatory mechanism in a social context where formal institutions for settling disputes are absent or lacking' (Selvadurai 1976:95). Indeed, the majority of the Mothers' Front members, who had incessantly petitioned politicians, hounded government bureaucrats, kept vigil outside army camps, and visited every police station in their region to no avail, were particularly intimate with alternative forms of mediation on behalf of their 'disappeared.' In fact, their resort to curses was just one manifestation of 'religious distress' which ran the gamut from beseeching gods and goddesses, saints and holy spirits with special novenas (Catholic masses), doing penances, taking vows, making offerings and donations, going on pilgrimages, and performing *bodhi pujas* (offerings to the Bo tree),[12] to visiting astrologers, palm readers and light readers (*anjanan eli*), placing charms, and chanting *vas kavi* (maleficent verses) and *seth kavi* (benedictory verses) over a period of months. Many of these rituals involved a mixture of invoking blessings on the 'disappeared', calling for his speedy return home, and calling also for the punishment of the perpetrators of 'disappearances'. The category 'perpetrator' spanned a wide spectrum, from friends, neighbours or relatives who were believed to have 'betrayed' the 'disappeared', to those who were directly involved in the abduction, as well as specific government officials who were ultimately deemed responsible for this reign of terror – senior police officers, government agents, parliamentary and provincial ministers and, of course, the president of the country. As Marx has so perceptively pointed out, 'religious distress is at the same time the expression of real distress and the *protest* against real distress' (quoted in Comaroff 1985:252, emphasis in original).

Gananath Obeyesekere (1975:20) points out the cathartic efficacy of cursing, which channels people away from 'premeditated crime into its (to us) symbolic counterpart – sorcery'; he notes nevertheless how amazed he was 'at the sheer sadism and vindictiveness of the curses' that were uttered by both priest and supplicant at renowned sorcery shrines in Sri Lanka.[13] Not surprisingly, then, sorcery is a privatised practice that is usually conducted in the greatest of secrecy. Though sorcery is a familiar practice and all classes of Sinhala Buddhists, and even some Sinhala Christians, resort to it, the bourgeoisie frequently portrays it as a practice of the lower classes, and thus, like the public display of excessive weeping, code it as 'unrespectable.' Yet although people could 'naturalise' women's tears as a manifestation of feminised sentimentality – which invoked refined sentiments, in turn – their responses to the unprecedented public vocalisation of women's curses were more complicated and nuanced.[14]

The media, particularly the Sinhala press, which had consistently sentimentalised these women's maternity, and, concomitantly, their suffering, sought to incorporate the Mothers' Front's curses within this continuum of maternalised suffering: 'The mothers first wept and wailed at the loss of their children. They sighed and moaned. After a while, those tears and sighs turned to anger. Then these mothers began to curse those who had deprived them of their children' (Kumaradasa Giribawa, *Irida Lankadeepa*, 28 June 1992). The concerted focus of the Sinhala press was on the sincerity and depth of feeling with which the mothers articulated their curses and the fact that much weeping and lamentation accompanied them; the press strove to engender feelings of pathos and empathy rather than, say, horror at what these women were wishing on the perpetrators of 'disappearances'. Even newspaper articles that reproduced some of the curses made by the members of the Mothers' Front were quick to stress the brittleness and vulnerability of these aged women and the sentimental responses they evoked: 'Tears welled up in the eyes of the onlookers who heard her sorrowful lamentation'[15] (*Divaina* 3 April 1992).

However, despite the attempts of the Sinhala press to sentimentalise the women's curses, the general public was much more discerning; they were able to differentiate between the pathos that was engendered by these women's laments, and the vengeful anger of their curses, which the public nevertheless interpreted as being morally defensible. As one female onlooker confided:

> I know that all religions say one cannot destroy hate with hate but I think these women are completely justified in wanting to take revenge (*pali ganna*) on these animals (*saththu*) who have done such terrible things to their children ... and to their entire families ... I know that the government is not going to do anything about it ... after all they are the ones who are behind it, right? So, where else can you look for justice but to your gods? If they took my son, I would have done the same thing. These poor women ...

Many poems sent to the newspapers that were written in support of these women also stressed the importance of avenging the crimes that had been perpetrated on these women and their kin. One verse (an excerpt from a longer poem) beseeched Lord Skanda (whom the women had invoked at Kataragama when on the *Pada Yatra*) in the voice of a mother:

> Use your divine vision, O Lord,
> to locate him who abducted my son
> Erase his name and identity and
> scatter his remains in all ends of the earth.[16]

Note how this curse calls for a similar 'disappearance' of the perpetrator of the 'disappearance' – the erasure of his name and identity, and, once he is killed, the dismemberment and burning of his body, once again thwarting identification.

The Sri Lanka Freedom Party (SLFP) also consistently sought to stress the moral righteousness of these women's curses; while constantly reminding the Mothers' Front members that their tears were a sign of weakness and enervation, the SLFP enthusiastically promoted the women's curses as a powerful political weapon of the weak. It is not surprising then that Asilin, along with many other members of the Mothers' Front, should take credit for the death of President Premadasa. His death was just one more incident in a long chain of events that the SLFP publicly credited the Mothers' Front with effecting: these included the bombing of the motorcade of Ranjan Wijeratne, Minister of State for Defence, who had been the most vociferous critic of the Mothers' Front; the sudden confessions of former Deputy Inspector-General of Police, Premadasa Udugampola, who had become notorious for his atrocities against all those suspected of being members of the JVP; and the unnerving of President Premadasa who, as SLFP leader Sirimavo Bandaranaike pointed out in her speech at the Mothers' Front's second convention in June 1992, had had himself bathed by seven virgins (on the advice of his Malayalee swami in Kerala, India) to ward off the women's curses made during the *Pada Yatra* held several months earlier.

Indeed, for a group of women that society had marginalised because of their class and gender for much of their life, these pyrrhic victories were very precious. They were not concerned that the trip to the Kaliamman Kovil may have been part of a carefully orchestrated political spectacle of which they were to be the chief performers; what mattered most was that they were finally being given a chance to do something concrete for their 'disappeared' – unlike their participation at the morning's meeting where politicians took turns to spout 'hot air' while they listened and wept. Once the women entered the Kaliamman Kovil, they noted, they felt more confident and purposeful. 'We knew what we had to do here ... not like when we were in the [meeting] hall just sitting and listening.' 'After all we have been doing these *pujas* [rituals] in many other *devales* [Hindu shrines] ... we were glad that we got an opportunity to come to this famous *devale* and do a *puja* as well' (comments of Mothers' Front members from Matara). In fact, when Bandula Gunewardena, a representative of the MEP (Mahajana Eksath Peramuna, a party that was supporting the Mothers' Front campaign) attempted to read out a *kannalawwa* to goddess Kali, the organisers had great difficulty in getting the attention of the women present: Gunewardena's voice could barely be heard over the lamentations, chanting and cursing of many women who continued with their own invocations despite a request for silence.

The participation of the Mothers' Front in publicised religious rituals posed an additional dilemma for Sri Lankan feminists who had now to contend not only with these women's mobilisation of their maternity but also their religiosity. As left activist and academic Jayadeva Uyangoda pointed out, the introduction by the Mothers' Front of 'voodoo in politics' (Uyangoda 1992b) was merely valorising women as the 'carriers and bearers of culture', as those who have a 'primary and initiating role in religious and magical rituals' (Uyangoda 1992a:4).[17] The unfolding of such a doubly stereotyped identity, the production of which I have interrogated elsewhere (de Alwis 1998), was further complicated here by these women's implicit faith in the efficacy of divine intervention over that of 'rationalist and enlightened traditions of politics' (Uyangoda 1992a:5). Moreover, by personalising politics and producing President Premadasa as the epitome of evil, noted Uyangoda, the SLFP and the Mothers' Front were not only leaving 'counter-democratic forces and structures unidentified and uncritiqued', but were also replicating the government's use of 'sinister substitutes' for 'open political competition, debate, discussion and electoral mobilisation' by exploiting and manipulating the 'religious emotions of the people' (Uyangoda 1992b:5).[18]

Although I share the concerns articulated by Uyangoda and other left and feminist academics and activists regarding the increasing authoritarianism of state and counter-state institutions, which has led to the debilitation of 'secularist foundations of political conduct' (Uyangoda 1992a:6), I am also troubled by Uyangoda's valorisation of the 'traditions of political enlightenment' that are posited as 'rational' and 'democratic' in opposition to the 'irrational' and 'dark' underworld of demons and sorcerers that has now 'burst its way into the light' and become 'public and acknowledged' (Uyangoda 1992a:5). Such a formulation replicates Christian and anthropological discourses on demonism that David Scott (1994) has so brilliantly deconstructed and historicised. In fact, it is just such a formulation that also enables the argument that those who participate in such 'demonic' practices are, by extension, 'less rational and more emotional' (see for example Kapferer 1983: Chapter 5), a label that Uyangoda himself has criticised when applied to the members of the Mothers' Front (Uyangoda 1992a:4).

Towards a Contingent Reading

The mobilisation of maternalised suffering and religiosity by the Mothers' Front marked out a crucial space – both conceptually and materially – within the political landscape of Sri Lanka. Here was a hitherto much-privatised practice that women were not only performing in public but were also using openly to speak ill of the president of the country. Indeed, the use of curses as public protest not only had no precedent in Sri Lanka but it could also circumvent emergency laws enforced by the state that were applicable to standard forms of political protest such as demonstrations and rallies.[19] To have banned people's right to religious worship, on the other hand, was something even an autocratic government that repeatedly defined itself as one with the best interests of the populace in mind would not have dared.[20] The presumption inherent in a curse, that it could bring about change through the intercession of a deity, also complicated efforts (for a believer such as President Premadasa) to stall such changes, for they now transcended the human. These women's curses, like their tears, thus set the terms of debate (now phrased in the idiom of religion). In the same way that the government had previously constituted its own fronts of weeping women, it now organised performances of counter-rituals and counter-utterances as it was pushed to counteract the Mothers' Front curses.

These women's curses, which were accompanied by much weeping and lamentation, did enable a certain sentimentalisation of maternalised suffering, but could not mitigate the threat that mothers posed in seeking to effect change (through divine intervention). Unlike maternalised tears, however, maternalised curses disrupted normative representations of Sinhala culture and tradition. A sanitised notion of Buddhism, which strove to deny and repress demonic beliefs and practices, was the premiss of Sinhala culture and tradition. A bourgeois norm of conduct, which I have termed 'respectability', could not circumscribe the Mothers' Front's performances of excess weeping or cursing (de Alwis 1998). The majority of these women, whose aged, ravaged bodies were marked as asexual, forestalled their reinscription within a modality of 'respectability'.[21] However, the rubric of 'motherhood', which both legitimised the Mothers' Front protests and evoked sentiment, simultaneously circumscribed this unfolding of 'un-respectability'; these women were not only speaking as mothers and wives but they were also calling for a return to 'normality'.

One could read the practices of the Mothers' Front, then, as engendering a fraught maternalism that was domesticated yet not respectable, that was demonic and threatening yet also sentimental and pathetic, that was poor and marginalised yet also racially dominant and exclusionary. In a context where an autocratic government and a nationalist militant movement had silenced left and feminist voices, it was the mobilisation of such a fraught maternalism that not only appropriated and defined a particular political space but also succeeded in winning the support of the Sinhala public and media. The contingent efficacy of such maternalised protest, however, must be understood in light of the very conditions of its possibility. In other words, the emotive power of tears and curses cannot be understood transparently; rather, they must be apprehended in relation to the cultural categories of 'respectability', 'domesticity' and 'suffering' that both enable as well as circumscribe such a maternalised politics. Although such a paradigm shift, I argue, enables a move out of the more familiar binaries of essentialisers versus empowerers, victims versus agents, through which such movements are frequently assessed, it still does not *determine* the efficacy of the Mothers' Front. It is for this reason that I find the concept of 'contingency' so useful.

William Connolly (1991:28), in his multifaceted characterisation of contingency, has called attention to the variable, uncertain, unexpected and irregular potentiality of this concept. My positing the efficacy of the Mothers' Front as contingent is precisely premised on the variable and unexpected possibilities presented by this concept. I wish to argue that at a particular moment in Sri Lankan history, at a time when the government had silenced other, more familiar and predictable voices of dissent, the maternalist politics of the Mothers' Front proved to be particularly effective. However, such a political as well as theoretical position does not preclude the retention of a critical voice and vision that call attention to the limitations of maternalist politics and understand the importance of striving for less limited formulations of political protest in the future.

Notes

1. The Janatha Vimukthi Peramuna (People's Liberation Front) comprised primarily nationalist Sinhala youth who wished to overthrow the government of the UNP (United Nationalist Party) on the grounds that it was corrupt, capitalist and classist. The rallying point for their uprising was the arrival of Indian forces in Sri Lanka (i.e., foreigners on Sinhala soil) to ensure an accord between the Sri Lankan state and the Tamil militants (primarily the Liberation Tigers of Tamil Eelam) who were fighting for a separate state in the northern and eastern regions of the country. This battle, which was begun around 1980, continues today.

2. The Sinhalese make up 74 per cent of the population, the Tamils 18 per cent, Muslims 7 per cent and Burghers (descendants of Dutch and Portuguese colonists) and other minorities 0.8 per cent. While the Sinhalese are predominantly Buddhists (69.3 per cent) and the Tamils predominantly Hindus (15.5 per cent), both communities, as well as other minorities, contribute to a 7 per cent population of Christians (primarily Catholics) in the island (*Serendib* 19(5): 49).

3. The Mothers' Front has been inspired by and shares much with similar organisations in Latin America, but I want to highlight here the importance of historical and material specificities rather than make comparisons between different movements.

4. Catholics also visit such shrines, and Gombrich and Obeyesekere (1988:142) report that they interviewed two Catholics along with 44 Buddhists.

5. The SLFP was the main opposition party during this period. Two of its members, who represented the districts of Matara and Hambantota in the parliament, founded the Mothers' Front. For a further discussion of the

influence of the SLFP in the Mothers' Front, see de Alwis (1997 and 1998).

6. This is a usual practice in Hindu places of worship. If the coconut breaks with the white kernel facing up, it is supposed to be a good sign, and if it faces down, an inauspicious sign. The latter omen, however, did not seem to bother other supplicants at this shrine (Gombrich and Obeyesekere 1988:142). One usually purchases the *puja watti* (offering basket) outside the temple and offers it to the deity; the basket includes coconut, some camphor, sticks of incense, fruits and flowers.

7. This is a very complicated conceit, which defies translation. Suffice it to say that lightning without rain is meant to suggest the extraordinariness of the punishment that should be meted out to the perpetrators.

8. For a brief description of this ritual see Wijesekera (1990), for an extended description and analysis see Gombrich (1981, cf. Leach 1971:690), and for a discussion of its origins see Obeyesekere (1984 especially pp. 293–6).

9. One of the Sri Lanka Freedom Party representatives in the Kalutara Provincial Council, Sumithra Priyangani Abeyweera, whose own father (an SLFP stalwart) was fatally shot by unknown assassins during this period, organised this protest. It commenced with a *bodhi puja* (offerings to the Bo tree) at the historic Buddhist temple at Kalutara and concluded with a *deva kannalawwa* at the shrine to Lord Vishnu in the Alutgama Kande Vihara complex. During the procession of the Mothers' Front from the Kalutara Bodhiya to the Vishnu Devale, the police forbade the group to carry their banner and insisted that the women walk in single file. As a news report pointed out, there were as many policemen present as there were mothers (*Divaina*, 4 July1992).

10. This is not the first time the president has publicly participated in this ritual (see *Lankadeepa*, 13 January 1992; *Island*, 22 March 1992). Yet the repetition of this ritual within such a short period and on such a grand scale suggests it was not a mere coincidence. This ritual is usually performed with just seven (grand)mothers, and with the chief (grand)-mother rather than a politician leading the chanting.

11. There is an extensive body of work on the various healing rituals associated with spirit possession. It includes the early contributions of Gooneratne (1865/66) along with many missionary and colonial accounts, e.g. Harvard (1823) and Tennent (1850), as well as anthropological studies by, *inter alia*, Kapferer (1979a, 1979b, 1983), Obeyesekere (1969, 1981, 1984), Wirz (1954), and Yalman (1964). Scott (1994) provides a nuanced historicisation and rigorous deconstruction of many of these accounts and studies. See also Jeganathan (1997) for an excellent problematisation of anthropological discourses that seek to posit a relationship between rituals associated with demonism and ethnic riots. For a description and discussion of various forms of sorcery, see for example, de Silva (1926), Obeyesekere (1975), Pertold (1925), Selvadurai (1976) and Wijetunga

(1919, 1922).

12. This is a relatively new form of Buddhist ritual that was a particular favourite of President Premadasa. For a useful description and discussion of this ritual, see Gombrich (1981), Gombrich and Obeyesekere (1988) and Seneviratne and Wickremaratne (1980).

13. Most formal rituals would involve the priest or priestess uttering the invocation/ curse while the supplicant repeated it after him/her. However, this would not preclude the supplicant articulating her/his own curses in private. The Mothers' Front, however, had no option other than private cursing, as they were denied access to the priests and priestesses associated with the Kaliamman shrine. The organisers of the Mothers' Front probably anticipated such an eventuality: hence their coming armed with their own curse which was written out in very elaborate and formal language like that used by a priest or priestess; such invocations can also be copied from liturgical texts as well as from mass-produced 'prayer books' that provide the appropriate invocations for different deities; for an example of the latter kind of text, see Somakirthi (1974).

14. The public performance of curses, out of a plethora of other possible forms of religious protest, was the only aspect of public spectacle that the members of the Mothers' Front initiated themselves, quite by accident. The women's unscripted and abandoned supplication to Lord Vishnu at Devinuwera and Lord Skanda at Kataragama during the *Pada Yatra* (Long March) organised by the Sri Lanka Freedom Party to protest against government atrocities, in March/April 1992, took both the SLFP and the media by surprise. The Mothers' Front, which had been one of many groups participating in the *Yatra*, soon became the centre of attention (see especially *Divaina*, 4 April 1992) and inspired its SLFP organisers to incorporate such *deva kaññalawwas* into the protest campaign of the Mothers' Front (the SLFP was planning to hold several of these *deva kaññalawwas* in different parts of the country but this plan never materialised, for some reason).

15. Note here that the reporter refers to this woman's curse as a lamentation (*vilapa*).

16. A.M.W. Atapattu, *Irida Lankadeepa*, 2 August 1992, my translation. For a discussion and analysis of the recent rise in the worship of Lord Skanda, see Obeyesekere (1977).

17. Such a notion is further reified in the work of anthropologists such as Kapferer (1983: Chapter 5, cf. Scott 1994: Chapter 4).

18. Sorcery is always directed at individuals, posits Uyangoda, though many of the curses I heard prove him wrong (see above). However, it is an undeniable fact that the SLFP consistently sought to present President Premadasa as the ultimate cause of all ills and deliberately chose to hold the *deva kaññalawwa* on his birthday.

19. Besides their efforts to ban demonstrations in February 1991, the state

also attempted to ban and later curtailed a protest march of the Mothers' Front organised in Kalutara on 3 July 1992 (see page 187 and note 9). On World Human Rights Day, 10 December 1992, the Organisation of Parents and Family Members of the Disappeared (OPFMD) organised a sit-down protest, and some Mothers' Front organisers like Mahinda Rajapakse joined them. The riot squad led a baton charge and tear-gassed them, leaving several leaders injured (*Island*, 11 December 1992).

20. Of course, it is not that the government did not toy with such an idea. After all, the gates of the Kaliamman Kovil were padlocked when the Mothers' Front first arrived (though the alternative media were quick to highlight such attempted lockouts as blatant and very public violations of human rights; see *Aththa*, 24 June 1992; *Divaina*, 6 July 1992), and the temple guards continued to deny women access to both the inner sanctum and the services of a priest or priestess (which nevertheless did not deter the mothers from what they came to do).

21. My argument about this bourgeois modality of respectability, which was premised on the articulation of a particular moral and normative way of being a woman, also highlights how discourses that sought to sexualise women could frequently disrupt women's respectability. The point I am making here, however, is that even though these aged women were marked as asexual, it did not necessarily follow that they could transcend their class positioning and thus inhabit a place of 'respectability'.

CHAPTER 14

'We Want Women to Be Given an Equal Chance'

Post-Independence Rural Politics in Northern Namibia

HEIKE BECKER

This chapter deals with the relation of state and society in the aftermath of the Namibian decolonisation war.[1] More specifically it discusses the process of women's representation in the reconstruction of local politics in the former war zone in northern Namibia. My argument focuses on post-war developments concerning chieftainship and the associated socio-legal institutions of customary courts. These courts are socio-political institutions that existed prior to the war, and for many years they have been the interstices between the state and society in rural Africa.

These institutions present a special problem for a gender analysis of post-conflict situations, especially in the case of the Southern African liberation wars, because of their nature as 'patriarchal institutions and traditions'. Mike Kesby (1996), for one, has found the reconstruction and gradual empowerment of 'traditional authorities' partly responsible for the post-war backlash against women in rural Zimbabwe.[2] Different national and local contexts may, however, result in rural socio-political institutions evincing varying gender politics. I argue that the specifics of the post-war state, its relation with society, and its gender politics, all impact on the gender politics of these institutions, which are at once a level of local government and a quasi-autonomous part of civil society.

In northern Namibia, national and local discussions of the Namibian constitution have contributed to changes in the gender composition of the customary courts and to the gender discourses of these institutions. The national constitution, which was adopted shortly before the country gained political independence in March

1990, makes ample legal provision for gender equality. I show how a rural community has translated these significant national political developments into changes at the local decision-making level and how they have benefited rural women.

My argument is based on the case of Ongandjera in southwestern Owambo, which shows how postcolonial political processes that work themselves out at the heart of political life in the capital are reflected in a rural area some 700 kilometres north of Windhoek. Ovamboland in the central north of the country was the main stage of the Namibian decolonisation war from 1966 to 1989.[3]

The Owambo area comprises seven linguistically and culturally closely related communities that, for the most part, have been politically organised as kingdoms for several hundred years. Colonial rule transformed the indigenous polities into local administrative organs dependent on the colonial state. Together they made up the larger administrative entity of Ovamboland. When South Africa succeeded the defeated former colonial power of imperial Germany in 1920 under the League of Nations' mandate system, the new rulers designed an elaborate system of indirect rule for the northern Namibian territories of Ovamboland, Okavango, Caprivi and Kaokoveld, authored largely by longtime Native Commissioner for Ovamboland C. H. L. ('Cocky') Hahn, who spent the entire first thirty years of South African rule in northern Namibia (1915–46).[4]

In 1968 Ovamboland became a separate homeland ('bantustan') following the recommendations of the 1962 Odendaal Commission, which was instrumental in imposing South Africa's 'separate development' apartheid policies on Namibia. An executive council, made up of one delegate from each of the seven Namibian Owambo 'tribes' with a chief councillor presiding, ran the homeland administration. Thus, the links between the Owambo traditional authorities and the colonial apartheid state remained extremely close.

Soon after independence, the new government, in an effort to transcend the apartheid-era ethnic-based administrative divisions, delimitated new local and regional boundaries. In 1992 it divided former Ovamboland into four of the thirteen new Namibian administrative regions. The boundaries of the new regions cut across older ethnic boundaries in certain instances. The new Omusati region, along with the other western Owambo polities of Ombalantu and

Uukolonkadhi-Eunda, as well as parts of the central Uukwambi area, fully incorporated Ongandjera.

Although the Namibian constitution does not make explicit provision for a system of chieftainship and customary courts, the Traditional Authorities Act of 1995 provides for these. A whole set of new policies, laws and practices curtails the coercive powers of traditional authorities, especially as compared to the pre-independence era. The authorities' main functions now relate to the administration of customary law and to cultural matters. Article 66 of the Namibian constitution acknowledges a parallel system of customary law and common law, subject to the condition that they comply with the provisions of the country's supreme law. Traditional authorities are clearly subordinated to state organs in matters of local and regional government (Article 12 of the Act, as amended in 1997). Furthermore, the provisions of the national constitution supersede, *inter alia*, 'any custom, tradition, practice or usage which is discriminatory or which detracts from or violates the rights of any person as guaranteed by the Constitution' (Article11(1)(a) of the Act). The explicit stipulation that requires traditional authorities to promote women to positions of leadership supplements the implicit prohibition of gender-based discrimination (Article 10(1)(g) of the Act).

War and Violence in Northern Namibia

Post-independence changes in the legal framework of rural politics cannot be understood without some knowledge of the northern Namibian experience of colonialism and the liberation war. The Namibian decolonisation war began in August 1966 with the first 'contact' between the South African Defence Force (SADF) and guerrillas of the People's Liberation Army of Namibia (PLAN) at Ongulumbashe in western Owambo. For the next twenty-three years, northern Namibia, and particularly Owambo, was the main setting of the war. Southern and central Namibia were only indirectly affected, mainly when in the 1980s young white and black men from those areas were conscripted into the then newly formed South West Africa Territorial Force (SWATF).

Little research into the impact of war and violence on society and culture in northern Namibia has been published as yet, in contrast to the substantial number of publications on armed decolonisation conflicts elsewhere in Southern Africa.[5] In the case of Zimbabwe, for instance, studies began to emerge within a few years of that country's independence (see, for example, Lan 1985; Staunton 1990; Kriger 1992; Bhebe and Ranger 1995). The reasons for this dearth are manifold and too complex to address in this chapter.[6] It would be very wrong, however, to conclude that the war did not have an enormous impact. This area was home to just over 600,000 people; estimates put the numbers of various colonial military and paramilitary forces at over 30,000 at the time the demobilisation started on 1 April 1989. An estimated 9,000 combatants in the guerrilla forces of the liberation movement, the South West Africa People's Organisation (SWAPO), opposed the colonial military and paramilitary forces (Preston 1997: 455–6).

No women were involved in combat in the apartheid security forces (Preston 1997:448), but from 1974 on, PLAN included women combatants. Initially the male-dominated SWAPO leadership resisted the inclusion of women fighters, and the number of women participating in actual combat always remained small, probably not exceeding a few hundred (see Shikola 1998:142). Most PLAN women provided support services such as driving and health care, and a few became commanders and political commissioners, but overall the guerrilla leadership remained a male domain (H. Becker 1995:149–50). No one has so far carried out an in-depth study of the social relations within PLAN. According to memories recorded in the decade following the end of the war, the conventional gendered division of labour was eroded in PLAN to a certain extent. Men took up tasks such as cooking and washing, and the small number of female commanders apparently succeeded in establishing their authority with their male comrades (H. Becker 1995:150; Shikola 1998:141). When the guerrillas moved across the border into Namibian territory from training camps in friendly nearby countries, however, it was the local population that provided cooking, shelter and other domestic chores. Local women performed such tasks in line with the conventional gendered division of labour.

From 1972 until 1989 Owambo was under a continuous state of emergency. A dusk-to-dawn curfew for the local people, who almost without exception supported SWAPO, provided cover for South

African war atrocities. Acts of nonsexual and sexual violence against women were prominent in these (see, for example, Herbstein and Evenson 1989:83; for sexual violence see, for example, Allison 1986:28,43; Herbstein and Evenson 1989:105; Hinz and Gevers 1989:13–14; König 1983:46–7). Many locals rendered material and moral support to the SWAPO fighters; the dangers they courted and their awareness of the atrocities generated high levels of tension for individuals, families and society as a whole in the war zone. The prevalence of feelings of insecurity and of the need for a reorientation of social identity are not in doubt.[7] Local political structures lost the respect of much of the population because many chiefs and headmen collaborated with the South African colonial regime. By the 1970s most Owambo had come to accept the churches and SWAPO as their main sources of authority, rather than the traditional authorities or the Ovamboland Bantustan authorities (Soiri 1996:50; Tötemeyer 1978:218).

Within the family, authority continued to erode even further. The sense of security that adults previously provided to youngsters, who owed respect and obedience to their elders, was lost when youngsters saw adults subjected to the whims of the colonial army. The fact that adults may have had ideas about the political and social situation but were afraid to discuss them with their children for fear of losing their lives exacerbated the loss of parental and familial authority. The unexplained brutality of life in the war zone made young people look for their own explanations and seek alternatives (Namhila 1997:31).

The war was the cause of social disintegration in contemporary Owambo and a high incidence of social problems like alcohol abuse and a steep increase of sexual violence against women and young children. Former exiles have expressed the shock they felt when witnessing such changes on their return to northern Namibia in 1989 (Namhila 1997:154). From the 1980s the war's brutalising effects on day-to-day life resulted in an unprecedented incidence of social and gender-based violence (Herbstein and Evenson 1989:94). In addition, the dusk-to-dawn curfew gutted social life, which had formerly helped to maintain the social organisation. In particular, the 'moonlight dances' (oudano) that earlier had brought young women and men together for all-night outdoor singing and dancing could no longer take place because of the curfew (interviews with Mirjam Kautwima,

Shipola Kukenge and Mukwaluwala Hitombo, Ongha, 18 May 1999). Young men sought new forms of relaxation, often related to an emerging culture of reckless drunkenness. This in turn, people say, caused a loss of respect for women, and may be at the root of the recent scourge of gender-based violence in northern Namibia. However, as the discussion of change in rural politics will show, the effects of the war and especially post-war changes have not been entirely to the detriment of women in the former war zone.

National and Local Gender Politics after Independence

Current changes concerning the participation of women in traditional authority structures are inextricably intertwined with the recent political history of Namibia. Current discourses on traditional structures in Owambo have partly adopted notions that originate in the country's national political discourse. *Omukwaniilwa* (King[8]) Jafet Munkundi argued in an interview (Uukwandongo, 26 July 1997) that the Traditional Authority of Ongandjera had begun to appoint women to leadership positions and to encourage women's participation in decision-making, 'because there is development, and the country is independent, and there is democracy. So we want women to be given an equal chance to men, and that women and men work together.'

Shortly after independence, rural women in northern Namibia began to lobby traditional authorities to change customary laws. In August 1993, more than a hundred women demonstrated against discriminatory customary inheritance laws at the highest Oukwanyama court at Ohangwena in eastern Owambo (*The Namibian*, 11 and 13 August 1993). This unprecedented event launched a chain of indigenous law reform efforts that within a couple of years improved women's rights to inherit land in all seven Namibian Owambo communities.

To women in northern Namibia, independence has come to mean far more than the political independence of Namibia; in the words of two retired teachers from Ongandjera: 'Everything changed for the better, and no one is discriminated against any longer' (interviews with Liina Mpanda and Lahja Angolo, Okahao, 20 July 1997). Another retired teacher, who in 1995 became the first female *elenga* (senior headwoman) in Ongandjera, also believed that women could now accede to leadership positions because decolonisation had opened the door to new ways for both women and men: 'With independence and the removal of the apartheid laws, things have changed. [Before independence] women in life have always been regarded as women for cooking and raising kids, and only men were involved in leadership structures' (interview with Martha Iileka, Etilyasa, 19 July 1997).

People's understanding of 'independence' and 'the constitution' has indeed changed gender representations and practices in Owambo. Although few Namibians know the wording of Namibia's supreme law,[9] its spirit of gender equality has reached an amazingly broad spectrum of the people. This is particularly true for the Owambo communities, where virtually everyone supports the SWAPO government. Further, it appears that the new norms and values not only challenge presumptions about gender and authority at the level of community organisation and politics, but also permeate the personal relations between men and women. As early as mid-1991, women in Ombalantu, bordering on Ongandjera, asserted during a group discussion that 'men feel threatened by the constitution' and that some would, albeit slowly, shift to less autocratic behaviour towards their wives precisely because of the equality statement enshrined in the constitution (H. Becker 1995:343).

It would be difficult to overrate the prominent role the Namibian constitution has played in the changes that are beginning to redress gender imbalances, despite the fact that the Standing Committee of the Constituent Assembly drew up the supreme law in only eighty days, between November 1989 and February 1990, without any significant popular consultation. Thus, unlike the process in South Africa during the negotiations to end apartheid, public lobbying by gender activists in Namibia hardly played a role.[10] Rather, by the time of Namibia's belated decolonisation, two decades of the international women's movement and Namibian women's own struggles at home and in exile had prepared the ground for an anti-sexist supreme law (H. Becker 1995:388–90).

The Namibian constitution prohibits any discrimination on grounds of sex (Article10) and provides affirmative action for women (Article 23). Although this is not laid down as an imperative, the constitution explicitly authorises measures such as the law governing local elections, which provides for affirmative action for female candidates. Some 40 per cent of all members of city, town and village councils are currently women and, in the absence of statutory affirmative action, almost a quarter of the members of the National Assembly (the first house of parliament) are women. Namibia compares well with the 12.7 per cent of female parliamentarians internationally. In contrast, only two (white) women held senior positions in national government service before independence, and just one woman was in a management position in the ethnic administrations (H. Becker 1995:94).

The government created a national machinery for the promotion of gender equality in August 1990 and adopted a national gender policy more recently. The most blatant discriminatory provisions in the general law, which were in the state-administered legal system and rooted in Western law, were abolished. The reform of legislation on civil marriages is the most outstanding success of law reform geared towards the realisation of gender equality. Other legal efforts that have benefited women include the introduction of three-month paid maternity leave in 1995 and an outstanding reform of the rape law adopted in February 2000. A new Act abolished the marital rape exemption and broadened the definition of the crime of rape to include violent sexual acts without penetration, as well as sexual violence against men and boys.

National Discourse on Gender and Tradition

There have also been setbacks. In April 1999 the Minister of Health officially withdrew a draft bill to provide for the decriminalisation of abortion that her predecessor had introduced almost three years earlier. The minister claimed that '99 per cent' of Namibians were against the decriminalisation of abortion and thus the bill could no longer be promoted. Leading representatives of the main Christian denominations welcomed this move, although women's organisations and especially the Namibian Reproductive Rights Alliance expressed their disappointment (*The Namibian*, 23 April 1999; 27 April 1999).

The most controversial gender debate in postcolonial Namibia took place in late 1995 and early 1996. The Married Persons' Equality Act No. 1 of 1996 did away with the husband's automatic 'marital power' and position as 'head of the family' which was vested in the husband in every civil law marriage contracted under the Roman Dutch Common Law. The drafting and parliamentary debate of the bill provoked a very controversial discussion in Namibian politics and society. Parliamentarians across the party political spectrum, authors of letters to Namibian newspapers, callers to the country's phone-in radio programmes, and members of the public who attended the nationwide hearings held to discuss the new law, opposed the reform in the strongest terms. Opponents argued 'African tradition' and the Bible in their cause, claiming that the commands of both African tradition and Christianity prevented equality between women and men (H. Becker 1996). It must be noted that male parliamentarians, letter writers and telephone callers made up the sole public opposition to the bill.[11] No women ever opposed the reform in public. In the end, President Nujoma threw his personal weight behind the contested reform, compelling all SWAPO parliamentarians to vote in favour of the new law, which the National Assembly finally passed despite the reservations of the National Council, the second house of Parliament, representing regional government delegates.

The debates around the Married Persons' Equality Bill exemplify contesting gender discourses in contemporary Namibia. The supporters of the bill employed the gender equality provisions of the Namibian constitution. Opponents argued that the bill would contravene god-given gender relations, which ancient African traditions had determined in the first place. The terms of the debate suggest a widespread perception in postcolonial Namibian society and politics that 'women's rights' and African tradition, particularly customary laws and politico-judicial institutions, are eternal foes. Proponents and opponents of gender equality do not contest the assumed facts of traditional gendered identities. Rather the contestations revolve around the moral values attached to these chosen versions of a strictly patriarchal past. The traditionalist discourse contests reforms to promote gender equality with nostalgia for the imaginary past. Those promoting gender equality, on the other hand, ascribe gender discrimination in Namibia to the very same 'centuries-old traditions' (see Becker 1995:52, 160, 170). Proponents and opponents of gender equality who take part in the postcolonial national public discourse appear to share a view of tradition as timeless and unchangeable. They imagine Owambo tradition in particular as highly patriarchal.

Gender, Power and Traditional Authority in Precolonial and Colonial Ongandjera

Contrary to current ideas about traditional gender relations, Ongandjera stands out among the Owambo communities as the polity that had a strong tradition of female rulers, who were known as *aakwaniilwa* (kings or queens; singular *omukwaniilwa*) in precolonial times until the 1860s (Williams 1991:133–5, 157–8, 192). According to an eminent oral historian of Ongandjera, these women ruled in full accord with both the community and their royal relatives. Some are said to have waged battles bravely and to have gone to war with their soldiers (interview with Petrus Amutenya, Okahao, 21 July 1997).

Although local history has much to say about them, the ruling queens of the past are largely forgotten today. Most local people have never heard of female *aakwaniilwa* ruling Ongandjera. A few have a vague idea that there once were queens, but cannot recall names or details of their reign. Old people's memories are not much different from those of very young men and women. However, some families still tell to their children stories about the queens of the past (discussion with male grade-12 students, Okahao, 23 July 1997).

Oral history suggests that male and female *omalenga* (counsellors and senior headmen or headwomen) assisted past Ongandjera kings and queens. By contrast, under colonial rule all *omalenga* were male. During the early years of colonial rule, there were still female *oomwene gwomikunda* (ward headmen or headwomen), but soon they became exclusively male (interviews with Aune Amos, Uukwalumbe, 22 July 1997; Festus Iitula, Okalondo, 19 July 1997, and Petrus Amutenya, Okahao, 21 July 1997). It seems intrinsic to the broader changes under colonial rule that women disappeared from positions of power. The emerging structures of colonial tribal authority evolved into all-male domains.

The system of indirect rule, which was based on the continued application of what the administration perceived as ordinary native law and custom and on the official recognition of indigenous rulers as tribal authorities,[12] proved crucial in the instauration of male rule. The colonial freezing and reinvention of native law and custom affected gender relations in Owambo greatly. The matrilineal kinship system survived largely intact, although it came under pressure partly for socio-economic reasons. Women's power and autonomy, however, suffered enormous blows. The efforts of colonial officials to prevent the migration of women out of Ovamboland exemplified the selective use of ostensibly traditional law. Officials prohibited women's mobility as presumably contravening traditional laws and customs.

Historian Patricia Hayes (1996:372) argues that such thinking was not simply imposed from above. She maintains that alliances between officials and conservative male elders, who in turn drew selectively on African cultural precedents concerning gender norms, reinforced these ideas. Oral history suggests that the colonial construction of gender did indeed build on and modify precolonial gender practices, representations and conflicts (H. Becker forthcoming); perhaps this explains why male Owambo so readily and eagerly took up colonial interpretations of tradition and custom. The colonials conceived of women as a social category whose invariable place was in tribal areas as agricultural producers; there they subsidised the system of cheap male migrant labour. In order to secure this arrangement, male tribal authorities were to keep women under control. Women's place, in line with this construction of gender, was confined to the domestic and tribal or traditional spheres of society, whereas men were able to enter the public, modern sphere, predominantly as migrant labourers. The arrangement prevented women from participating in public life, and their marginalisation in the colonial public sphere extended to the socio-political and judicial tribal institutions.

The colonial origins of the prevailing forms of gendered community decision-making are now largely forgotten. In the contemporary view, there has long been 'an Owambo law that women were not recognised' (discussion with male community members, Okahao, 22 July 1997). People say that, rather than the colonial state, the Lutheran missionaries implanted Christian norms that perpetuated and enhanced the pattern:

> Nobody knows whether there was a law, but the thing was just there that women did not get involved in decision-making and rather remained at home.... It is something inherent in Owambo tradition that women were not recognised. The arrival of Christianity simply perpetuated this.... When the Finnish missionaries came to Okahao [the Ongandjera capital], the female missionaries encouraged women to become recognised [but not the male missionaries]. That's the same in Finland, that women are

under men, and that there are no women decision-makers in Finland. (Interview with Liina Mpanda and Lahja Angolo, Okahao, 20 July 1997)

Before decolonisation, local public forums such as sessions of customary courts were open only to men. On the other hand, women stayed away not only because they were not invited, but also because they felt that they had nothing to contribute (interviews with Kornelia Iyambo, Okalondo, 19 July 1997 and Aune Amos, Uukwalumbe, 22 July 1997). One elderly woman elaborated on women's earlier exclusion from community decision-making within the broader context of gender representations and practices:

> It was like a traditionally sanctioned practice. It came from our culture that women were seen as incapable of thinking and thus bringing about something. Even in the house the marital power was vested in the husband. Women had no say, even where the men were wrong. This was reflected in our laws. Women were looked upon as children, as if they had no brains. Men were the only important people. (Interview with Martha Iileka, Etilyasa, 19 July 1997)

Some locals have also argued that 'in the past, women were not recognised by the colonial government' (discussion with male community members, Okahao, 22 July 1997). This was particularly true in the time of Native Commissioner 'Cocky' Hahn, when administration officials called only men to tribal gatherings where they announced orders and policies. This practice changed when Harold Eedes became Native Commissioner of Ovamboland in 1946 (interview with Petrus Amutenya, Okahao, 24 July 1997). However, perceptions of power and authority remained suffused with gender assumptions because the colonial administration itself was all-male. The same was true for the Owambo ethnic second-tier ('bantustan') administration until independence in 1990.

The colonial administration's gender politics heavily affected local concepts of gender and political authority. Colonial discourses and practices constructed women and decision-making bodies as mutually exclusive. The procedures and substance of local political decision-making bodies, which in their present form are a rather recent innovation (interviews with Petrus Amutenya, Okahao, 21 July 1997 and Festus Iitula, Okalondo, 19 July 1997), and specific gender representations and practices, which are also of recent origin (see

H. Becker 1995:78–105 and forthcoming), all converged to marginalise women.

After Independence: Women in Traditional Authority Positions

As late as April 1995 no women held office within the traditional authority structures of Ongandjera. This situation began to change with the appointment of two women as *omalenga* in late 1995 and early 1996. Office bearers of the traditional authority, including the present *omukwaniilwa*, as well as female and male residents, agreed that it was good to have women in traditional authority positions, 'because by nature people are equal', as a group of local men argued. Women were particularly enthusiastic about having female office bearers in the traditional authority. They saw this as more than an abstract notion of equality, believing that headwomen and female chiefs made a difference in decision making because they would introduce a woman's point of view. Customary courts frequently hear rape cases, for instance, and survivors often feel more comfortable with proceedings there than in the state courts. Thus traditional authorities have begun to assume a significant role in trying to curb the increasing incidence of gender-based violence in the aftermath of the war (H. Becker 2000:50–1).

Yet the local discourse about women in positions of authority is not without contradictions. Men have repeatedly claimed that women are reluctant to assume elected leadership positions 'because a woman is afraid of what the people will say about her' (interview with Jason Tshehama, Uukwalumbe, 22 July 1997). Male community members insist that women lack the courage to take decisions, although women from the community counter that men tend not to accept the decisions women take. In order to arrive at an assessment of changing gender relations in post-independence rural politics, it is important to look beyond the appointment of a few headwomen. The overarching question is how women and men participate in the most important public forums of the community, namely sessions of customary courts.

Until decolonisation, hearings of customary courts in Ongandjera were all-male affairs. Women were present in specified situations only, for example when they themselves were a party or witness to a court case. Only in 1989 did the Traditional Authority decree that women and men were equally invited to attend court hearings. It appears that women in Ongandjera have taken this call seriously. But although most of those who attended public events like the hearings of customary courts in 1997 were women (discussion with female community members, Okahao, 21 July 1997; interview with Jason Tshehama, Uukwalumbe, 23 July 1997), women were only marginally involved in the actual decision making. Again, informants said that women feared to expose themselves: 'These days women outnumber men at court hearings and meetings. But when there is a court case, women are too shy and afraid to participate in the decision making, because the accused might harm her later. The few men who are there make the decisions' (interview with Jason Tshehama, Uukwalumbe, 23 July 1997).

The Ongandjera king himself was concerned that women would not discuss any matters in front of men (interviews with Jafet Munkundi and Andreas Shaanika Ndakokamo, Uukwandongo, 26 July 1997). This concurs with common statements that, because of their oppression in the past, women would hardly speak before men, even at home in the presence of their husbands. Despite claims to the contrary, there are indications that male opposition to women's participation in leadership roles and public decision making may be stronger than we were led to believe. A group of women in Okahao, the Ongandjera capital, complained that many men were indeed rather unhappy with women taking up community responsibilities, as they feared that 'the women are colonising us'. Not surprisingly, male opposition to outspoken women may silence many women, especially when this is compounded with the threat of domestic violence (discussion with female community members, Ogongo (Uukwambi), 7 September 1995).

Postcolonial Local Discourses on Gender and Tradition

Contrary to perceptions of an unchangeable patriarchal African tradition, which are so common in national, postcolonial discourse, people in Ongandjera have challenged colonial representations of gender. This raises questions about the specific conditions that have been conducive to such changes in post-war northern Namibia.

We must be clear, first, that the changes have not come about as the consequence of direct state intervention. The vaguely worded affirmative action provisions of the Traditional Authorities Act No. 17 of 1995 were not known to anyone in Ongandjera in 1997. Rather, a new local discourse on gender has emerged completely independently of the state; this new local discourse of gender argues that if women serve as government ministers, they can also act as traditional leaders. Local women, and some men, now dismiss claims that there is an antagonism between African tradition and constitutional gender equality. Unlike many urbanites on both sides of the traditional-versus-constitutional divide, such rural people do not regard the traditional system as separate in any way from wider postcolonial Namibian society.

The local gender equality discourse is thus rooted in the intense identification of Oshiwambo-speaking Namibians with 'our new Namibia', and the changes wrought by the country's new dispensation. The timing of Namibia's decolonisation late in the twentieth century has facilitated the positioning of the gender equality debate as a prominent feature on Namibia's national agenda since 1990 (H. Becker 1995:388–9). Most Owambos' long-standing support of, and identification with, SWAPO, first as a liberation movement and now as the ruling party, have encouraged a local gender equality debate. Since Namibia gained independence in 1990, many Owambo women as well as office bearers in traditional authorities have taken up the gender equality discourse. To an extent these traditional authorities' institutions have altered earlier patriarchal discourses.

There can be no doubt that the efforts on the part of the Owambo traditional authorities to provide democratic reforms are geared toward regaining acceptance from the local population and improving relations with the SWAPO government. Research conducted shortly after the end of the war found that attitudes towards traditional authorities in Owambo were 'generally negative'. The feeling prevailed 'that some leaders had "sold out" to the SADF and South African regime' (Pendleton, Lebeau and Tapscott 1993:66). Analysts have emphasised that the local population in Owambo directed anti-colonial resistance against both the South Africans and the traditional authorities, which they saw for the most part as the colonial regime's stooges (Soiri 1996:50; Tötemeyer 1978:218).

Born in 1919, Uushona Shiimi was the Ongandjera king from 1949 to 1972; he was a prominent example of a chief closely aligned with the colonial regime. The administration carefully groomed him as a leader to their liking. Today local people remember Uushona for his harsh and often unfair penalties and for his use of forced labour on road construction. His close collaboration with the colonial regime made him highly unpopular with the people of Ongandjera (interviews with Samuel Mateus Hango, Epumbu, 21 and 24 July 1997, Martha Iileka, Etilyasa, 19 July 1997, and Petrus Amutenya, Okahao, 24 July 1997). As the first Chief Councillor of the Ovamboland administration from 1968 until the time of his death, Uushona Shiimi played a major part in the South African efforts to create Namibian self-governing homelands (see Tötemeyer 1978:104–5).

Such discredited positions put strong popular pressure on the Owambo traditional authorities to reform their structures and policies. Striving for more gender balance in decision making, widely recognised as a crucial element in the new Namibia, may well be part of conscious efforts to improve their standing. Perhaps the recognition accorded Namibian traditional authorities by the state, in contrast to the treatment of similar authorities in postcolonial Zimbabwe and Mozambique, acted as an inducement to initiate change.

Postcolonial changes in traditional rural politics appear to be embedded in efforts to revive elements of traditional culture, thereby challenging both their former proscription by the missions and the distorted colonial versions. The postcolonial revival has begun to bring to the fore the prominent role women played as performers of oral traditions and in the transmission of oral history (interview with Jason Amukutuwa, Elim, 13 May 1999), and as ritual leaders, particularly in the female initiation ceremonies locally known as *efundula, ohango* or *olufuko* (see H. Becker 1998).

Conclusion

Although prominent apologists for grossly unequal gender relations in Namibia, as in other southern African countries, employ the theme of an ancient African tradition, which muted women in the family and community, rural residents in post-war northern Namibia seek new traditions that incorporate new values and more longstanding cultural elements. Rural women who want to see their lives changed for the better after the end of the war have taken up national constitutional notions of gender equality. As a result of the postcolonial redefinition of gendered traditional politics, women have become visible in local public forums from which they were excluded in the colonial past.

Namibia's postcolonial gender discourses and policies are a relative success story, attributable in part to the relatively strong state that emerged from the Namibian decolonisation conflict. During the first decade of independence, the postcolonial state and prominent sections of society collaborated successfully in efforts to promote gender equality. Namibian women in politics have not contented themselves with the role of ardent but submissive party supporters. Unlike in other southern African countries, such as Botswana, Zambia and Zimbabwe (see Geisler 1995), in Namibia there are no dancing and ululating women praising the virtues of dependent wifehood and dismissing independent women as prostitutes. Nor is Namibia another case of men rendering women socially invisible after independence and sending them back to the hearth after participating in nationalist struggles, an oft-lamented fact in other countries. As this chapter has shown, not only are Namibian women visible in national politics, but the notion of gender equality has also had significant repercussions among rural communities in the former war zone in northern Namibia.

Notes

1. Piteimo Hainyanyula of the Centre for Applied Social Sciences (CASS) at the University of Namibia assisted the research. When it was carried out, in 1997, I was a senior researcher with CASS. The Swedish International Development Agency (SIDA) provided generous financial assistance.
2. 'Traditional Authority' is the official term for the institution of chieftainship in Namibia, set in law in the Traditional Authorities Act of 1995. I use the term in inverted commas initially in this chapter to highlight the problem of labelling institutions 'traditional' that are of decidedly colonial origin.
3. Ovamboland was the colonial name for the area, and I use it in this chapter when referring to the colonial context. In other contexts I refer to the area as Owambo.
4. The German and South African colonial authorities deemed the southern and central parts of Namibia essentially 'white man's country' and open to white settlement, in contrast to the northern territories. Fittingly, the

southern and central area was known from 1906 as the 'police zone'. Pockets of 'native reserves' within southern and central Namibia were subject to direct colonial rule during both German and South African colonial times. For a history of Namibia under South African rule see Hayes *et al.* (1998).

5. The project on war-affected people carried out in the early 1990s centred on the integration of former exiles and combatants. It hardly touched upon the experience of the *ovakalimo* in northern Namibia; *ovakalimo* were the 'stayers', those who did not go into exile (see Preston 1993).

6. Namibian society and politics receive very little attention in academic and media circles, including those in neighbouring South Africa. International media reports on the war in the Congo, for instance, frequently ignore the Namibian defence forces' involvement. The same is true for reports on the AIDS epidemic in southern Africa which tend to focus on South Africa, Zimbabwe and Botswana only. It appears that unlike Botswana, which has an equally small population, the media, the academy and the wider public regard Namibia as insignificant.

7. Kaleni Hiyalwa (2000) recounts the impact of the war on ordinary rural life in a novel, *Meekulu's Children*, set in Owambo during the 1970s and 1980s.

8. *Omukwaniilwa* (oshiNdonga) is a gender-neutral term that refers to every male and female member of the royal families of the Owambo kingdoms. Thus, the most appropriate translation is 'royal'. However, I translate it as 'king' or 'queen' when it refers to the supreme ruler of a kingdom.

9. The text of the Namibian constitution is available in English only.

10. Gender activists in Windhoek held two well-attended public meetings during this period to discuss the constitutional proposals, but it is doubtful whether the Members of the Constituent Assembly actually considered their suggestions (see H. Becker 1995: 237–41).

11. The male Deputy Speaker of the National Assembly, Zephania Kameeta, made a powerful plea for the passing of the bill, however (*Debates of the National Assembly*, 31 October 1995, Vol. 2:169-172). A vocal NGO coalition also called for the speedy passing of the bill.

12. Whenever the administration deemed it fit, this was combined with interference. Interventions ranged from the ordinary influence of administrators who made sure that 'the different tribal heads have more or less come to look to the Native Affairs Staff for advice and guidance in determining their affairs' (U.G. 33/1925, quoted in Olivier 1961:195) to the deposal of intransigent chiefs, effected by military force. Relevant examples are the 1917 death of the Kwanyama king Mandume yaNdemufayo in battle with the Ovamboland Expedition despatched by Pretoria to remove him; and the deposal of King Iipumbu yaShilongo of Uukwambi in 1932. In both cases the administration replaced the kingship with a system of headmen-in-council.

Bibliography

Agger, I. (1989) 'Sexual Torture of Political Prisoners: an Overview', *Journal of Traumatic Stress*, Vol. 2, pp. 305–318.

Akina Mama wa Afrika (1995) *African Women*, London Women's Centre, London.

Albertyn, C. (1994) 'Women and the Transition to Democracy in South Africa', in F. Kaganas and C. Murray (eds.) *Gender and the New South African Legal Order*, Juta and Co, Johannesburg.

Albertyn, C. *et al.* (1999) *Engendering the Political Agenda: a South African Case Study*, UNRISD, Dominican Republic.

Ali, N. M. (1999) 'Gendering Asmara 1995: Women and the Sudanese Opposition in Exile', paper prepared for The Aftermath: Conference on Women in Post-War Reconstruction, University of the Witwatersrand, Johannesburg, South Africa, July 20–22.

Allison, C. (1986) 'It's Like Holding the Key to Your Own Jail', in *Women in Namibia*, World Council of Churches, Geneva.

Amadiume, I. (1986) *Male Daughters, Female Husbands*, Zed Books, London and New York.

AVEGA (1999) *Agahozo: Survey On Violence Against Women In Rwanda*, Kigali, December.

Banerjee, P. (2001) 'Between Two Armed Patriarchies: Women in Assam and Nagaland', in Manchanda, R. (ed.) *Women, War and Peace in South Asia: Beyond Victimhood to Agency*, Sage, New Delhi.

Becker, D. (1995) 'The Deficiency of the Concept of Posttraumatic Stress Disorder When Dealing with Victims of Human Rights Violations', in R. Kleber, C.R. Figeley. and P. B. R. Gersons (eds.) *Beyond Trauma: Cultural and Societal Dynamics*, Plenum Press, New York.

Becker, H. (1995) *Namibian Women's Movement 1980 to 1992: From Anticolonial Resistance to Reconstruction*, IKO-Verlag für Interkulturelle Kommunikation, Frankfurt.

Becker, Heike (1996) 'Married Persons' Equality Bill: What Some of our Lawmakers Have to Say', *Sister Namibia*, Vol. 8, No. 1, pp. 7–8.

Becker, H. (1998) 'Efundula Past and Present. Female Initiation, Gender and Customary Law in Northern Namibia', paper presented at the Gender, Sexuality and Law Conference, Keele University (UK), 19–21 June 1998.

Becker, H. (2000) 'Gender and Peaceful Conflict Resolution in Historical and Contemporary Perspective: a case study from Northern Namibia', UNESCO Project: Women and a Culture of Peace in Africa, Windhoek.

Becker, H. (forthcoming) *Gender, Power and Traditional Authority: Four Namibian Case Studies* (working title), Namibia Scientific Society, Windhoek.

Behrend, H. (1991) 'Is Alice Lakwena a Witch? The Holy Spirit Movement and Its Fight against Evil in the North', in H. B. Hansen and M. Twaddle (eds.) *Changing Uganda: The Dilemmas of Structural Adjustment and Revolutionary Change*, James Currey, London.

Bennet, O., J. Bexley and K. Warnock (eds.) (1995) *Arms to Fight, Arms to Protect: Women Speak about Conflict*, PANOS Oral Testimony Series, London.

243

Bhebe, N. and T. Ranger (eds.) (1995) *Society in Zimbabwe's Liberation War*. Volume Two, University of Zimbabwe Publications, Harare.

Braam, T. and Webster, N. (2000). 'Mainstreaming Violence Against Women: Tshwaranang's Organisational Strategy Into The New Century', Johannesburg, Tshwaranang Legal Advocacy Centre to End Violence Against Women.

Brownmiller, S. (1975) *Against Our Will: Men, Women and Rape*, Bantam Books, New York.

Burt, M. R. and B. L. Katz (1987) 'Dimensions of Recovery from Rape: Focus on Growth Outcomes', *Journal of Interpersonal Violence*, Vol. 2, pp. 57– 81.

Caringella-MacDonald, S. (1988) 'Marxist and Feminist Interpretations on the Aftermath of Rape Reforms', *Contemporary Crises*, pp. 125–44.

Carrillo, Roxanna (1991) }*Violence against Women: An Obstacle to Development*, New Brunswick, Center for Women's Global Leadership.

Chaterjee, P. (1987) 'The Nationalist Resolution of the Women's Question', in K. Sangari and S. Vaid (eds.) *Recasting Women: Essays in Colonial History*, Kali, New Delhi.

Cockburn, C. (2001) 'The Gendered Dynamics of Armed Conflict and Political Violence', in C. Moser and F.C. Clark (eds.) *Gender, Armed Conflict and Political Violence*, Zed Books, London.

Collins, B.G. and M.B. Whalen (1989) 'The Rape Crisis Movement: Radical or Reformist?' *Social Work*, January, pp. 61–3.

Comaroff, J. (1985) *Body of Power, Spirit of Resistance*, University of Chicago Press, Chicago.

Connolly, W. E. (1991) *Identity/Difference: Democratic Negotiations of Political Paradox*, Cornell University Press, Ithaca.

Coomaraswamy, R. (1997) 'Women of the LTTE', *Frontline*, Chennai, January 10.

Cordero, I. (1998) 'Women in War: Impact and Response', in S. Stern (ed.) *Shining and Other Paths: War and Society in Peru 1980–1995*, Duke University Press, Durham.

Custers, P. (1987) *Women in the Telegana Uprising*, Naya Prakashan, Calcutta.

Dahl, S. (1993) 'The Trauma of Rape: a Description of the Stressors', *Nordisk Sexologi*, Vol. 11, pp. 144–164.

Das, V. (1995) *Critical Events*, Oxford University Press, Bombay.

de Alwis, M. (1997) 'Motherhood as a Space of Protest: Women's Political Participation in Contemporary Sri Lanka', in A. Basu and P. Jeffrey (eds.) *Appropriating Gender: Women's Activism and the Politicization of Religion in South Asia*, Routledge, London and New York.

de Alwis, M. (1998) 'Maternalist Politics in Sri Lanka: A Historical Anthropology of its Conditions of Possibility', PhD thesis, University of Chicago. Ann Arbor, UMI Dissertation Services.

de Silva, W.A. (1926) 'Sinhalese Magic and Spells', *Journal of the Royal Asiatic Society (Colombo Branch)*, Vol. 30, No. 79, pp. 193–203.

DeWolf, S. (1995) *The Central Role of Mozambican Women in Claiming Recognition of the Human Rights of Refugees: Observations from Tongagara Camp, Zimbabwe*, Christian Care, August.

di Leonardo, M. (1985) 'Morals, Mothers, and Militarism: Antimilitarism and Feminist Theory', *Feminist Studies*, Vol. 11, No. 3, pp. 599–617.

Dubisch, J. (ed.) (1986) *Gender and Power in Rural Greece*, Princeton University Press, Princeton.

Earthaction (1994) 'Defend the Ogoni People in Nigeria', *Alert*, No. 3.

Ehrenreich, B. (1997) *Blood Rites: Origins and History of the Passions of War*, Virago, London.

Elshtain, J. B. (1981) *Public Man, Private Woman*, Princeton University Press, Princeton.

Elshtain, J. B. (1983a) 'On Beautiful Souls, Just Warriors, and Feminist Consciousness', in J. Stiehm, (ed.) *Women and Men's Wars*, Oxford University Press, Oxford.

Elshtain, J. B. (1983b) 'On "The Family Crisis"', *Democracy*, Vol. 3, No. 1.

Elshtain, J. B. (1987) *Women and War*, Basic Books, New York.

Embassy of Eritrea (c.1994) Research and Information Section. Typescript.

Enloe, C. (1998) 'All the Men Are in the Militias, All the Women Are Victims: The Politics of Masculinity and Femininity in Nationalist Wars', in L. A. Lorentzen and J. Turpin (eds.) *The Women and War Reader*, New York University Press, New York.

Enloe, C. (1989) *Bananas, Beaches and Bases: Making Feminist Sense of International Politics*, University of California Press, Berkeley.

Eno, J. (2000) 'The Sierra Leone Experience', paper prepared for the International Conference on the Transformation of Conflicts in Africa and the Perspectives of African Women, Afard/Alert International, Dakar, 23–6 May.

'Eritrean Government Takes Women Soldiers from Frontlines' (2000) Channel Africa, 11 March, Internet Posting from <dehai-news> listserv.

'Eritrean POWs, Including Women, Wait for War's End' (1999) Internet Report from Mekele, Ethiopia, 29 June, <dehai-news> listserv.

'Eritrean Women Soldiers Leave Frontline, But Are Ready to Return' (2000), Agence France Presse, 11 March, Internet, Visafric News Section.

Fisher, I. (1999) 'Proven as Combat Soldiers, Eritrean Women Seek Equality in Society', *New York Times International* (Internet), 26 August.

Frazier, P.A. (1990) 'Victim Attributions and Post-rape Trauma', *Journal of Personality and Social Psychology*, Vol. 59, pp. 298–304.

Freire, P. (1979) *Pedagogy of the Oppressed*, Seabury Press, New York.

Gahama, J. *et al.* (1999) 'Burundi', in A. Adedeji (ed.) *Comprehending and Mastering African Conflicts*, Zed Books, London.

Galloy, M. R. (2000) 'Femmes, Conflits et Paix au Congo', paper prepared for the International Conference on the Transformation of Conflicts in Africa and the Perspectives of African Women, Afard/Alert International, Dakar, 23–6 May.

Gautam, S. *et al.* (2001) 'Where There Are No Men: Women in the Maoist Insurgency in Nepal', in R. Manchanda (ed.) *Women, War and Peace in South Asia: Beyond Victimhood to Agency*, Sage, New Delhi.

Geisler, G. (1995) 'Troubled Sisterhood: Women and Politics in Southern Africa. Case studies from Zambia, Zimbabwe and Botswana', *African Affairs*, Vol. 94, pp. 545–78.

Gilliam, A. (1991) 'Women's Equality and National Liberation', in C. Mohanty, A. Russo and C. Torres (eds.) *Third World Women and the Politics of Feminism*, Indiana University Press, Bloomington.

Gilmore, I. (1999a) 'Women Hold the Line in Africa's Forgotten War', *Issue*, No.1437, 2 May.

Gilmore, I. (1999b) 'Africa's Forgotten Battleground', *Weekly Mail and Guardian* (Johannesburg), 10 May.

Goldblatt, B. and Meintjes, S. (1998) 'South African Women Demand the Truth' in M. Turshen and C. Twagiramariya (eds.) *What Women Do in War Time: Gender and Conflict in Africa*, Zed Books, London.

Gombrich, R. (1981) 'A New Theravadin Liturgy', *Journal of the Pali Text Society*, Vol. 9, pp. 47–73.

Gombrich, R. and Obeyesekere, G. (1988) *Buddhism Transformed: Religious Change in Sri Lanka*, Princeton University Press, Princeton.

Gooneratne, D. de S. (1865/1866) 'On Demonology and Witchcraft in Ceylon', *Journal of Royal Asiatic Society (Ceylon Branch)*, Vol. 4, pp. 1–117.

Goswami, R. and D. Indranee (1999) 'Women in Armed Conflict Situations', in the summary report of a study by NorthEast Network, Shillong, India (unpublished).

Gray, L. and M. Kevane (1999) 'Diminished Access, Diverted Exclusion: Women and Land Tenure in sub-Saharan Africa', *African Studies Review* Vol. 42, No. 2, pp.15–39.

Grinker, L. (1992) 'The Main Force: Women in Eritrea', *Ms*, Vol. 2, No. 6, pp. 46–51.

Groenenberg, M. (1993). *Psychotherapeutic Work with Traumatized Female Refugees from Different Cultures*, from the Proceedings of an European Consultation initiated and organized by the UNHCR and Pharos Foundation for Refugee Health Care, Utrecht, 17–19 June 1993.

Hale, S. (1996) *Gender Politics in Sudan: Islamism, Socialism, and the State*, Westview Press, Boulder.

Hale, S. (1999) 'Post-war Eritrean Women: The Soldier, the Party, and the National Union of Eritrean Women', paper prepared for The Aftermath Conference on Women in Post-War Situations, Johannesburg, 20–22 July 1999.

Hale, S. (2000) 'The Soldier and the State: Post-Liberation Women – The Case of Eritrea', *Frontlines Feminisms*, Garland Press, New York.

Harrison, G. (1996) 'Democracy in Mozambique: the Significance of Multi-party Elections', *Review of African Political Economy*, No. 67, pp. 19–35.

Hartsock, N. (1982) 'Prologue to a Feminist Critique of War and Politics', in J. Stiehm (ed.) *Women's Views of the Political World of Men*, Transnational Publishers, New York.

Harvard, W. M. (1823) *A Narrative of the Establishment and Progress of the Mission to Ceylon and India*, London.

Hassim, S. (1991) 'Gender, Social Location and Feminist Politics in South Africa', *Transformation*, Vol. 15, pp. 65–82.

Hassim, S. (1999) 'From Presence to Power: Women's Citizenship in a New Democracy', *Agenda*, Vol. 40.

Hatch, C. (2000) 'Women of War', *Christian Science Monitor*, 8 March.

Hayes, P. (1996) '"Cocky" Hahn and the "Black Venus": the Making of a Native Commissioner in South West Africa, 1915–46', *Gender and History*, Vol. 8, No. 3, pp. 364–92.

Hayes, P. *et al.* (eds.) (1998) *Namibia under South African Rule: Mobility and Containment, 1915–46*, James Currey, Oxford.

Herbstein, D. and J. Evenson (1989) *The Devils Are Among Us: The War for Namibia*, Zed Books, London and New York.

Herman, J.L. (1992) *Trauma and Recovery: The Aftermath of Violence. From Domestic Abuse to Political Terror*, Basic Books, New York.

Hinz, M. and N. Gevers (1989) *Koevoet Versus the People of Namibia*, Working Group Kairos, Utrecht.

Honwana, A. (1997) 'Sealing the Past, Facing the Future: Trauma Healing in Rural Mozambique' in *The Mozambican Peace Process in Perspective*, Accord, London.

Horn, P. (1991) 'Post-Apartheid South Africa: What About Women's Emancipation?' *Transformation*, Vol. 15, pp. 25–39.

Houseman, J. (1982) 'Mothering, the Unconscious and Feminism', *Radical America*, No.16, November–December.

Human Rights Watch (1995) 'Nigeria: the Ogoni Crisis: a Case-Study of Military Repression in Southeastern Nigeria', *Human Rights Watch/Africa*, Vol. 7, No. 5.

Huntington, S. (1968) *Political Order in Changing Societies*, Yale University Press, New Haven.

Ibeanu, O. (1997) 'Oil, Conflict and Security in Rural Nigeria: Issues in the Ogoni Crisis', African Association of Political Science, Occasional Paper Series, Vol. 1, No. 2.

Interview with Comrade Prachanda (2000) 'Red Flag on the Roof of the World', *Revolutionary Worker*, 20 February; website http://www.mcs.net/~rwor

Jajo, Chanmaya (1999) 'Women and Regional Histories', in *Report on the North East Regional Workshop, Guwahati, June 24–25, 1999*, organised by Women's Core Group All India Coordinating Forum of Adivasi/ Indigenous Peoples (unpublished).

Jayawardena, K. (1987) *Feminism and Nationalism in the Third World*, Zed Books, London and New York.

Jega, A. (2000) 'General Introduction: Identity Transformation and the Politics of Identity under Crisis and Adjustment', in A. Jega (ed.) *Identity Transformation and Identity Politics Under Structural Adjustment in Nigeria*, Nordiska Afrikainstitutet,

Stockholm.

Jeganathan, P. (1997) 'After a Riot: Anthropological Locations of Violence in an Urban Sri Lankan Community', PhD Dissertation, University of Chicago. Ann Arbor: UMI Dissertation Services.

Jenkins, C. (1999) 'Eritrea's Women Fighters', BBC News, East Africa, 22 July.

Kakwenzire, J. (1999) 'Women in Post-war Reconstruction: the Case of Uganda', Abstract Book of the Conference on Women in the Aftermath of War, Johannesburg, 20–22 July.

Kanapathipillai, V. (1986) 'The Survivors' Experience', in V. Das (ed.) Mirrors of Violence: Communities, Riots and Survivors in South Asia, Oxford University Press, New Delhi.

Kannabiran, V. and T. Lalitha (1987) 'The Magic Time: Women in the Telegana People's Struggle', in K. Sangari and S. Vaid (eds.) Recasting Women: Essays in Colonial History, Kali, New Delhi.

Kapferer, B. (1979a) 'Emotion and Feeling in Sinhala Healing Rites', Social Analysis, Vol. 1, pp.153–76.

Kapferer, B (1979b) 'Entertaining Demons: Comedy, Interaction and Meaning in a Sinhalese Healing Ritual', Social Analysis, Vol. 1, pp. 108–52.

Kapferer, B. (1983) A Celebration of Demons: Exorcism and the Aesthetics of Healing in Sri Lanka, Indiana University Press, Bloomington.

Kassim, S. (1991) 'The Law and Violence Against Women in Tanzania', in African Women: Transformation and Development, Institute for African Alternatives, London.

Kesby, M. (1996) 'Arenas for Control, Terrains of Gender Contestation: Guerrilla Struggle and Counter-insurgency Warfare in Zimbabwe, 1972– 1980', Journal of Southern African Studies, Vol. 22, No. 4, pp. 561–84.

Key, E. (1909) The Century of the Child, G. P. Putnam's Sons, New York and London.

Klingebiel, S. et al. (1995) 'Promoting the Reintegration of Former Female and Male Combatants in Eritrea: Possible Contributions of Development Co-operation to the Reintegration', Reports and Working Papers, Deutsches Institut für Entwicklungspolitik.

König, B. (1983) Namibia: The Ravages of War, International Defence and Aid Fund for Southern Africa, London.

Koss, M. P. and B. R. Burkhart (1989) 'A Conceptual Analysis of Rape Victimisation: Long Term Effects and Implications for Treatment', Psychology of Women Quarterly, Vol. 13, pp. 27–40.

Kruks, S., R. Rapp, and M. Young (eds.) (1989) Promissory Notes: Women and the Transition to Socialism, Monthly Review Press, New York.

Leach, E. (1971) 'Sinhalese "Milk Mothers" (kiri amma)', Man (n.s.), Vol. 6, No. 4, p.690.

Lebowitz, L. and S. Roth (1994) '"I Felt like a Slut": the Cultural Context and Women's Response to being Raped', Journal of Traumatic Stress, Vol. 7, pp. 363–90.

Lloyd, G. (1984) The Man of Reason: 'Male' and 'Female' in Western Philosophy, Methuen, London.

Lloyd, G. (1986) 'Selfhood, War and Masculinity', in C. Pateman and E. Gross (eds.) Feminist Challenges, Northeastern University Press, Boston.

Lorentzen, L. A. and J. Turpin (eds.) (1998) The Women and War Reader, New York University Press, New York.

Lunde, I. and J. Ortmann (1992) 'Sexual Torture and the Treatment of Its Consequences', in M. Basoglu (ed.) Torture and Its Consequences: Current Treatment Approaches, Cambridge University Press, Cambridge.

Magaia, L. (1988) Dumba Nengue: Run for Your Life (Peasant Tales of Tragedy in Mozambique), Africa World Press, Trenton.

Mahamane, Z. (1999) 'Femmes Touareg du Niger, Suite à la Rébellion', ACAS Bulletin, 55/56, 52–4.

Malibongwe Collection (1990) Malibongwe Conference Papers and African National Congress In-House Seminar Papers, 1989 and 1990.

Manchanda, R. (2000) 'Redefining and Feminising Security', unpublished paper presented at a seminar, Discourses on Human Security, organised by the Sustainable Development Policy Institute, Islamabad, May 24–26.

Manchanda, R. (2001a) 'Guns and Burqua: Women in the Kashmir Conflict', in R. Manchanda (ed.) Women, War and Peace in South Asia: Beyond Victimhood to Agency, Sage, New Delhi.

Manchanda, R. (ed.) (2001b) Women, War and Peace in South Asia: Beyond Victimhood to Agency, Sage, New Delhi.

Martin-Baro, I. (1989) 'Political Violence and War as Causes of Psychosocial Trauma in El Salvador', International Journal of Mental Health, Vol. 18, No. 1, pp. 3–20.

McCallin, M. (1991) The Psychological Well-being of Refugee Children: Research Practice and Policy Issues, International Catholic Child Bureau, Geneva.

McKay, S. R. (1998) 'The Psychology of Societal Reconstruction and Peace', in L.A. Lorentzen and J. Turpin (eds.) The Women and War Reader, New York University Press, New York.

Meijer, M. (1985) 'Some Aspects of Oppression in the Torture of Women', in J. Smeulers (ed.) Tortures, Medical and Psychosocial Aspects, De Tijdstroom, Lochem.

Meintjes, S. (1998) 'Gender, Nationalism and Transformation: Difference and Commonality in South Africa's Past and Present', in R. Wilford and R.L. Miller (eds.) Women, Ethnicity and Nationalism: The Politics of Transition, Routledge, London.

Meintjes, S. (2000) 'The Aftermath: Women in Post-war Reconstruction', Agenda, Vol. 43, pp. 4–10.

Metzger, D. (1976) 'It Is Always the Woman Who is Raped', American Journal of Psychiatry, Vol. 133, pp. 405–7.

Meyer, C. B. and S. E. Taylor (1986) 'Adjustment to Rape', Journal of Personality and Social Psychology, Vol. 50, pp. 1226–34.

Mladjenovic, L. (1999) 'Notes from the Trip to Macedonia', Women for Peace, Women in Black, Belgrade.

Moore, D. (2000) 'Levelling the Playing Fields and Embedding Illusions: "Post-Conflict" Discourse and Neo-Liberal "Development" in War-torn Africa', Review of African Political Economy, Vol. 83, pp. 11–28.

Mukamulisa, M. T. and A. Mukarubuha (2000) 'L'Expérience rwandaise', paper prepared for the International Conference on the Transformation of Conflicts in Africa and the Perspectives African Women, Afard/Alert International, Dakar, 23–26 May.

Musengezi, C. (2000) 'Interview with Nancy Saungweme', in C. Musengezi and I. McCartney (eds.) Women of Resilience: The Voices of Women Ex-Combatants, Zimbabwe Women Writers, Harare.

Namhila, E. N. (1997) The Price of Freedom, New Namibia Books, Windhoek.

Neugebauer, M. (1998) 'Domestic Activism and Nationalist Struggle', in L. A. Lorentzen and J. Turpin (eds.) The Women and War Reader, New York University Press, New York.

Nnoli, O. (1978) Ethnic Politics in Nigeria, Fourth Dimension Press, Enugu.

Nnoli, O. (1987) 'Revolutionary Violence, Development, Equality and Justice in South Africa', Africa Today, Vol. 34, Nos. 1 and 2.

'No Easy Walk to Freedom' (1998), BBC News, Crossing Continents, 2 December.

Nordstrom, C. (1991) 'What John Wayne Never Told Us', unpublished paper.

Ntwarante, A. and G. Ndacasiyaba (2000) 'L'Expérience du Burundi', paper prepared for the International Conference on the Transformation of Conflicts in Africa and the Perspectives African Women, Afard/Alert International, Dakar, 23–26 May.

NUEW (1994a) 'Constitution of the National Union of Eritrean Women', typescript.

NUEW (1994b) 'National Union of Eritrean Women', Eritrean Relief and Rehabilitation

Association, reprinted from *The Horn of Africa Bulletin*, Vol. 6, No. 5, September–October 1994.

NUEW (1999) 'National Report – On The Implementation of the African and Global Platform for Action for the Advancement of Women (a Summary)', National Union of Eritrean Women, Eritrea.

Obeyesekere, G. (1969) 'The Ritual Drama of *Sanni* Demons: Collective Representations of Disease in Ceylon', *Comparative Studies in Society and History*, Vol. 11, No. 2, pp. 174–216.

Obeyesekere, G. (1970) 'Religious Symbolism and Political Change in Ceylon', *Modern Ceylon Studies*, Vol. 1, No. 1, pp. 43–63.

Obeyesekere, G. (1975) 'Sorcery, Premeditated Murder, and the Canalization of Aggression in Sri Lanka', *Ethnology*, Vol. 14, No. 1, pp. 1–23.

Obeyesekere, G. (1981) *Medusa's Hair*, University of Chicago Press, Chicago.

Obeyesekere, G. (1984) *The Cult of the Goddess Pattini*, University of Chicago Press, Chicago.

Osaghae, E. (1995) 'The Ogoni Uprising: Oil Politics, Minority Nationalism, and the Future of the Nigerian State', *African Affairs*, Vol. 94, No. 376.

Parpart, Jane L. and Kathleen A. Staudt (eds.) (1989) *Women and the State in Africa*, Boulder, Lynne Rienner.

Papic, Z. (1999) 'War in Kosova, Feminist Politics and Fascism in Serbia', *Women for Peace*, Belgrade, Women in Black.

Pendleton, W., D. Lebeau and C. Tapscott (1993) *A Socio-Economic Assessment of the Oshakati/Ondangwa Nexus*, Namibian Institute for Social and Economic Research, Research Report 10, Windhoek.

Pertold, O. (1925) *Inquiries into the Popular Religions of Ceylon, Part I: Singhalese Amulets, Talismans and Spells*, publication of the Philosophy Faculty of Karlovy University, Prague.

Pillay, A. (2000) 'Coalition Building for Peace in Africa', *Agenda*, Vol. 43, pp. 32–5.

Pillay, A. and C. Bop (1999) 'Coalition Building in Africa to Challenge Gender Based Violence in the Aftermath of Conflict', working document prepared for the meeting of the African Women's Anti-War Coalition, Misty Hills, South Africa, 23 July.

Preston, R. (1997) 'Integrating Fighters after War: Reflections on the Namibian Experience, 1989–1993', *Journal of Southern African Studies*, Vol. 23, No. 3, pp. 453–72.

Rajasingham-Senanayke, D. (2001) 'Ambivalent Empowerment and Tamil Women in the Sri Lankan Conflict', in R. Manchanda (ed.) *Women, War and Peace in South Asia: Beyond Victimhood to Agency*, Sage, New Delhi.

Reid, C. (1982) 'Reweaving the Web of Life', in P. McAllister (ed.) *Reweaving the Web of Life: Feminism and Non Violence*, New Society, Philadelphia.

Report of the Working Group on Women's Gains and Losses, Conference on Women in the Aftermath of War, Johannesburg, 20–22 July 1999 (unpublished).

Reports from the Battlefield: 'Fury of Women Unleashed' (1998) *The Worker*, February; see website http://www.maoism.org/misc/nepal

Romero, S. (1985) 'A Comparison Between Strategies Used on Prisoners of War and Battered Wives', *Sex Roles*, Vol. 13, Nos. 9/10, pp. 537–47.

Rowbotham, S. (1983) *Dreams and Dilemmas*, Virago Press, London.

Ruddick, S. (1980) 'Maternal Thinking', *Feminist Studies*, Vol. 6, No. 2, pp. 342–67.

Ruddick, S. (1984) 'Preservative Love and Military Destruction: Some Reflections on Mothering and Peace', in J. Trebilcot (ed.) *Mothering: Essays in Feminist Theory*, Rowman and Allanheld, Atlantic Highlands, NJ.

Ruddick, S. ([1989]1995) *Maternal Thinking: Towards a Politics of Peace*, Beacon Press, Boston.

Sachitanandam, S. (2001) 'Women's Participation in Popular Movements in the North and the East', in S. Fiaz and R. Samaddar (eds.) *Peace Process in Sri Lanka: Peace*

Audit Report 2, Southeast Asia Forum for Human Rights Paper Series 8, Kathmandu, April.

Sajor, I. L. (ed.) (1998) *Common Grounds: Violence against Women in War and Armed Conflict Situations*, Asian Centre for Women's Human Rights, Quezon City, Philippines.

Samaddar, R. (1999) *Those Accords, A Bunch of Documents*, Southeast Asia Forum for Human Rights Paper Series 4, Kathmandu, September.

Scarry, E. (1987) *The Body in Pain: The Making and Unmaking of the World*, Oxford, Oxford University Press

Schreiner, O. (1978) *Woman and Labour*, Virago, London.

Scott, D. (1994) *Formations of Ritual: Colonial and Anthropological Discourses on the Sinhala Yaktovil*, University of Minnesota Press, Minneapolis.

Selvadurai, A. J. (1976) 'Land, Personhood, and Sorcery in a Sinhalese Village', *Journal of Asian and African Studies*, Vol. XI, Nos. 1–2, pp. 82–101.

Seneviratne, H. L. and S. Wickremaratne (1980) '*Bodhi-puja*: Collective Representations of Sri Lanka Youth', *American Ethnologist*, Vol. 7, No. 4, pp. 734–43.

Sharoni, S. (1998) 'Gendering Conflict and Peace in Israel/Palestine and the North of Ireland', *Millenium Journal of International Studies*, Vol. 27, No. 4, pp.1061–89.

Shikola, T. (1998) 'We Left Our Shoes Behind', in M. Turshen and C. Twagiramariya (eds.) *What Women Do in Wartime: Gender and Conflict in Africa*, Zed Books, London.

Sideris, T. (1998) 'Violation and Healing of the Spirit: Psycho-Social Responses to War of Mozambican Women Refugees', unpublished doctoral thesis, Rand Afrikaans University, Johannesburg.

Sideris, T. (1998) 'Women and Apartheid: collective trauma and social reconstruction', *The Way Supplement*, Vol. 93, pp. 80–92.

Smith, A. D. (1999) 'United Front: Eritrea; in Africa's biggest but least-known war, men and women fighting, and dying, side by side in the trenches', *The Independent* (London), 27 November.

Soiri, I. (1996) *The Radical Motherhood: Namibian Women's Independence Struggle*, Nordiska Afrikainstitutet Research Report No. 99, Uppsala.

Somakirthi, P. (ed.) (1974) *Deva Kannalawwa* (*Appeals to the Deities*), Modern Books, Nugegoda.

Sooka, Y. (1999) Keynote Address to The Aftermath: Conference on Women in Post-war Situations, University of the Witwatersrand, Johannesburg, South Africa, July 20-22.

Sorenson, B. (1998) 'Women and Post-conflict Reconstruction: Issues and Sources', *Occasional Paper* No. 3, the War-torn Societies Project, Geneva, UN Research Institute for Social Development.

Stacey, J. (1983) 'The New Conservative Feminism', *Feminist Studies*, Vol. 9, pp. 559–83.

Stiefel, M. (1999) *Rebuilding After War: Lessons from the War-torn Societies Project*, War-torn Societies Project, Geneva.

Sveaass, N. and E. Axelsen (1994) 'Psychotherapeutic Interventions with Women Exposed to Sexual Violence in Political Detention: a Presentation of Two Therapies', *Nordisk Sexologi*, Vol. 12, pp. 13–28.

Swiss Peace Foundation (1995) *War Against Women: The Impact Of Violence On Gender Relations*, Report of the 6th Annual Conference of the Swiss Peace Foundation, 16/17 September, 1994, Berne, Swiss Peace Foundation.

Swiss Peace Foundation (1998) *Bulletin, No. 3*, September.

Tennent, J. E. (1850) *Christianity in Ceylon*, John Murray, London.

Tötemeyer, G. (1978) *Namibia Old and New: Traditional and Modern Leaders in Ovamboland*, C. Hurst and Co, London.

Tucker, N. (1999) 'Zimbabwe: Supreme Court Revokes Women's Rights', *Houston Chronicle*, 14 April.

Turpin, J. (1998) 'Many Faces: Women Confronting War', in L. A. Lorentzen and J. Turpin (eds.) *The Women and War Reader*, New York University Press, New York.

Turshen, M. (1999) 'West African Workshop on Women in the Aftermath of Civil War', *Review of African Political Economy*, Vol. 26, No. 79, pp. 123–33.

Turshen, M. (2000) 'The Political Economy of Violence Against Women in Uganda', *Social Research*, Vol. 67, No. 3, pp. 805–24.

Turshen, M. (2001) 'The Political Economy of Rape: an Analysis of Systematic Rape and Sexual Abuse of Women During Armed Conflict in Africa', in C. Moser and F. Clark (eds.) *Gender, Armed Conflict and Political Violence*, Zed Books, London.

Turshen, M. and O. Alidou (2000) 'Africa: Women in the Aftermath of Civil War', *Race and Class*, Vol. 41, No. 4, pp. 81–92.

Turshen, M. and C. Twagiramariya (eds.) (1998) *What Women Do in Wartime: Gender and Conflict in Africa*, Zed Books, London and New York.

UN (1995) *The World's Women: Trends and Statistics*, United Nations, New York.

UN (1996) *Platform for Action and the Beijing Declaration*, United Nations, New York.

UN (1998) 'The Causes of Conflict and the Promotion of Durable Peace and Sustainable Development in Africa', report of the Secretary-General to the United Nations Security Council, 16 April.

US Committee for Refugees (2000) *World Refugee Survey 2000*, Immigration and Refugee Services of America, Washington, DC.

Uyangoda, J. (1992a) 'Tears and Curses', *Pravada*, Vol. 1, No. 7, pp. 4–5.

Uyangoda, J. (1992b) 'Voodoo in Politics', *Pravada*, Vol. 1, No. 7, pp. 5–6.

Van Willigen, L. H. M. (1984) 'Women Refugees and Sexual Violence', *Medisch Contact*, Vol. 50, pp. 1613–14.

Verbatim Reports (1999) Conference on The Aftermath: Women in Post War Reconstruction, Johannesburg, 20–22 July (unpublished).

Vieux-Chauvet, M. (1968) *Amour, Colère et Folie*, Galimard, Paris.

Vincent, L. (2000) 'The Politics of Crime in South Africa', *Africa World Review*, February–July, pp. 38–43.

Wijesekera, N. (1990) *The Sinhalese*, M. D. Gunasena, Colombo.

Wijetunga, W. P. (1919) 'Some Sinhalese Customs and Folklore: Omens and Prognostications', *Ceylon Antiquary and Literary Register*, Vol. 5, Part 11, October, pp. 88–90.

Wijetunga, W. P. (1922) 'Some Beliefs among the Sinhalese', *Ceylon Antiquary and Literary Register*, Vol. 7, Part 3, January, pp. 150–4.

Wilford, R. and R. Miller (eds.) (1998) *Women, Ethnicity and Nationalism: The Politics of Transition*, Routledge, New York.

Williams, F.-N. (1991) *Precolonial Communities of Southwestern Africa: A History of Owambo Kingdoms 1600–1920*, National Archives of Namibia, Archeia 16, Windhoek.

Wilson, A. (1991) *Women and the Eritrean Revolution: The Challenge Road*, Red Sea Press, Trenton.

Wirz, P. (1954) *Exorcism and the Art of Healing in Ceylon*, E. J. Brill, Leiden.

Wood, K. and R. Jewkes (1998) '"Love is a Dangerous Thing": Micro-dynamics of Violence in Sexual Relationships of Young People in Umtata', *CERSA – Women's Health*, Medical Research Council, Pretoria.

World Bank (1998a) *Haiti: The Challenges of Poverty Reduction*, World Bank, Washington, DC.

World Bank (1998b) *Post-conflict Reconstruction: The Role of the World Bank*, World Bank, Washington, DC.

Yalman, N. (1964) 'The Structure of Sinhalese Healing Rituals', in E. B. Harper (ed.) *Religion in South Asia*, University of Washington Press, Seattle.

Young, R. M. (1996) 'Evolution, Biology and Psychology from a Marxist Point of View', in I. Parker and R. Spears (eds.) *Psychology and Society: Radical Theory and Practice*, Pluto Press, London.

Index